KT-178-327

Westbourne Library
Alum Chine Road
Bournemouth BH4 8DX
Tel: 01202 761845

Kingwell (1)

- You can return this item to any Bournemouth
  library but not all libraries are open every day.

- Items must be returned on or before the due
  date. Please note that you will be charged for
  items returned late.

- Items may be renewed unless requested by
  another customer.

- Renewals can be made in any library, by
  telephone, email or online via the website.
  Your membership card number and PIN will be
  required.

- Please look after this item - you may be charged
  for any damage.

www.bournemouth.gov.uk/libraries

BOURNEMOUTH

410051930

For Dad

GLADIATORS

FROM SPARTACUS TO SPITFIRES: ONE-ON-ONE COMBAT THROUGH THE AGES

BEN HUBBARD

First published in Great Britain in 2011 by Futura

Copyright © Omnipress 2011

The moral right of the author has been asserted.

A CIP catalogue record for this book
is available from the British Library.

ISBN 978-0-7088-6696-2

Typeset in Great Britain by Omnipress Limited
Printed and bound in Great Britain

Futura
An imprint of
Little, Brown Book Group
100 Victoria Embankment
London EC4Y 0DY

An Hachette UK Company
www.hachette.co.uk

www.littlebrown.co.uk

The views expressed in this publication are those of the author.
The information and the interpretation of that information are
presented in good faith. Readers are advised that where ethical
issues are involved, and often highly controversial ethical issues
at that, they have a personal responsibility for making their own
assessments and their own ethical judgements.

Contents

SAMURAI

MEDIEVAL TOURNAMENTS

DUELLING

BOXING

GUNMEN

FIGHTER PILOTS

Introduction

One-on-one combat is as old as the history of human beings. Millions of years ago a disagreement, a dispute about a point of honour or a power struggle would have led our ancestors to punch the matter out. Many bouts must have been sudden and savage – a disagreement over a scrap of meat, a place next to the fire, a mate. Perhaps some fights were prearranged, organised for a particular location and fought according to some prehistoric rules and protocol. It is hard to imagine fights to the death were organised for bare hands alone. As the bare-knuckle boxers of the nineteenth century would discover, it is difficult to batter a man to death with fists, as the soft bones in the hand break long before the harder ones in the head.

Instead, for serious mortal combat, early humans would have fought with the best available weapons – a favourite stick or mammoth bone. This was until two million BC, when there was a breakthrough in weapons technology in the Oldavai Gorge, Tanzania – the first stone axe. This was perfect for crushing animal bones and extracting the rich marrow. It could also pulverise a human skull with very little effort.

By 6,000 BC stone axes and wooden clubs would give way to spears and copper swords. Whole armies would be equipped with this modern weaponry to protect the first cities of ancient Mesopotamia. Kings and priests ruled these cities and temples were built for worship.

Soon great bouts of one-on-one combat between gods and monsters crept into mythology. Gilgamesh was the Mesopotamian king of the city of Uruk, but his oppressive rule angered the gods. To punish him they created Enkidu – a primitive man covered with hair – to kill him, and a terrible battle ensued: '…in the street they attacked each other, the public square of the land. The doorposts trembled and the wall shook.' In the end Enkidu acknowledged Gilgamesh's superior strength and the two became friends.

Several millennia later, the ancient Greek gods behaved like naughty adolescents and fought each other vicariously through mortals on Earth. The heroes of Greek mythology fought with a stern code of honour and bravery that influenced every aspect of Greek culture. Probably the best-known one-on-one bout was fought between Hector and Achilles in Homer's *The Iliad*:

> *[Achilles] eyed his fair flesh over and over to see where he could best wound it, but all was protected by the goodly armour…save only the throat where the collarbones divide the neck from the shoulders, and this is a most deadly place: here then did Achilles strike him as he was coming on towards him, and the point of his*

spear went right through the fleshy part of the neck.

Homer, *The Iliad*, translated by Samuel Butler

One-on-one combat between two champions in front of lines of facing armies was one of the great rituals of ancient warfare. The Greeks added rules and regulations to another of their rituals – boxing. Boxing was an Olympic event performed in the heat of the midday sun. The rules were simple – two men would stand and slug each other until one had conceded defeat, or was knocked out. The boxers protected their hands with soft ox-hide thongs, but by the fourth century BC the thongs had become tough and hard, designed to cut and lacerate. By the time the Romans supplanted the Greeks as rulers of the ancient world, leather boxing wraps had been replaced with spiked gloves that could puncture flesh and break bone.

Roman boxing matches were to the death, but were only one minor event on a day-long bill of bloodshed and butchery. The gladiator games took the notion of one-on-one combat to the death and turned it into a popular form of entertainment. Up to fifty thousand spectators cheered and bellowed for blood from the stands of Rome's Colosseum.

The games were presented and paid for by the emperor, as part of the imperial system of 'bread and circuses.' It was assumed that if the one million citizens of Rome were kept happy with food and entertainment it would prevent them from becoming a rebellious one million-strong mob. No expense was spared to provide new, novel and exotic forms of bloodshed. The carnage began in the morning, with the hunting of wild and rare animals shipped in from the far reaches of the empire. Lunchtime was reserved for the public execution of criminals, disobedient slaves and other so-called enemies of Rome. Some of the hapless condemned were torn limb from limb by wild animals, others had molten lead poured down their throats and many were crucified and then set alight.

But the executions were only a prelude to the afternoon's entertainment – the gladiator fights. The gladiators were also condemned men but were given the chance to fight for their lives in the arena. The people and emperor decided if a fallen gladiator would be allowed to live or die, by giving the thumbs-up or down. Gladiators could improve their chances by fighting with a bravery and honour deemed worthy of Rome, although this did not ensure survival.

Bravery and honour were also the most important elements of the samurai *bushido*, or 'way of the warrior.' *Bushido* demanded that a warrior devote himself to training, self-sacrifice and above all, his master. The Japanese samurai showcased his *bushido* virtues on the battlefield in mounted archery duels with enemy warriors.

If a samurai failed in his duty or disgraced himself he was expected to commit *seppuku* – suicide by disembowelment. *Seppuku* was performed by plunging a blade into the abdomen and then making a deep cut from left to right. The bravest warriors allowed their entrails to hang from the wound as they died. *Seppuku* is believed to be one of the most painful ways to die, and for this reason, a samurai often recruited a second to behead him. It was suggested a flap of skin be left on the neck to stop the head falling on the ground and rolling away.

Many of the *bushido* values were shared by the code of chivalry which formed the basis for jousts in medieval Europe. Here, mounted knights would thunder towards each other to unhorse the other for glory, valour and to impress spectating ladies. These jousts were the refined version of the more brutal tournaments that came before them. In these free-for-all brawls, two lines of mounted knights, foot soldiers and spearmen charged at one another in a mock-battle. The aim was to capture other knights without injuring or killing them in the process. Those who managed to disentangle themselves from the fray chased each other across the countryside and continued on in smaller battles. Devious knights would gang up and set ambushes for lone wanderers, and 'accidental' killings were frequent.

Chivalric values sanctified the barbarity of the earlier tournaments, making them safer and more civilised until their peak in the seventeenth century. But chivalry would live on in the duel of honour, a supposedly civilised form of one-on-one combat performed by gentlemen. Duels arose from a perceived insult or slur upon another's honour and were fought with swords or pistols. Gentlemen were notoriously prickly and would issue a challenge at the slightest provocation. Offences ranged from name-calling to one man's dog attacking another's.

The duels were often fought in a secret location and heavily regulated by protocol and etiquette. The weaponry and terms of the duel were decided before the event and seconds were on hand to make sure the bout was fair, honourable and gentlemanly at all times. But there was no disguising the barbarity behind Britain's most infamous duel. James Douglas, Duke of Hamilton and Lord Charles, Baron Mohun were two aristocrats who hacked and stabbed at each other dementedly, and nearly severed their fingers trying to grab each other's blades. The country was so appalled at the contest that it began to turn its nose up at duelling altogether.

Instead, gentlemen of England during the Age of Enlightenment became interested in a less fatal form of one-on-one combat – boxing. Academies sold the sport to aristocrats as a classical pursuit, fought in the tradition of Greek and Rome. Gloves were used in practice sessions, so bruised and blackened faces would not raise eyebrows at gentlemen's clubs. But despite great effort to keep the sport in the domain of gentlemen, there was no getting around the fact that brawls, punch-ups and fisticuffs were still common in many taverns in less salubrious working-class areas. So boxing largely fell out of favour in Britain – but by the twentieth century it had reached fever pitch on the other side of the Atlantic.

Working-class pugilists were often the celebrated heroes of boxing in the United States and early fights were promoted as minority grudge matches. An Irishman would fight an Italian, for example, and punch-ups between zealous fans would erupt across the venue floor. Race supplanted cultural heritage as the backdrop to America's domination of the sport. The country's white majority was horrified when a black man, Jack Johnson, won the heavyweight title in 1908, and outraged when he started wearing tailored suits, racing sports cars and having relationships with white women. A desperate search for 'a great white hope' to defeat Johnson ensued, and ex-heavyweight champion James J. Jeffries even came out of retirement to: 'Demonstrate that a white man is king of them all.'

It was not until 1919 that the next popular white boxer emerged; working-class slugger Jack Dempsey. Dempsey won the title by knocking down the champion Jess Willard seven times, breaking his jaw, ribs and cheekbone, and punching out six of his teeth. Dempsey's popularity was partly due to his rugged frontier-town image – he was a man's man from the heart of the American West.

Only a few decades earlier the American West had been ruled by gunmen, lawmen and outlaws alike. Pistol duels were common in the small towns of the Wild West, although they were seldom the 'high noon' gunfights of Hollywood legend. Instead, whiskey-soaked card players would trade insults in a saloon bar and end up going for their guns. But even at close range most gunmen failed to hit each other, and instead often ended up hitting a bystander or breaking a thumb trying to cock their revolver. Nevertheless, gunfighting legends such as John Wesley Hardin, who once shot a man for snoring too loudly, live on in popular culture.

The gunfighting period lasted only around thirty years and by the turn of the century modernisation had made the Wild West obsolete. Horses and carts were replaced with the motor car, gas lamps were replaced with streetlights and the clunky single-action revolver gave way to rapid-fire automatics that didn't need to be cocked.

There was certainly no place in the Wild West for the aeroplane; a startling new technology that in 1903 took the world by storm. It was not long before these flying machines were put to military use. At first pilots could do little more than fling bricks and grenades and wave at each other. But after a breakthrough mechanism allowed a machine gun to fire through the plane's propeller, the fighter pilot was born. World War I dog-fights were sold to the public as chivalrous duels between knights of the sky, and to begin with their bouts were ruled by etiquette and a gentlemanly code of conduct. Pilots were 'invited' to duel with a couple of warning shots, and those shot down behind enemy lines were wined and dined and treated like guests of honour.

But it didn't take long for such noble ideals to fade and be replaced by the fighter pilot's best dog-fighting tactic – ambush and attack from behind. Advances in technology affected no other form of one-on-one combat as much as the fighter plane. Pilots had to adapt to sudden changes in a plane's weaponry and speed, and also those of the enemy. Today's technologies such as tail-mounted radar, rear-firing missiles and helmet-mounted sights have all but made dog-fighting obsolete. Remote-controlled drone planes have also revolutionised pilot safety by simply removing him from the sky altogether.

The story of one-on-one combat is tied to advances in technology. The tools of battle have evolved from the first stone axe to the modern fighter jet. Humans have further tried to influence one-on-one combat by giving it rules and regulations and wrapping it in etiquette and protocol. But beneath this civilising façade lies man's primeval core. One-on-one combat is an expression of his deep-seated instinct to fight another over what he deems important – people, possessions, power and honour.

GLADIATORS

Introduction

Ancient Rome was built on a foundation of aggressive expansion, extraordinary self-belief and a catalogue of virtues that would inform every move it made. It was by adhering to these virtues – training, firmness, endurance, contempt of death, love of glory and the desire to win – that the Roman legions steamrolled their way across the known world, and crushed those who resisted underfoot. But it was not all just for blood and glory – it was for Rome. And Rome was the greatest city in the world. It had it all – clean drinking water, public baths and toilets; food, drink and goods from around the world; cheap, affordable slaves; theatre and chariot racing; and of course, the Colosseum.

The Colosseum was where Rome showed its dominion over man and beast, and what happened to those who opposed it. It was where the serious entertainment took place. And going to the Colosseum was an all-day affair. During the morning events animals such as ostriches, rabbits, zebras and bulls were hunted around an artificial forest set by men with bows, arrows and spears. This was followed by one-on-one combat between men and wilder animals – lions, tigers, bears and rhinoceros. Lunchtime was set aside for the public executions. Sometimes ferocious animals attacked people tied to frames. At other times the condemned were made to wear shirts soaked in pitch, crucified, and then set alight. But the afternoon was when the real action took place – the gladiator fights.

With such an array of good things on offer, Rome naturally felt the rest of the world would want a slice. Luckily Rome was a brand of civilisation that could be franchised out – and Romans were happy to help other cultures open their own branch. So when Rome dispatched its mighty legions to conquer two thirds of the ancient world, its reasons were twofold: to increase the wealth of Rome and to give foreigners the chance of a lifetime – to become Roman.

To achieve this, the Roman army followed a tried and tested method – crush and conquer new countries, make slaves and gladiators of those who opposed, rebuild each new territory into a small replica of Rome, and offer the subjected people Roman citizenship. There were benefits. Existing towns and cities would be modernised to feature the latest advances in Roman infrastructure. In addition, Rome offered protection, prosperity and peace. As long as the people kept this peace (known in imperial times as the *Pax Romana*), paid their taxes, and provided troops for the army, Rome didn't really mind what they got up to. They were even free to worship foreign gods, as long as they offered up the odd dedication to the divine leader.

It was expected of new citizens that they liked the Roman brand, and if they didn't, then dissent or opposition was certainly not tolerated. Warriors who opposed Rome were either executed, sold as slaves, or sentenced to the gladiator school. Here they joined the ranks of the *infamis*, the disgraced, who made up the lowest echelon of Roman society. Their outlook was not optimistic; hundreds of thousands lost their lives in Roman amphitheatres. But there was also a slim chance for the *infamis* to redeem themselves, to show they did, in the end, understand and accept the Roman brand. To do this they had to show the *virtus* that each Roman legionaire carried in his heart, the ideals that had made Rome great – strength (*fortitudo*), training (*disciplina*), firmness (*constantia*), endurance (*patientia*), contempt of death (*contemptus mortis*), love of glory (*amor laudis*) and the desire to win (*cupido victoriae*).

If gladiators fought following these virtues, they had a chance of leaving the arena alive. It was up to the crowd and emperor to decide. They turned their thumbs to indicate whether a defeated gladiator should live or die. Those who won the favour of the people went on to become the admired, loved and lusted-after rock stars of the ancient world. They won fame, fortune and the greatest prize of all: freedom.

GLADIATORIAL GAMES

The gladiatorial games were about appeasement and control. The Emperor of Rome would buy his people's affections with 'bread and circuses' – free handouts of grain and exhibitions of lavish, wholesale butchery. Then, with the mob's thirst for blood sated, the emperor was able to behave in whatever way he saw fit. Often this meant squandering the Empire's wealth to indulge every sick whim and twisted fantasy. Many had large appetites for the violence of the arena. Claudius enjoyed watching the expressions of gladiators as they died. Others gratified their urges by becoming actively involved: Nero dressed in the skin of a wild animal and attacked the genitals of men and women tied to stakes; Caligula enjoyed forcing the sick, elderly and disabled to fight to the death.

Commodus (AD 161–192) took this participation a step further, by actually fighting in the Colosseum as a gladiator. An athletic, fair-headed man, Commodus dressed in the skin of a lion, carried a club and likened himself to the mythical demigod Hercules. In the arena he drove chariots and hunted animals, and was regarded as a crack shot with a spear or a bow. Commodus also considered himself one of the greatest gladiators who ever lived and littered Rome with effigies of himself. He ordered the head be removed from the Colossus of Nero and replaced with a likeness of himself. He then had the statue adorned with a club, lion skin and bronze lion at its feet, and fitted with the inscription: 'The only left-handed fighter to conquer twelve times one thousand men.' Commodus had Rome officially renamed, *Colonia Lucia Annia Commodiana*, or 'Colony of Commodus.'

But the Emperor's contests in the arena were farcical at best. Commodus used a wooden sword to fight his opponent, who would not for one second have considered harming his emperor. Instead, it was outside the amphitheatre that Commodus was at his most deadly. Here, he paid for his extravagant lifestyle by extorting money from the Roman aristocracy. Some were blackmailed with charges of treason and others had to pay for their lives. Many nobles were simply executed for their fortunes. Cassius Dio, a senator during Commodus' rule, describes his emperor thus: 'Commodus, taking a respite from his amusements and sports, turned to murder and was killing off the prominent men...Commodus was guilty of many unseemly deeds, and killed a great many people.'

Dio also accuses Commodus of turning Rome 'from a kingdom of gold to one of rust and iron.' Many modern historians agree with this judgement and consider Commodus' reign the beginning of the end of the Roman Empire.

Ironically Rome's borders were all but conflict-free while Commodus was emperor. But the decline of the Roman Empire did not begin at its outer reaches;

instead the rot started at its core. With Commodus as emperor this was a perilous time for anybody who lived in the capital city. Commodus had little hesitation in killing any person at any time, even his sister Drusilla who had conspired to assassinate him. When he was not plotting the execution of a Roman senator or aristocrat, Commodus turned his palace into a gladiatorial training ground. Here, unlike his bouts in the ring, Commodus used a steel blade against his opponents, as Dio reports:

> ...*he used to contend as a gladiator; in doing this at home he managed to kill a man now and then, and in making close passes with others, as if trying to clip off a bit of their hair, he sliced off the noses of some, the ears of others, and sundry features of still others.*
>
> Cassius Dio, *Roman History*, translated by Earnest Cary

Contests and Costume Changes

On the day of the games Commodus' lion skin and club were carried before the litter which bore him to the Colosseum. He would then go through a series of costume changes. He arrived in a white silk toga to greet the senators, then donned a purple robe and gold crown to sit in the royal box, before entering the arena barefoot in a simple tunic to perform. The lion skin and club, when not in use, sat on a gilded chair next to the emperor in the royal box.

It was from his box that Commodus would participate in the first event of the day, the animal hunts. On one particularly successful morning, the emperor killed one hundred bears by throwing spears from the balustrade. This activity had been made somewhat easier as the arena had been split into four parts with dividing walls, but his efforts left Commodus exhausted. After drinking down a measure of wine from a cup shaped like a club, Commodus looked to the audience, who, on cue, shouted: 'Long life to you!' On another occasion Commodus took to the arena floor to hunt a group of herbivores. He went on to slay a few wilder beasts, including a tiger, hippopotamus and elephant, which had been ensnared for him in nets.

Commodus often introduced the afternoon event, the gladiator fights, by appearing on the bill. He entered the arena dressed as a *secutor* (see page 76) and sometimes even let the audience choose his opponent – although it was no surprise that Commodus won all of his contests. He rewarded himself handsomely for these bouts, taking a gladiatorial fee of one million sesterces. This was a colossal sum by anyone's standards, especially for a gladiator, who at best could charge fifteen thousand sesterces for his services.

After Commodus' dalliance, the real gladiator fights began, watched with keen interest by their 'gladiator' emperor who encouraged them to increasingly violent levels of brutality and slaughter. On one occasion when some of the victorious gladiators hesitated in finishing off their defeated opponents, an incensed Commodus ordered that all of the combatants be shackled together as Dio's account records: 'Thereupon the men so bound fought man against man, and some killed even those who did not belong to their group at all, since the numbers and the limited space had brought them together.'

On another occasion, Commodus ordered that every man in the city missing a foot to illness or misfortune, be rounded up and brought to the arena. Here, they were dressed like serpents from the knees down and given sponges to throw at Commodus. Dressed as Hercules, Commodus then battered the men to death with his club, calling the spectacle the 'slaying of the giants.'

After each of Commodus' events the crowd was obliged to shout out: 'Thou art lord and thou art first, of all men most fortunate. Victor thou art, and victor thou shalt be; from everlasting, Amazonian, thou art victor.'

But many people missed out on the emperors' events because they were too scared to attend – nobody was safe when Commodus was around. At one stage many stayed away because of a rumour that Commodus was preparing to shoot a few of the spectators in a re-enactment of Hercules' sixth task: the killing of the Stymphalian birds. No-one believed Commodus was above such an act, least of all the senators, who lived in constant fear of death. One of these was Cassius Dio, who recounted a particularly close shave:

> *And here is another thing that he did to us senators which gave us every reason to look for our death. Having killed an ostrich and cut off his head, he came up to where we were sitting, holding the head in his left hand and in his right hand raising aloft his bloody sword; and though he spoke not a word, yet he wagged his head with a grin, indicating that he would treat us in the same way. And many would indeed have perished by the sword on the spot, for laughing at*

him (for it was laughter rather than indignation that overcame us), if I had not chewed some laurel leaves, which I got from my garland, myself, and persuaded the others who were sitting near me to do the same, so that in the steady movement of our arms we might conceal the fact that we were laughing.

But, in the end Commodus shared the fate of many of Rome's tyrannical emperors. After he announced he would inaugurate the year 193 as a consul dressed like a gladiator, the people were outraged. His advisers had a wrestler strangle the emperor to death in his bath. Commodus was declared an enemy of the state by the senate, his statues torn down and the name of Rome restored to the city.

Emperors and Gladiators

The history of gladiators is inextricably linked with the story of Rome and its emperors. Gladiators, unlike the other combatants in this book, had no choice but to fight. They were mostly prisoners of war and slaves who had only one way of staying alive – by killing every opponent and winning the favour of the crowd.

It was then up to the crowd to give a defeated gladiator the thumbs up or down, and for the emperor to make the final decision. Clever emperors always tried to please the crowd. The games were the emperor's gift to his people and a way of distracting them from the difficulties of his rule. But a cheering crowd at the Colosseum could just as easily become an angry mob, and the relationship between the emperor and his people – played out in the Colosseum's arena – lived forever on a knife's edge.

The victims in this political drama were of course the gladiators, who were forced to kill – or be killed – for Rome's entertainment. And these hapless souls had only one shot at walking away alive – by showing the crowd that they had fought with the same honour and bravery that had made Rome the mightiest empire in the ancient world.

MODERN MORALITY

But the gladiator games were not just about fighting well and restoring one's honour, they were about entertainment. And this entertainment consisted of the violent slaughter of people and animals.

The Romans' apparent love of bloodshed is difficult to comprehend alongside the ideals and morals of the modern world. It also typically provides a source of anguish and outrage for authors writing about the games. Many of those penning a gladiatorial history do not hold back their disgust, but compare the gladiator games to the extermination camps of Nazi Germany or the atrocities of Genghis Khan. Historians such as Michael Grant and J. P. V. D. Balsdon demand that readers feel repelled by the 'nastiest blood-sport ever invented' and the 'callous deep-seated sadism which pervaded Romans of all classes'.

But while encouraging the 'boo, hiss' response, these commentaries do not invite discussion about the pathos of the games, nor do they ask the question which so baffles our modern-day sensibilities – why? 'Why' is not something addressed by writers and historians of the day either, although many, like the Roman senator Tacitus, admit to the Roman appetites:

> *There are the peculiar and characteristic vices of this metropolis of ours, taken on, it seems to me, almost in*

the mother's womb – the passion for play actors and
the mania for gladiatorial shows and horse-racing
Tacitus, Annals, translated by Church and Brodribb

It is, of course, folly to examine the gladiatorial games using modern morality. And it is short-sighted to believe the gladiatorial games were some sort of ancient one-off; an ugly episode blotting an otherwise pristine copybook. The public enjoyment of bloodshed has been a staple throughout human civilisation, up to and including the present day. The animal hunts, which took up the morning slot of the gladiator games, continued to be staged by Christian Roman emperors until the early sixth century, one hundred years after gladiators had been banned. 'Sport' such as bear-baiting continued through the medieval age, as did bullfighting, which is still enjoyed today in some parts of Spain. Despite recent calls for it to be banned, fox hunting is still a staple of the English gentry, while dog- and cock-fighting are enjoyed by gamblers worldwide, albeit in less salubrious settings.

Public executions, which filled the lunchtime agenda in Roman amphitheatres, also continued long after the fall of Rome. During the 1793 Reign Of Terror, French citizens crowded to see thousands of noble heads removed by guillotine. In 2006, the 'private' hanging of Iraqi dictator Saddam Hussein was recorded by camera phone and within minutes uploaded to the internet for public consumption. It can still be watched today. While gladiator fights represent a certain peak on the graph of one-on-one combat, the rest of its history is certainly not a flat line. In the medieval age, knights battled it out in collective brawl called a *melee*. From the sixteenth century, tens of thousands of Europeans were killed in duels. Today, while fights to the death are not organised for public consumption, millions are entertained by the modern-day equivalents – boxing and cage-fighting among them. Maybe in one thousand years, contemporary writers will write about these sports with the same disdain and disgust as today's authors do of Roman ones.

BLOODSTAINED BEGINNINGS

There is little agreement on the exact origins of the gladiator fights, but historians agree they are not Roman. It is also widely accepted that the fights were connected to the spilling of human blood during funeral ceremonies.

Human sacrifice as part of a funeral ceremony was not uncommon in the ancient world. When archeologist Leonard Woolley discovered the Mesopotamian city of Ur in 1992, he stumbled upon 'death pits'. These royal tombs, dating from around 2,600 BC, were sites of mass-sacrifice, where the king and queen had been buried with their servants. Dozens of bodies of men, women and animals were found neatly arranged, as if they had ingested poison lying in a prearranged position ready to follow their dead monarchs to the afterlife.

In the eleventh century Viking chiefs were sometimes buried with a slave girl, who had often volunteered to be sacrificed. This slave girl or *thrall* spent several days drinking heavily, sleeping with the men of the village and performing rituals, before being stabbed to death on the chief's funeral pyre. It is thought humans were also sacrificed during Mycenaean funerals, and in the *The Iliad* Homer describes Achilles honouring the fallen Patroclus in this way:

> *Then he completed the grim task he had in mind, killing twelve noble sons of the brave Trojans with his bronze blade, and setting the pyre alight so the pitiless flames would spread. Then he gave a groan, and called his dear friend by name: 'All hail to you, Patroclus, though in the House of Hades. See how I keep the promises I made. Twelve noble sons of brave Trojans, the fire will devour with you. But the dogs, not the flames, shall feed on Hector, son of Priam.*
>
> Homer, *The Iliad*, translated by Samuel Butler

The Ancient Greeks believed that blood of the living spilt on the graves of fallen warriors would aid them on their journey to the afterlife. Festus, a second century BC Roman scholar, suggests that the first gladiator fights were actually developed as a less cruel substitute for the human sacrifice carried out on the tombs of great warriors. Early examples of such fights have been found in Campania, southern Italy. In the town of Paestum, two fourth century BC tomb frescos depict a pair of fighters protected by helmets and greaves, attacking each other with spears. In the background there is also a referee or official overseeing the proceedings, suggesting something organised rather than a brawl. Campania, which was first colonised by the Greeks, was also an early site of gladiator schools and amphitheatres.

MUNERA

The earliest Roman gladiator fights took place at the funerals of wealthy citizens. This type of funeral was called a *munus* (plural *munera*), which refers to a duty performed by a dead person's family. This posthumous obligation fulfilled two purposes – to help a relative on their journey to the afterlife and to raise the profile of the family hosting it. A *munus* was a large, expensive event, funded privately by a family, but enjoyed by a crowd.

The first recorded *munus* in Rome took place in 264 BC, and was held to honour an aristocrat called Iunuis Brutus Pera. At this funeral three pairs of gladiators fought in the Forum Boarium, a market square. The gladiators were called *bustuerii* after *bustum*, meaning funeral pyre. Nearly fifty years later in 216 BC, a three-day *munus* was held for consul Marcus Ameilius Lepidus. Twenty-two pairs of gladiators performed at this *munus*, which took place in the larger Forum Romanum. Then, in 183 BC a much grander *munus* took place for Publius Liciniusin. This *munus* lasted for three long days, featured sixty pairs of gladiators, and provided free handouts of meat to the spectators.

In the years to come *munera* grew in size and popularity. As Rome expanded its empire, its aristocrats grew wealthier, and the *munera* held by their families became more extravagant. The public attitude also changed, and it was expected that a *munus* would be a spectacular event with food provided. High profile Romans eager to curry favour with the masses, were happy to oblige.

LUDI

During the Roman Republic *munera* were privately funded and were not regulated by the state. Instead the state provided its own public games called *ludi*, usually held to give thanks to the gods or commemorate a military victory. *Ludi* were introduced in the fourth century BC and included theatre (*ludi scaenici*) and chariot racing (*ludi circenses*). The theatre mostly consisted of Roman mime – a type of bawdy slapstick played out for laughs. The chariot racing, was by comparison, a passionately loved and deadly serious spectator sport. The Etruscan king Tarquin Priscus founded the Circus Maximus to house the chariot racing. Its first *ludi* was the *ludi Romani*, which ran for several days in a row. Originally built of wood, the Circus was a large U-shaped arena, with stepped-seating for 150,000 people.

The racing itself involved four teams – the reds, blues, greens and whites – which inspired fanatical loyalty from their fans. Charioteers drove teams of two to four horses around the central *spina* barrier for seven laps to complete a race. Each race was a furious, high-octane event where charioteers used their reins to tie themselves into their chariots and did their best to encourage accidents among the other racers. Fatalities – equine and human alike – were common.

Spectating itself came with its own perils. Fires were known to break out in the circus, including the Great Fire of Rome, which destroyed two-thirds of the city in AD 64. A further danger for spectators was added when wild animals were introduced to the Circus Maximus. As a new addition to the *ludi* strange and exotic creatures were snatched from the far reaches of the Roman Empire to thrill and amaze Roman audiences. These beasts represented the power of Rome, and its dominion over nature. The more unusual and terrifying the creature, the more popular it was. Public favourites included lions, tigers, elephants, bears, wild goats, dogs and camels.

Circus organisers paid handsomely to have these animals from northern Africa and the near East lured into cages and transported to the capital. After some weeks spent caged aboard wagons and ships the animals arrived at their destination half-crazed with fear, starvation and exhaustion. It is little wonder that when exposed to the glare and hullaballoo of the Circus, some animals were known to snap and attack the audience.

Pompey the Great was one of the first senators to parade elephants at the Circus in 79 BC. It was a piece of shameless self-promotion to showcase his power over the mightiest foreign creatures. But instead of parading submissively around the Circus perimeter, the elephants charged at the iron grilles protecting the alarmed audience. To stop further such incidents Julius Caesar, Pompey's contemporary and arch-rival, ordered a protective moat be dug between the Circus floor and the spectator stand. Emperor Nero later ordered that this moat be filled in.

Despite the odd hiccup the audience loved the spectacle of the animals. The poet Claudian describes the appeal of foreign animals to Roman citizens:

> ...beasts that are the joy of the rich amphitheatre and the glory of the woods. Whatsoever inspires fear with its teeth, wonder with its mane, awe with its horns and bristling coat – all the beauty, all the terror of the forest is taken.

Before long it was decided to present these 'terrors of the forest' in the environs of their natural habitats, albeit artificially created. Whole forest 'sets' made of trees, bushes and logs were built in the Circus to provide a stage for the *venatio*, or animal hunt. The animals were released from their cages into the manmade forest and then hunted down by the *venatores* with spears, bows and arrows.

The *venatio* provided a further symbol of Rome's control over nature and was so popular it became a permanent fixture of the games until the sixth century AD. However, despite all attempts to make animals behave as if they were in a natural setting, they did not always play ball. In AD 281 Emperor Probus celebrated his military victories by holding a *venatio* at the Colosseum, which he had dressed like a forest and readied 200 lions, 200 leopards and 300 bears for release into it. The results left Probus discombobulated, as he describes:

> *All of these were slaughtered as they came out of the doors of their dens, and being killed in this way they afforded no great spectacle. For there was none of that rush on the part of the beasts which takes place when they are let loose from cages. Besides, many, unwilling to charge, were dispatched with arrows…all of which beasts, it is clear, made a spectacle more vast than enjoyable.*

CAESAR'S ACCESSION

Lions were a particular favourite of the people, a point not lost on Julius Caesar, who imported four hundred lions for a *venatio* in the Circus Maximus. Caesar knew the power of Rome lay in pleasing its people, and nothing pleased the people more than a good show. As well as the *ludi*, Caesar ruthlessly exploited *munera* to bolster support from his already adoring Roman public. However, the nervous senate denied Caesar's request to use more than three hundred and twenty pairs of gladiators at a 65 BC *munus* he held for his father, who had actually died twenty years earlier.

But Caesar would not be denied his ambition – in 48 BC he was made dictator and could do as he pleased. Rich from his campaigns in Gaul, Caesar held an extravagant *munus* for his deceased daughter Julia in 46 BC. According to historian Cassius Dio, those who fought and died at the *munus* included one equestrian (a Roman aristocrat lower on the social ladder than a patrician), the son of a Praetor (a commander or magistrate) and several of Caesar's own soldiers. As Julia had died eight years earlier, the religious and honorary significance of this *munus* was tenuous. Christian writer Tertullian later said of the *munera*: 'This class of public entertainment has passed from being a compliment to the dead to being a compliment to the living.' This had been true for a long time in Republican

Rome, arguably since the inception of the *munera*. There was no disguising the true meaning of the *munera* now – it was a king's gift to his subjects, some cheap thrills to pacify the populous. Caesar knew better than anybody that it was the people who had the final say in Rome; the people who were only ever one grievance away from becoming a mob. It was the support of his armies and the Roman public that had taken Caesar to the top.

The problem was that he had overlooked a different mob angrily scheming under his own nose – the senate. On the Ides of March 44 BC a group of senators, fearing Caesar had become a tyrant, assassinated him in the senate building. It was said the dictator tripped several times as he tried to avoid the senators' twenty-three stab wounds, slipping in the blood that also blinded his eyes. But the conspiring senators had underestimated Caesar's appeal – the people loved him. So in the end, while attempting to restore Rome to the glory of its republican days, the senate had actually sealed the deal for a new type of ruler – the emperor.

BREAD AND CIRCUSES

Happily, for Caesar's heir Octavian and his successors, the murdered dictator had already created the blueprint for imperial rule: To control your people simply buy their affections with *panem et circenses* – bread and circuses.

Octavian, or Augustus as he became, was only too happy
to oblige. In 2 BC Augustus made a massive increase in
grain distribution, upping the number of *plebs frumentaria*
or 'people of the grain' to 200,000 – one fifth of Rome's
population. He then set about organising *munera* of
a kind never seen before in the ancient world. These
spectacular extravaganzas spared no expense to provide
new and novel way of slaying man and beast. They were
the gladiator games as we commonly know them today –
a festival of killing held in an amphitheatre and watched
by thousands.

While *munera* passed had been exploited for political
gain by ambitious aristocrats, the gladiator games would
now and forever afterwards be intrinsically bound up
with the imperial cult; the thing that made the emperor
a divine entity to be worshipped across the empire. And
this worship and loyalty would in turn be rewarded by the
emperor. It was no secret that in 26 BC the games were
organised, paid for, and in honour of Augustus, but it was
a point the emperor felt was worth underlining. *Res Gestae
Divi Augusti* (the things done by the Divine Augustus) was
an autobiographical list of the emperor's achievements
inscribed on two bronze pillars outside his mausoleum.
One column describes the spectacles he organised:

> *Three times I gave shows of gladiators under my name
> and five times under the name of my sons and grandsons;*

in these shows about 10,000 men fought. Twice I furnished under my name spectacles of athletes gathered from everywhere, and three times under my grandson's name. I celebrated games under my name four times, and furthermore in the place of other magistrates twenty-three times... Twenty-six times, under my name or that of my sons and grandsons, I gave the people hunts of African beasts in the circus, in the open, or in the amphitheatre; in them about 3,500 beasts were killed.

To make certain that no ambitious aristocrat, senator, general or any other potential usurper could compete with his spectacles, Augustus put heavy restrictions on everybody else's games. From 22 BC, privately sponsored games would only be allowed twice yearly, with a cap of one hundred and twenty gladiators and a total cost 25,000 denarii. Of course there were no such restrictions on the emperor's games, which by comparison could sometimes include thousands of gladiators and cost nearly 170,000 denarii.

Augustus' games were held during scheduled dates in December and March, with each show running for around six days. Each day at the games followed a set order of events, which became the norm for all subsequent games for the next four hundred years. The morning featured the *venatio* and fights between animals and gladiators, known as the *bestiarii*. Then, a period of time was set aside in the middle of the day for public executions, followed by the eagerly anticipated people's favourite – the gladiator fights. The link between the games and the imperial cult was further cemented by the emperor's presence at the spectacles. Here, in the arena, a complicated and fragile political relationship was formed between the emperor and the attending crowd. Freedom of expression had always been considered a Roman right and the games provided a suitable venue to do it in.

Although now, in Imperial Rome, with an all-powerful emperor at the helm it was not considered wise to express too loudly, as consul Gaius Asinius Pollio neatly sums up: 'I'm saying nothing. It's not easy to inscribe lines against a man who can proscribe.'

Nevertheless, many Romans, feeling protected within the crowd, let loose their displeasure at the games. Demands for cheaper bread or lower taxes would quickly pick up momentum and become a loud group chant which echoed around the arena. At other times the chants reflected the crowd's desire for a gladiator to live or die. These included shouts of *mitte* (let him go) or *Iugula!* (kill him). The crowd also indicated whether they thought a fallen gladiator should be finished off or allowed to live, by sticking out a hand and turning their thumbs. In the arena it was customary for a defeated gladiator to hold up his index finger, if he could, to plead for mercy. His opponent would look questioningly to the emperor's box – should I kill him, or not? The emperor would then look to the crowd before delivering his decision, a thumb up, or a thumb down. Clever emperors always took their cue from the crowd and obeyed their wishes. However, not all of Rome's emperors were clever; several were of dubious intelligence and others were dangerously insane.

But whatever the emperor's mental state, the gladiatorial games were about theatre and he was expected to fulfill a role, one which Augustus played with aplomb. This required the emperor to participate enthusiastically in the games while retaining the poise and dignity befitting the imperial office. Many emperors fluffed it.

Tiberius

After a promising start as a military general, Augustus' adopted son Tiberius kicked his aristocratic duties to the curb, and stomped off to self-exile in Rhodes.

After Augustus' death, the senate had to gently coax Tiberius into the emperor's chair, and even then he appeared to sulk through the duration of his reign. While Tiberius' life is mired in conjecture and controversy, he is most remembered as an unlikeable and reluctant ruler. The writer Tacitus filled up six books of his annals on Tiberius, who he summed up thus:

> *Tiberius Nero was of mature years, and had established his fame in war, but he had the old arrogance inbred in the Claudian family, and many symptoms of a cruel temper, though they were repressed, now and then broke out…he had no thoughts but of wrath, hypocrisy, and secret sensuality.*

Upon becoming emperor, Tiberius quickly alienated the senate (who he described as 'men fit to be slaves') and then did the same with his public. He first upset the populace by making his disdain for their beloved games clear. He also refused to attend them. He went on to further limit the budget and number of gladiators allowed in non-imperial games but did not organise his own spectacles to fill the void.

After ostracising himself from his people and peers, Tiberius retired to rule from Capri. It was here, according to contemporary writers, that the emperor went about fulfilling his most cruel and obscene impulses, often carried out in the dungeons and torture chambers of his many luxury villas.

Many modern scholars, however, feel Tiberius was a misunderstood and unfairly condemned man. It would certainly be no surprise if the various writers of the day had given Tiberius a heavily biased obituary, after all, he seemed to have a gift for making people hate him. But one thing was for sure, by his death Tiberius was almost unanimously disliked. The senate refused to give Tiberius divine honours and the people shouted 'To the Tiber with Tiberius' – the gravest of Roman indecencies usually reserved for the corpses of convicted criminals. Ironically, Rome prospered under Tiberius, who expanded its borders and stuffed its coffers full to overflowing.

While some think Tiberius was a reasonable emperor he was certainly not a savvy politician. He had not observed the rule of bread and circuses, he had not played the role of gladiatorial patron and participator, he had not, in short, played the game.

Caligula

There would no question of Caligula's love of the games – he was a zealous believer in the importance of drama and theatre. A self-professed singer and dancer, Caligula acted his way out of an early grave on Capri where he spent six years with his grandfather Tiberius.

Despite the multitude of abuses Tiberius hurled at Caligula, in return he: 'Behaved with such obsequiousness to his grandfather and all about him, that it was justly said of him, "There never was a better servant, nor a worse master".' This behaviour almost certainly prevented Tiberius from having his grandson executed, as he was wont to do of many others that surrounded him. Tiberius himself, while encouraging Caligula to participate in his perversions, seemed aware of his grandson's shortcomings, noting that he: 'Was destined to be the ruin of himself and all mankind' and that in Caligula, he, Tiberius: 'Was rearing a hydra for the people of Rome, and a Phaeton for all the world.'

Initially Emperor Caligula won the people's favour by holding large lavish games, which included extensive gladiator fights and *venationes*. But after around a year alarm bells began to ring. This was the amount of time it had taken Caligula to spend the colossal fortune of

27,000 million sesterces left in Rome's coffers by Tiberius. From then on, Caligula became the kind of unhinged tyrannical nightmare that the former republican senators could have only imagined in their most tortured slumbers.

First Caligula set about making the people refill Rome's empty purse. He levied taxes on anything he could think of, including food, marriage and prostitution. Then he seized the estates of rich aristocrats, created a brothel in his palace made up of citizen's wives and children, and auctioned off the lives of gladiators at the games.

Caligula's behaviour at home became increasingly erratic and perverse. He was said to live in incest with all three of his sisters and kept his sister Drusilla by his side in the manner of a wife, even though she was married to consul Cassius Longinus. When Drusilla died Caligula ordered a period of public mourning, during which it was a capital offence to laugh, bathe or eat with family members. Caligula was not as fond of his other sisters and treated them appallingly, according to writer Suetonius he: 'frequently prostituted them to his catamites'.

Caligula was also in the habit of inviting to dinner noble men and their wives, who he would 'examine very closely, like those who traffic in slaves.' He would then leave the room, send for the woman he found most desirable, and then return to give the diners a graphic account of what had taken place.

Aside from his sexual appetites, with both women and men, his constant female companion was Caesonia, described by Suetonius as 'neither handsome nor young, and was besides the mother of three daughters by another man.' He often exhibited Caesonia to his soldiers, either naked or sometimes dressed up in military garb. When she gave birth to a daughter, Caligula declared it his and named her Julia Drusilla; a child he apparently respected for her unusual tendency to scratch the face and eyes of other children.

Caligula's madness was both random and pointed. He was described as tall, gangly and pale with thinning hair, and it was a capital crime for any person to look down at his balding pate from above. As such he resented any man with a full head of hair, and frequently ordered such men to shave their hair into ridiculous looking styles. Not all hirsute men got off so lightly, as Suetonius recorded:

> *There was one Esius Proculus, the son of a centurion. of the first rank, who, for his great stature and fine proportions, was called the Colossal. Him he ordered to be dragged from his seat in the arena, and matched with a gladiator in light armour, and afterwards with another completely armed; and upon his worsting them both, commanded him forthwith to be bound, to be led clothed in rags up and down the streets of the city, and,*

after being exhibited in that plight to the women, to be then butchered.

Suetonius, *Lives of the Twelve Caesars*, translated by Thomson and Forester

It was at the games and other public events that Caligula's insanity became visible. He was heard to remark once at the Circus Maximus, dissatisfied at the crowd's reaction to the races: 'I wish the Roman people had but one neck.' Anyone and everyone was fair game at these events, as Suetonius describes:

> *In the spectacles of gladiators, sometimes, when the sun was violently hot, he would order the curtains, which covered the amphitheatre, to be drawn aside and forbad any person to be let out; withdrawing at the same time the usual apparatus for the entertainment, and presenting wild beasts almost pined to death, the most sorry gladiators, decrepit with age, and fit only to work the machinery, and decent house-keepers, who were remarkable for some bodily infirmity.*

At another gladiator fight, a knight who Caligula had condemned to be thrown to the lions began screaming out his innocence. Caligula calmly had him dragged out of the arena to have his tongue ripped out before bringing him back in to continue the spectacle.

But there was a limit. Caligula had forced many senators to commit suicide and was rumoured to be planning to make his favourite horse Incitatus consul (Incitatus already had its own house equipped with servants to which it would 'invite' dignitaries to dine). A conspiracy was formed and once again a Caesar of Rome was stabbed to death by the senate in conjunction with the praetorian guard (the royal bodyguard in charge of protecting the emperor).

Claudius

It was the commotion of Caligula being murdered with his family (Suetonius: 'His wife Caesonia was killed with him, being stabbed by a centurion; and his daughter had her brains knocked out against a wall.') that caused Claudius, Caligula's uncle, to hide in fear. Legend has it that the praetorian guard found him trembling behind a palace curtain and immediately proclaimed him emperor.

It was the continued support of the army which propped up Claudius' reign, although sometimes he had to buy this loyalty. The senate and nobility were mistrustful, but the people loved him. Claudius was intelligent and well-read. He knew the importance of bread and circuses and immediately set about distributing grain to the people and providing them with large elaborate games. Claudius was also an enthusiastic participant in the games and did certainly not see the need to hide his enthusiasm behind a veneer of imperial dignity, as Suetonius explains:

> *In any exhibition of gladiators, presented either by himself or others, if any of the combatants chanced to fall, he ordered them to be butchered, especially the*

> *Retiarii, that he might see their faces in the agonies of death. Two gladiators happening to kill each other, he immediately ordered some little knives to be made of their swords for his own use.*

Claudius' reputation for cruelty and tyrannical behaviour was not unfounded. He had senators, knights and his own wife Messalina executed. He then married his power-mad niece Agrippina and, on her behest, groomed her son Nero for the throne instead of his own son Britannicus. In return Agrippina went on to murder Claudius with a meal of poisonous mushrooms.

Nero

Nero was only seventeen when he was declared emperor by the praetorian guard and made his intentions clear – he would rule as a just and generous emperor in the style of Augustus. For the first five years he kept to his word. Nero reduced taxes, banned capital punishment and even ordered that none should be slain in the arena, not even convicted criminals.

In their place Nero organised poetry competitions and encouraged theatre and athletic events. He would actively participate himself, as a singer, musician and charioteer. Then in AD 59 he ordered the execution of his mother Agrippina, followed by his wife Octavia in AD 62. Perhaps seeing that there were no consequences for his actions, Nero appeared to spin entirely out of control, plunging headfirst into a cesspool of vice, degeneracy and insanity.

He often spent the evenings walking the streets with an entourage of gladiators, where he would start fights and indulge his sexual appetites with men, boys and women alike. He created lakeside festivals where guests on rafts floated towards each other, arranged by 'age and experience in vice.' On the shore would be brothels, filled with noble ladies and prostitutes, lit up in the darkness and accompanied by bands of musicians. At one such event Nero married a Greek man call Pythagoras, taking on the role of the bride, as Tacitus describes:

> *The bridal veil was put over the emperor; people saw the witnesses of the ceremony, the wedding dower, the couch and the nuptial torches; everything in a word was plainly visible, which, even when a woman weds darkness hides.*

According to Suetonius, in another marriage to a man called Doryphorus, Nero took his nuptials a step further, and from the honeymoon chamber: 'Went so far as to imitate the cries and lamentations of a maiden being deflowered.' Nero's actions divided Rome – the senate and Roman aristocrats were quaking in their boots, but the masses quite liked him, as Tacitus explains: 'These and the like sentiments suited the people, who craved amusement, and feared, always their chief anxiety, scarcity of corn, should he be absent.'

Nero made sure citizens were provided with a healthy supply of corn and grain. He also gave them circuses – eagerly awaited entertainment for the many unemployed and bored Roman citizens. The cost of these spectacles was high, but trifling matters like public spending and other mechanisms of the empire were of little consequence to Nero, who spared no expense in indulging himself. And the empire was so successful in its tried and tested systems of rule, that it simply chugged along like a reliable old boiler. The Roman Empire was managed by ten thousand bureaucrats, who kept the engine room well oiled, regardless of the emperor's involvement. This was a lucky break for Nero, whose mind was concerned with other matters.

Gladiator fights and executions were now firmly back on the agenda. Nero built a new amphitheatre and set about organising bouts between condemned criminals and fights between women. Nero also invented a new way of participating in the arena. Suetonius explains:

> *He so prostituted his own chastity that after defiling almost every part of his body, he at last devised a kind of game, in which, covered with the skin of some wild animal, he was let loose from a cage and attacked the private parts of men and women, who were bound to stakes.*

FLAMES AND RUINATION

Then, disaster struck. In AD 64 a fire started in the Circus Maximus and burned for nine days long, destroying most of the city. According to legend Nero had laid the fire and played his fiddle while it burned, but in reality he was at his villa at Antium, 35 km (22 miles) away. Nevertheless, fingers were pointed at Nero, who had been openly discussing plans for a reconstruction of Rome. The fact that Nero's golden palace was being designed to cover a whole third of the devastated city was seen as further evidence of his guilt.

Nero tried to deflect these accusations by blaming the Christians and set about persecuting them, which earned him the title of 'antichrist.' Tacitus describes Nero's reign of terror:

> *Accordingly, an arrest was first made of all who pleaded guilty; then, upon their information, an immense multitude was convicted, not so much of the crime of firing the city, as of hatred against mankind. Mockery of every sort was added to their deaths. Covered with the skins of beasts, they were torn by dogs and perished, or were nailed to crosses, or were doomed to the flames and burnt, to serve as a nightly illumination, when daylight had expired. Nero offered his gardens for the spectacle, and was exhibiting a show in the circus, while he mingled with the people in the dress of a charioteer or stood aloft on a car. Hence, even for criminals who deserved extreme and exemplary punishment, there arose a feeling of compassion; for it was not, as it seemed, for the public good, but to glut one man's cruelty, that they were being destroyed.*

It had to end somewhere. The senate and nobility had long wanted to be rid of Nero. He had spent 2,000 million sesterces on his extravagances and was in danger of bankrupting Rome. He had also made the fatal mistake of alienating his own legions by appearing on stage playing the parts of pregnant women and gladiators about to be executed. For an emperor of Rome, this was just not done. The head of the praetorian guard joined sides against Nero with general Galba in Spain. Nero had now successfully alienated the senate, the nobility and the army.

The senate issued an edict that Nero should die a slave's death: on a cross and under the whip. With this death warrant issued, Nero fled Rome and committed suicide. But, while the senators and nobility of Rome celebrated Nero's death, Tacitus reported that: 'The degraded populace, frequenters of the arena and the theatre, the most worthless of the slaves, and those who having wasted their property were supported by the infamous excesses of Nero' were upset by the news. Apparently there were many for whom the vice and corruption of the emperor was of little concern – what was of consequence was their entertainment.

Nero was only the fifth emperor of Rome, and another four centuries of megalomaniacal rule was to follow, supported in turn by ever more grand and spectacular gladiator games. These games would increase on an unprecedented scale when the Emperor Vespasian began constructing an arena that was worthy of Rome – the Colosseum. Completed in AD 80 this amphitheatre of death would house fifty thousand spectators and encourage an altogether new age of killing and craziness that would forever stain the annals of human civilisation.

Who Were the Gladiators?

It was in AD 117 that Rome reached its zenith. Emperor Trajan had conquered the disputed territory of Parthia and marched his legions into Mesopotamia; the first Mediterranean ruler to do so since Alexander the Great. But the sight of this new country depressed the emperor. Gazing over the large swath of arid land before him, he realised it was all too big and far away from Rome; the empire had gone as far as it could go.

From that point on, Rome would stop expanding its borders, and do its best to control the territories within its empire. Rome felt it had offered many conquered people a good deal in allowing them to become Roman and enjoy the success of its empire. Of course, some had opposed these plans and tried to stem the terrible tide of the unstoppable Roman legions.

Those prisoners of war not executed were either sold as slaves or forced to join a gladiator school (*ludus*). In the early years of the empire, slaves who had been disobedient or were accused of a serious crime, such as murder, were also bundled off to a *ludus* to await their fate. Being trained as a gladiator was, ironically, the best option for these condemned souls, as it at least gave them a chance to stay alive. But to justify the cost of training a gladiator, a new recruit had to be physically worthy, and it helped if he was good looking. Those who did not fit the criteria were sentenced to death by wild beasts (*ad bestias*) or death by the sword (*ad gladium*), which was shorthand for whatever method of execution was popular at the time.

That these men were being handed out different varieties of the same thing – a painful death sentence – was of no consequence to the Romans. Gladiators represented the lowest echelons of society who, through birth or action, had forfeited their right to stay alive. They were the disgraced, or *infamis*, lower even than actors and certainly not worthy of civil liberties. Calling someone a gladiator, as Cicero often did of his political opponents, was considered the ultimate insult.

It is curious then, that battling gladiators were trained to display the Roman *virtus* expected of an upstanding Roman citizen – strength (*fortitudo*), training (*disciplina*), firmness (*constantia*), endurance (*patientia*), contempt of death (*contemptus mortis*), love of glory (*amor laudis*), and the desire to win (*cupido victoriae*). These were the qualities Romans had used to conquer the known world, the qualities that had made Rome great. Therefore, by exhibiting these qualities gladiators could earn prizes, fame, freedom, and paradoxically, respect. Gladiators who behaved like cowards, were sent to the bottom. This hypocrisy did not go unnoticed by commentators of the time, such as Tertullian:

> *Next taunts or mutual abuse without any warrant of hate, and applause, unsupported by affection....* *The perversity of it! They love whom they lower; they despise whom they approve; the art they glorify, the artist they disgrace.*

Other writers make their condemnation of the games clear, such as the writer Seneca:

> *Man, an object of reverence in the eyes of men, is now slaughtered for jest and sport... and it is a satisfying spectacle to see a man made a corpse.*

It is perhaps comforting to modern sensibilities that some were opposed to the arena's bloodshed, but they were in the minority, and even despite their proclamations would still actually attend the games. What is even stranger, considering popular feeling towards those who fought as gladiators, are the great numbers of free men who volunteered to become one. In fact, by the first century AD it is thought free men made up half of the gladiator ranks in Rome. Citizens, senators and even emperors appeared in the arena, after Augustus made it law that they could.

There were several reasons why free men chose this life. Some of them were freed gladiators, wanting to win a large enough purse to start a new life. Others had retired from the army and found it difficult to adapt to peaceful civilian life. Some may simply have needed the money. But others must have wanted to experience the excitement, glamour and glory of the arena. However, those nobles and emperors who wanted to fulfill such desires were met with scorn and derision.

Roman writer Juvenal describes the case of Roman aristocrat and tribune Gracchus, who disgraced himself by appearing in the arena without a helmet, which members of the Roman gentry did to disguise themselves:

> *To crown all this [scandal], what is left but the amphitheatre? And this disgrace of the city you have as well — Gracchus not fighting as equipped as a 'murmillo', with buckler or falchion (for he condemns — yes, condemns and hates such equipment). Nor does he conceal his face beneath a helmet. See! he wields a trident. When he has cast without effect the nets suspended from his poised right hand, he boldly lifts his uncovered face to the spectators, and, easily to be recognised, flees across the whole arena. We can not mistake the tunic, since the ribbon of gold reaches from his neck, and flutters in the breeze from his high-peaked*

*cap. Therefore, the disgrace, which the Secutor had to
submit to, in being forced to fight with Gracchus, was
worse than any wound.'*

Juvenal, Satires, translated by G. G. Ramsay

TRAINING BEGINS

Whatever walk of life a gladiator recruit harked from they left it behind at the *ludus* gates. First they had to swear an oath (*sacramentum gladiatorium*) agreeing: 'To endure to be burned, to be bound, to be beaten, and to be killed by the sword.' The free men then signed a contract stating the duration of their gladiator employment, the type of gladiator they would fight as, and how often they would appear in the arena. The free men then joined the other recruits to become part of the gladiator family (*familia gladiatoria*) and were subject to a life of training within the *ludus* walls (it is thought some free men were able to sleep outside of the *ludus*, but others were not allowed and some chose not to).

From AD 80 there were four main *ludi* in Rome that were managed by imperial functionaries instead of the usual *lanista*, the gladiator manager who also often ran a *ludus*. The *Ludus Gallicus* trained heavily armed gladiators, such as *samnites* and *mumillones*. The Ludus Dacicus trained Dacian prisoners of war, while the Ludus Matutinus trained the *bestarii* (animal fighters) and *venatores* (animal hunters).

The *Ludus Magnus* was the biggest school, with areas large enough for gladiators on horseback (*equites*) and in chariots (*essidari*) to train. The *Ludus Magnus* was connected directly to the Colosseum by a long underground tunnel. There were more than one hundred *ludi* located across the foreign lands of the Roman Empire, although the exact number is unknown.

NOVICUS

Every new recruit (*novicus*) would undergo an examination by a *medici* and the *lanista*. Each man's health, physical condition and physique was thoroughly checked. This determined whether a recruit was up to hours of rigorous training and which type of gladiator they were best suited as. Next the *novicus* was shown around the *ludus*.

A typical *ludus* was built around a central courtyard and included a large kitchen and mess hall; baths; an armoury where the weapons were locked away at night; a prison for those gladiators who tried to escape; and the gladiator quarters, small, windowless cells around 5 by 3 metres (16 by 10 feet) in size and shared by two men. Sometimes there was also an oval yard designed to imitate the arena floor, surrounded by raised seating for up to three thousand spectators. Here fans could come and watch their favourite gladiator train, or look out for new potential during the off-season.

For a *novicus* each day followed a strict routine. His cell would be unlocked at dawn and the first meal of the day eaten in the mess hall. Gladiators ate a high-energy protein diet that included a type of barley porridge. After breakfast the *novicus* was led to the central courtyard for the training and drills that filled the majority of the day. Some of the training time would be spent practising thrusting and slashing strokes with a wooden sword or staff (*rudis*) against a 2 metre (6.5 foot) high pole (*palus*). Specialist trainers called *doctores* would also teach a *novicus* to fight as their particular gladiator type, ie, a *retarius* would be trained by a *Doctores Retiarii*. Heavier weapons than normal were used in these sessions, to build up strength and stamina.

Aside from training and eating, it was made sure the gladiators were kept clean and healthy and at their physical peak. They were allowed to have women back to their cells on occasion, when the *lanista* or *ludus* manager allowed it. It was in the *lanista*'s interest that his gladiators were in good fighting shape, as this would allow him to charge top dollar for their appearance in the arena. The price to rent a gladiator for the games ranged from 1,000 sesterces to 15,000 sesterces, depending on his quality. But if the gladiator was slain, the *lanista* could charge the organiser of the games up to hundred times that fee. For this reason, a gladiator bloodbath was an expensive affair – although by the same token allowing a gladiator to be killed was considered a symbol of generosity.

The *lanista*, however, while not wanting to lose a commodity, made money whether his gladiator lived or died. Although it was considered respectable for a nobleman to own and rent out gladiators, *lanistae* were reviled in Roman society, as historian Auguet describes:

> *In the eyes of the Romans he was regarded as both a butcher and a pimp. He played the role of scapegoat; it was upon him that society cast all the scorn and contempt aroused by an institution which reduced men to the status of merchandise or cattle.*
>
> R. Auguet, *Cruelty and Civilization*

COMPETITION AND CAMARADERIE

Each *ludus* was made up of a hierarchy of fighters and rivalry between gladiators was constantly encouraged. Those that had won a match in the arena could call themselves a *veteranus*. The best fighter in a *ludus* took the title *primus palus* (first pole), the second best *secundus palus* (second pole) and so on.

Outside of training there was a strict policy of segregation, keeping apart the different types and ranks of fighter until the time of combat. But despite this policy of segregation, bonds were formed between gladiators in the *ludus*. These relationships must have been a strange mix of competition and camaraderie. After all, a gladiator's best friend in the *ludus* could be the man he was charged with fighting to the death the next day.

The gladiators of a *ludus* also formed unions called *collegia*, to look after, as much as possible, gladiatorial rights. These *collegia* made sure fellow gladiators had a proper burial and that any money or property they owned was forwarded on to their families.

BREAKING POINT

While some gladiators fought their way up to *primus palus*, winning acclaim, freedom and a healthy retirement purse, they were in the minority. Most gladiators did not make it past their thirtieth birthday. For many prisoners of war and slaves, the *ludus* was the last stop before a violent and anonymous end on the sands of the arena before a hostile crowd of thousands baying for their blood. The pressure suffered by these doomed souls while being transported to the arena is unimaginable. For some the fastest exit out was the only option left open, as Seneca writes:

> *Lately a gladiator, who had been sent forth to the morning exhibition, was being conveyed in a cart along with the other prisoners; nodding as if he were heavy with sleep, he let his head fall over so far that it was caught in the spokes; then he kept his body in position*

long enough to break his neck by the revolution of the wheel. So he made his escape by means of the very wagon which was carrying him to his punishment.

But taking one's life was not something easily carried out, especially for the *novicus*, who was kept in chains at all times except for within the training yard. It was not uncommon for young recruits to quickly hit breaking point, and they were therefore closely monitored. For this reason, opportunities to take one's life were few and far between, and suicide required a desperate level of initiative. Seneca describes one such case:

For example, there was lately in a training-school for wild-beast gladiators a German, who was making ready for the morning exhibition; he withdrew in order to relieve himself – the only thing which he was allowed to do in secret and without the presence of a guard. While so engaged, he seized the stick of wood, tipped with a sponge, which was devoted to the vilest uses, and stuffed it, just as it was, down his throat; thus he blocked up his windpipe, and choked the breath from his body. That was truly to insult death!

ANCIENT ROCK STARS

For most gladiators the chances of winning a fortune was small. Most of the gladiator's fee went into the *lanista*'s pocket, with the fighter themselves taking a cut of around twenty per cent. A seasoned *veteranus* who had won his freedom but decided to return to fight, could negotiate much bigger sums under the terms of his contract.

Occasionally a gladiator who had won the favour of the crowd and emperor was handsomely rewarded. Nero, never one to worry about the bill, was known to be particularly generous, according to Suetonius: 'He gave the gladiator Spiculus properties and residences equal to those of men who had celebrated triumphs.'

Even those who were not made rich could still win adoration and acclaim by performing courageously and displaying the necessary Romans *virtus* in the arena. In fact many gladiators achieved a rock star status – admired by men and loved by women. The poet Martial sings the praises of one such gladiator, Hermes in an epigram:

> *Hermes, the age's delight to the Sons of Mars…Hermes, schooled in all weapons…Hermes, gladiator and trainer both…Hermes, the confusion and terror of his own school…Hermes, proud with the warrior's spear… Hermes, threatful with the sea-trident… Hermes, the darling and passion of gladiators' women.*

It is clear from the graffiti found on the walls of Pompeii that gladiators made the hearts of many women flutter. These scrawls include: 'Celadus makes the girls swoon' (*Celadus, suspirium puellarum*) and 'Crescens the Netter of young girls by night' (*Cresces retiarius puparum nocturnarum*).

It was not uncommon for the *lanista* of a *ludus* to send slave girls to a gladiator's cell, if he had fought well. Other female visitors included those from the ranks of the Roman nobility. One such story describes Faustina, the wife of Emperor Marcus Aurelius, who became instantly inflamed by a gladiator she had seen in a procession. After a time she decided to admit her passion to Marcus Aurelius, who consulted the priests on the matter. They advised that the gladiator in question should be killed so Faustina could bathe in his blood and then have sex with her husband. Faustina carried out the prescribed action, which seemed to do the trick as her love abated. But the child born from the bloody union of that night turned out to be heir apparent Commodus, who: 'Was born a gladiator, not really a prince; for afterwards as emperor he fought almost a thousand gladiatorial bouts before the eyes of the people.'

In another story Juvenal recounts the love of senatorial wife Eppia for the gladiator Segius. Eppia, apparently gives up her 'soft downy pillows' and 'wailing children' to follow Sergius and his touring *familia gladiatoria* to Alexandria in Egypt. Juvenal finds this curious for two reasons – one because of the torturous sea journey to Egypt, which was to be avoided if all possible, and two, because Sergius was not much to look at:

> *Was it good looks and youthfulness set Eppia on fire? What did she see in him to endure being classed with the gladiators? After all, her Sergius had already begun to smooth his throat, an injured arm presaged retirement; and his face was seriously disfigured, a furrow chafed by his helmet, a huge lump on the bridge of his nose, and a nasty condition provoking a forever-weeping eye. He was a gladiator, though...that's why she preferred him to children and country, Husband and sister. They love the steel.*

FEMALE GLADIATORS

Some Roman women took their gladiatorial love a step further and decided to fight in the arena. While the majority of women gladiators were forced to fight against their will, some free women, including those of noble birth, did so too. While it seems remarkable that a wealthy Roman woman would demean herself by appearing alongside the *infamis*, it is possible they escaped this label by not accepting payment.

The appearance of women must have caused a certain amount of consternation, as in AD 11 Augustus put restrictions on female gladiators, forbidding any free woman under twenty to appear in the arena. Nevertheless the trend continued well into the days of the empire. Nero's tribute games to his mother featured women fighting as gladiators, driving chariots and hunting animals. Emperor Domitian, who loved novelty in the arena, arranged for night time fights between female gladiators and dwarfs to be held by torchlight.

A marble relief depicting two female gladiators was discovered in modern day Turkey. Dating from between the first and second century AD, the relief shows 'Achillia' and 'Amazone' in combat and armed with *gladii* (the short sword of the gladiator), large shields, leg greaves and *manica* (arm protectors). The gladiators are both wearing loin cloths instead of tunics and neither has a helmet, which is maybe to show the audience they are not men. The fight between Achillia and Amazone must have been important enough to warrant an expensive artwork to be commissioned, but the sight of female gladiators offended the sensibilities of many Roman males. This was certainly true of Emperor Septimus Severus, who banned female gladiators in around AD 200. The Roman male position is scornfully summed up by Juvenal:

> *Who has not seen the dummies of wood they slash at and batter, whether with swords or with spears, going through all the moves?*

These are the girls who blast on trumpets in honour of Flora. Or, it may be, they have deeper designs, and are really preparing for the arena itself. How can a woman be decent, sticking her head in a helmet, denying her sex she was born with? Manly feats they adore, but they wouldn't want to be men, poor weak things (they think), how little they really enjoy it! What great honour it is for a husband to see, at an auction where his wife's effects are up for sale, belts, greaves, manica and plumes! Hear her grunt and groan as she works at it, parrying, thrusting; See her neck bent down under the weight of her helmet. Look at the rolls of bandage and tape, so her legs look like tree trunks. Then have a laugh for yourself after the practice is over, amour and weapons are put down, and she squats as she uses the vessel.

Ah, degenerate girls of the line of our praetors and consuls, tell us, whom have you seen got up in any such fashion, panting and sweating like this? No gladiators wench, no tough strip-tease broad would ever so much as attempt it.

Types of Gladiators

The first gladiators were based on foreign warriors who had been defeated in battle by the Roman legions. The armour and weaponry of these warriors was sent back to the capital to be used in the staging of *munera*. This gave Roman citizens the chance to see the armaments and fighting styles of their beaten enemies. The earliest gladiators therefore took on ethnic names such as Thracian and Gaul, but these evolved over time as their once subjugated namesakes became permanent fixtures of the Roman Empire.

One of the original gladiator types was the *samnite*, based on the Samnite people defeated by Rome in the fourth century BC. The *samnite* gladiator was equipped with a large rectangular shield, short 50 cm (1.6 foot) *gladius* sword, a wide leather belt, a visored helmet with a plume and one leg greave.

Over time the *samnite* would evolve into the *secutor* (meaning 'chaser') who fought wearing a smooth round helmet, with two small eye holes. The helmet was deliberately designed to limit the *secutor*'s field of vision, requiring him to get in close to an opponent to properly attack him. However even a trident point would not pass through the eye holes of a *secutor* helmet. It was for this reason the *secutor* was usually pitted against the *retarius* (net fighter), who carried a trident.

The Romans believed that two equally matched but differently armed gladiators should meet each other in combat. This could mean a heavily armoured gladiator with limited movement was paired with a lightly protected but more agile counterpart. The point was to make the fight fairer and more interesting for the spectators. It also meant people could have a favourite type.

The *retarius* was often considered one of the sillier types and often scorned and criticised. This is maybe because, armed only with a trident, fishing net, and a metal shoulder guard called a *galerus*, the *retarius* was often forced to duck, dive and run away from his opponent rather than stand and fight. He was therefore often chased by the *secutor*, who needed to get close to be effective.

The *retarius* was also chased by the heavily armed *mumillo* (sea fish), who had a stylised fish crest on his helmet, carried a large rectangular shield and was further protected by a leg greave and a *manica* on his arm. The *murmillo*, who probably evolved from the heavily armed Gaul, was a favourite of Emperor Domitian. One spectator at the Colosseum was misfortunate to find this out the hard way, as Suetonius recounts:

> *A householder who said that a Thracian gladiator was a match for the murmillo, but not for the giver of*

the games, he caused to be dragged from his seat and thrown into the arena to dogs, with this placard: 'A favourer of the Thracians who spoke impiously'.

It was common for a *murmillo* to be paired with the lightly armed Thracian, who fought with a 40 cm- (1.3 foot-) long curved scimitar, a small, circular shield and a distinctive crested helmet. Often the more heavily armed gladiators of the same kind would fight each other, such as the *holomachus*, protected by greaves, a shield and large crested helmet, and carrying a lance and *gladius*. On occasion he would battle with a *dimachaerus*, who carried no shield, wore only light armour and used two scimitars for attack.

An altogether different kind of gladiator were the *equites*, who fought each other from horseback with lances, throwing spears and swords. The *sagittari* were mounted archers, whose skill on horseback and with a bow made them a favourite with the crowd. The essedari battled each other from horse-drawn war chariots in the style of Celtic warriors from Britain.

NOVELTY ACTS

The *andabatae* were criminals that had not been trained at a *ludus*, but were instead intended as a sort of gladiatorial comic relief. Two *andabatae* would fight on horseback armed only with a *gladius* and wearing helmets without eye holes, meaning they were fighting blindfolded. They would therefore stagger around the arena floor slashing at each other until one was fortunate enough to chance upon a killing blow. Sometimes the *andabatae* fought from horseback, in a sadistic precursor to the medieval joust.

Fights between the *praegenarii* was another gladiatorial novelty act intended to warm up the crowd. The *praegenarii* were dressed like gladiator clowns and fought each other with the wooden *rudis* used in gladiator training. Often the *praegenarii* were dwarves, or men with physical disabilities or missing limbs.

The gladiators who fought against the wild animals were called *bestarii* and those who hunted them were called *venatores*, who used spears and bow and arrows on foot or on horseback. *Naumachiae* were gladiators who performed in simulated naval battles (see page 84).

The luckiest type of fighter was called a *rudiarius* – a freed gladiator. This freedom was granted by the emperor or organiser of the games to a gladiator who had fought with particular *virtus*, or one that had won many contests in a row. In a special ceremony the *rudiarius* would be given the wooden training *rudis* as a symbol of his freedom and allowed to walk from the arena. This occasion was rare, but a great crowd-pleaser when it happened.

Although a celebrated free man, a *rudiarius* was not allowed to become a Roman citizen, but his children could. If he did not have enough money to retire, a *rudiarius* could have his pick of positions. These could include working for the emperor or Roman noble as a bodyguard; training new gladiators as a *doctores*; working in the arena as a referee; or returning to a *ludus* as a gladiator. *Rudiarii* returning to the arena always attracted a big crowd, and Emperor Tiberius is known to have offered 100,000 sesterces to any *rudiarius* who returned to fight.

A famous example of a returning gladiator is Flamma, who was awarded the *rudis* four times, but every time chose to remain a gladiator. His gravestone in Sicily features the following inscription:

> *Flamma, secutor, lived 30 years, fought 34 times, won 21 times, fought to a draw 9 times, defeated 4 times, a Syrian by nationality. Delicatus made this for his deserving comrade-in-arms.*

THE ARENA

Gladiator fights were intended to be public spectacles from the time of the first Roman *munera*. As these events grew larger and more extravagant, purpose-built arenas were constructed in which to hold them. In Rome in the first and second centuries BC *munera* were mostly presented in the Roman Forum, where some limited makeshift seating was erected for growing numbers of the public. Julius Caesar built the first wooden Roman amphitheatre, which provided seating for spectators around a central elliptical-shaped arena where the action was staged. The first stone amphitheatre was constructed in Rome in 29 BC by Titus Statilius Taurus, although it was later destroyed in the great fire of AD 64.

Arenas sprang up in other Roman provinces in the days of the late republic. In 70 BC an oval arena was built in Pompeii that could seat twelve thousand people. Further afield amphitheatres were built in Lyon, France and Merida in Spain. As Rome became an empire, foreign Roman towns and cities would prove their dedication to the emperor cult by building increasingly impressive amphitheatres. In Arles, France a massive stone amphitheatre was constructed featuring an arena 69 by 38 metres (226 by 125 feet) in area, and seating for twenty-three thousand spectators. In El Djem in modern day Tunisia, a monumental amphitheatre was constructed with seating for forty thousand people in AD 232.

By the third century there were over two hundred amphitheatres across the Roman Empire. Every one of these buildings took their design from the largest amphitheatre of the ancient world and mother of them all – the Colosseum.

The Colosseum

The Great Fire of Rome in AD 64 had cleared the way for rebuilding, both physically and symbolically. Rome had undergone a period of civil war after Nero's suicide in AD 68, which left the city bruised and divided. In AD 70 Emperor Vespasian began the construction of the *Amphitheatrum Flavium*, on what was a lake in the grounds of Nero's hated golden palace. The new amphitheatre was designed to close the lid on the horrors of Nero's reign and once again celebrate the majesty of Rome. Ironically the Colosseum took its common name from the bronze statue of Nero – the *Colossus Neronis* – that stood close by.

Thousands of slaves and prisoners of war were used to drain the lake and remove tens of thousands of tons of earth. Solid rock foundations were then laid between 4 and 12 metres (13 and 39 feet) deep. Over 100,000 tons of travertine blocks were imported to build the structure, along with 300 tons of iron to clamp it all together. Many thousands of tons of marble were also used to line the building's façade and carve dozens of statues. The statues decorated the Colosseum's upper arches, at the top of the building's 50 metre- (164 foot-) high outer wall. When completed in AD 80 the Colosseum was a marvel of archways, steps, seating and Doric and

Corinthian columns, built around seven concentric rings that encircled the central elliptical arena. The arena measured 87 by 55 metres (285 by 180 feet) and was surrounded by a 5 metre- (16 foot-) high wall, above which rose several tiers of seating.

The seating was divided by class and rank, which observed Rome's social hierarchy. Closest to the arena was the Emperor's box, with the organiser's box situated across the arena on the opposite side. The seating next to these boxes was reserved for the vestal virgins and the senators, some of whom had regular seats decorated with carved plaques. Above them sat the knights and visiting dignitaries, followed by Roman aristocrats and citizens. The following tier was for poorer Roman citizens, as well as slaves and foreigners. The final rows were reserved for women – the wives, daughters and mothers of Roman senators and nobles.

This curious arrangement was perhaps explained by the sudden and all encompassing passion that could apparently strike a Roman woman of rank upon seeing a gladiator. After all, it had happened before (see the case of Eppia, see page 72). A similar affliction was not in store for the vestal virgins, who had sworn a vow of chastity. If this vow was broken the offending virgin was punished by being buried alive in an underground chamber called the Campus Sceleratus, with only enough food and water to last a few days.

While the crowd sat and enjoyed whatever appeared on the sand-covered arena floor, the real workings happened directly underneath it in the hypogeum. This was an elaborate series of tunnels, passageways and cells, where the animals and people to be executed were kept until making their entrance. This entrance would be facilitated by a system of ropes, pulleys and lifts, that would pull animals and humans from the hypogeum through thirty-six different trapdoors onto the arena floor. This meant, for example, a man tied to a frame could appear as if by magic in the centre of the arena. Then, animals could emerge from trapdoors dotted around the arena, ready to make their attack. They also allowed whole sets of trees and bushes to be quickly brought up to the top for the *venatio*, or a staged story from mythology; which were sometimes used as a novel way of executing slaves and criminals.

The Colosseum was also used to stage sea battles, called *naumachiae*. These only took place during the reign of Emperor Titus (AD 79–81), and in AD 81 Domitian became emperor and built the hypogeum, rendering *naumachiae* impossible. Cassius Dio recounts the *naumachiae* at the Colosseum's inauguration:

> *Titus suddenly filled this same theatre with water and brought in horses and bulls and some other domesticated animals that had been taught to behave in the liquid*

element just as on land. He also brought in people on ships, who engaged in a sea-fight there, impersonating the Corcyreans and Corinthians.

The flooding of the arena would have helped immensely with the cleaning of blood and visceral left behind. Following the construction of the hypogeum all that could be done to perish the sights and smells was to add a new layer of sand to the arena floor. As a result, the stench in the Colosseum became unbearable, especially on a hot day without a breeze. To counter the smell, jets of perfumed water were pumped up from tanks in the hypogeum and sprayed over the crowd through a sprinkler system.

The baking sun was kept off those in the higher tiers with an awning system of large sails that were suspended on large poles. Roman sailors were used to put together the rigging and hoist out the sails. These did not cover the seats nearest to the arena, but the senators occupying these seats stayed cool under large parasols. On one occasion, the spectators were denied the cooling awning and made to sit in the searing heat by the very man charged with organising their comfort – Emperor Caligula (see page 48). This would have been harsh medicine for the undeserving crowd, who may have been sitting in the sun for several days running. The inauguration games of the Colosseum were long indeed, lasting for over one hundred days.

A Day at the Games

The Colosseum's inaugural games followed a set sequence of events that had been tried and tested for some centuries, albeit now performed on a much larger scale. Trumpets heralded the start of the morning's animal events. Wild beasts, such as lions, tigers, panthers and leopards would bare their teeth, growl and pace the inside of their cages, which were lined up along the arena wall. Other animals such as bears, bulls and rhinoceros could suddenly appear through trapdoors on the sandy arena floor.

Some of the *bestarii* ready to do battle with these wild beasts were dressed as gladiators, and armed with swords, shields and helmets. Others fought in a tunic, armed only with a spear. Many of the animals, kept starved and locked up under the arena for days, would leap at the *bestarii* without provocation. Others cowered and slunk back into the furthest corners of their cages. These reluctant participants were forced out by attendants carrying torches of burning straw.

Sometimes animals were forced to fight with each other instead of with a *bestarius*. Different pairings were tried – a bull against an elephant, a lion against a crocodile, a leopard against a tiger, a buffalo against a rhinoceros. Rhinoceros were particular crowd pleasers, because they could be relied upon to be unpredictable. The poet Martial describes the people's pleasure when a rhinoceros that was being paraded around the arena bolted suddenly and gorged a nearby bull. Then the beast became calm and passive, until goaded back into a rage once more:

> *At length the fury we once knew returned. For with his double horn he tossed a heavy bear as a bull tosses dummies from his head to the stars…He lifted two steers with his mobile neck, to him yielded the fierce buffalo and the bison. A panther fleeing before him ran headlong upon the spears.*
>
> Martial, *De Spectaculis*, translated by T. R. Glover

The *bestarii* were often followed by animal athletics and circus acts, such as bull-riding and elephant dancing. Next was the animal hunt (*venatio*), the last event of the morning schedule. First, a set of trees and bushes emerged from below the arena. Then flocks of harmless herbivores such as ostriches and rabbits would be let loose to run frantically through the makeshift forest. Horse-riding bowmen (*sagatarii*) would ride after them and let loose their arrows among the flock. Then the most savage animals, such as lions and panthers appeared. More *venatores* would hunt them down, with spears, swords and on occasion, their bare hands. Emperor Commodus was a great lover of the *venatio*, and would enter the arena to hunt personally, or otherwise fling spears from the emperor's box.

The animal events would often not go according to plan. Martial describes one such occasion, when a pregnant boar was speared by a *venatore*:

> ...*a light spear having pierced a pregnant she-boar, one of her litter leaped forth from the wound of its wretched mother...was this a delivery? She would willingly have died wounded by more weapons, that this sad way to life might have been opened to all her young ones... nor did the litter lie still-born, but ran about while its mother was falling. Oh! how great invention is evoked by sudden chances!*

MIDDAY MAYHEM

Lunchtime was set aside for the public executions of slaves and criminals. For many Romans, this was a signal to leave the Colosseum and relieve themselves in the public toilets outside and take a bite to eat in the many nearby bars. To many, the executions were seen as bloodshed too far, a pointless spectacle that was without honour, as writer Seneca describes:

The men have no defensive armour. They are exposed
to blows at all points, and no one ever strikes in vain…
There is no helmet or shield to deflect the weapon.
What is the need of defensive armour, or of skill? All
these mean delaying death…The spectators demand
that the slayer shall face the man who is to slay him in
his turn; and they always reserve the latest conqueror
for another butchering. The outcome of every fight is
death, and the means are fire and sword. This sort of
thing goes on while the arena is empty.

But Martial offers a popular opposing view, that the executed man has been given his just deserts and his death restores the natural order:

Finally he met with the punishment he deserved; the
guilty wretch had plunged a sword into his father's throat
or his master's, or in his madness had robbed a temple of
its secret gold, or laid a cruel torch to Rome.

While many Roman citizens of rank and privilege considered the executions base and unnecessary, emperors like Commodus and Claudius, couldn't get enough. Claudius in particular was said to enjoy watching the expressions on people's faces as they died.

But the executions could become too repetitive for even the most bloodthirsty spectators, so the organisers thought up new ways to keep the slaughter interesting. One type of execution popular during the reign of Nero was the *tunica molesta*, a shirt covered in pitch or soaked in some other flammable substance. The victim was made to wear the shirt before being crucified, and set alight while on the cross.

Another form of execution pitted one condemned man armed with a *gladius* against an unarmed man. The armed man would be forced to chase and catch the other (or be encouraged to do so by attendants carrying hot branding irons), and stab him to death. He was then made to hand the *gladius* to the next condemned man entering the arena, who would in turn begin the chase. This continued until the last man standing was finished off by a *ventore*.

At the end of such an event two men dressed as mythological figures would enter the arena – Charon the ferryman, carrying a two handled mallet, and the god Mercury, who brandished a long rod of iron with a red-hot end. As the pair walked among the corpses, Mercury would poke them with his smoldering point and Charon would bash them with his hammer. This would ensure that nobody was shamming. Sometimes the executions followed a story from mythology, like that of Prometheus. Prometheus was the Greek Titan who stole fire from Zeus to give to humans. He was consequently punished by having his liver devoured by an eagle, for eternity. Martial describes the rendition of Prometheus for the arena, an eagle in this instance being replaced by a wild boar:

As first, bound down upon the Scythian rock, Prometheus with ever-renewed vitals feasted the untiring vulture, so has Laureolus, suspended on no feigned cross, offered his defenseless entrails to a Caledonian bear. His mangled limbs quivered, every part dripping with gore, and in his whole body no shape was to be found... This criminal had surpassed the crimes of ancient story, and what had been fabulous, was in his case a real punishment.

ENTER THE GLADIATORS

An afternoon at the areana brought the event everybody had been waiting for and the amphitheatre would be brimming with excitement. First a procession entered, led by servants carrying the gladiator's weapons and followed by trumpeters, scribes to take down the details of the day, blacksmiths to keep the weapons sharp, and the organiser of the games.

Then the trumpets announced the arrival of the gladiators, who would enter the arena dressed in colourful tunics and loin cloths. The gladiators then showed their muscles and prowess, by stretching and sparring with one other. After a period the gladiators left and the weapons were brought back in for inspection. Emperor Commodus often entered the arena personally to ensure the swords were sharp.

Then the arena was finally deserted, leaving the crowd in silent anticipation as it waited for the first pair of duelling gladiators. The spectators would not stay hushed for long, as the amphitheatre's musicians signalled the start of combat. Music accompanied every stage of the fight, following closely the peaks and troughs of battle, much like the score from a modern day film.

For the gladiators themselves, the long hours of attacking a *palus* and their respective drills with a *doctores* became suddenly relevant. It is perhaps understandable to wish that every gladiator fought the good fight and died heroically. But the figures alone register this impossible. When Emperor Trajan conquered Dacia he held games that lasted for one hundred and twenty-three days, during which over ten thousand gladiators were killed. Some gladiatorial contests would have been short, brutal and involved terrified men crying and soiling themselves. But others would have literally fought to the death, their deepest survival instincts allowing them any brutality to stay alive.

A battle concluded with one of the gladiators raising their index finger in submission. If the gladiator had fought valiantly and in accordance with the Roman *virtus* he was sometimes spared. If the crowd made a united chant of *mitte* (let him go) and the emperor agreed, the gladiator was granted a *missio*, or reprieve, and allowed to leave the arena alive. If the emperor (there are recorded cases of Caligula and Domitian rejecting the crowd's wishes) did not grant a *missio*, then the defeated gladiator was still expected to die with honour. To do this he would wrap his arms around his opponent's legs and allow him to administer a fatal thrust between his shoulder blades. The victor would then approach the emperor's box to be rewarded with a laurel wreath and a purse; the contents of which were determined by the emperor's generosity.

The defeated gladiator would be carried out on a stretcher and stripped of his weapons and armour, which would be recycled at the *ludus*. It is thought the average gladiator fight lasted for around twenty minutes, but there were other occasions when gladiators spent hours fighting. During these lengthier bouts, the referee would call for short breaks to let the exhausted gladiators catch their breath. There is a famous example of such a contest which took place during the Colosseum's inauguration. The two gladiators were the Gallic slave Priscus and a free man Versus. The story is described by Martial:

> As Priscus and Versus each drew out the contest and the struggle between the pair long stood equal, shouts loud and often sought discharge for the combatants. But Titus obeyed his own law (the law was that the bout

go on without shield until a finger be raised). What
he could do, he did, often giving dishes and presents.
But an end to the even strife was found: equal they
fought, equal they yielded. To both Titus sent wooden
swords and to both palms. Thus valor and skill had
their reward. This has happened under no prince but
you, Caesar: two fought and both won.

Martial's gushing tone probably reflects the good
feeling in the crowd caused by the emperor's decision
– both gladiators leaving as free men through the *Porta
Sanavivaria* (The Gate of Life).

Titus had another crowd-pleasing finale that brought
the day at the Colosseum to an end. Cassius Dio
explains:

He would throw down into the theatre from aloft little
wooden balls variously inscribed, one designating some
article of food, another clothing, another a silver vessel
or perhaps a gold one, or again horses, pack-animals,
cattle or slaves. Those who seized them were to carry
them to the dispensers of the bounty, from whom they
would receive the article named.

Spartacus

Much of our information about gladiators comes from sources such as funerary inscriptions, mosaics from ancient Roman houses and weapons and armour from preserved archeological sites, like the city of Pompeii. Occasionally a writer or commentator from the time describes the feats of heroic gladiators, such as Martial's account of Priscus and Versus. But most of the gladiators remain faceless and unremembered and their stories forgotten.

However, there is one better-known gladiator, whose legacy has survived the test of time. Spartacus was the slave gladiator who wanted nothing more than to escape Rome and the tyranny of the arena and return to his homeland of Thrace.

Spartacus belonged to a *ludus* in Capua, which was mostly made up of Gauls and Thracians. Spartacus was a former Roman legionary who had deserted, been caught, sold as a slave and sentenced to the *ludus*. According to the writers Plutarch and Florus, the *ludus* at Capua was particularly harsh, keeping its gladiators locked up in cramped confinement for the majority of every day.

Then, in AD 73 something unexpected happened – seventy-eight gladiators stole knives from the kitchen, overpowered the guards and jumped the *ludus* walls. The men leading the escape were the Gauls, Crixus and Oenomaus, and the Thracian Spartacus. As luck would have it, the escaped men chanced upon a wagon that was loaded with gladiatorial weapons. Now properly armed, the gladiators set up camp on top of Mount Vesuvius.

A small Roman force of three thousand legionnaires was sent to deal with the gladiators, who at that stage were not considered any kind of threat. Their commander, praetor Gaius Claudius Glaber set up camp at the bottom of the mount. This, in effect, laid siege to the rebel hideout as there was only one narrow path leading up to the top. Plutarch describes the action that followed:

> *The top of the hill, however, was covered with a thick growth of a wild vine, and Spartacus' men cut off the usable branches, and wove them into strong ladders of such strength and length that when they were fastened at the top they reached along the face of the cliff to the plain below. They descended on these to the plain below...The Romans did not know these things; and therefore their enemies surrounded them, threw them into confusion through the suddenness of their attack, put them to flight, and seized their camp.*

Plutarch, *Life of Crassus*, translated by Bernadotte Perrin

News soon spread of Spartacus' victory and tens of thousands of slaves flocked to join him. This new gladiator army wasted no time in attacking the Roman camps and towns around Campania, defeating any force that confronted them. By this stage Spartacus' army was no mere rabble of badly equipped slaves, but a well-armed and experienced fighting force, trained in the gladiator tradition by Spartacus and Crixus.

After a period of terrorising the Italian mainland, Rome began to take the gladiator army seriously and dispatched legions under the commands of consuls Gellius and Lentulus. At this time Crixus broke away from the main rebel force, taking with him the Gauls and the German gladiators. Gellius wasted no time in destroying Crixus' small army, but his legionaries were no match for Spartacus who had already defeated the hapless Lentulus. This was all worrying news for the senate, who realised there was a real threat that Spartacus might attack Rome itself. In response, the war against the rebel army was handed over to some real Roman muscle – the celebrated general and Roman aristocrat Marcus Licinius Crassus.

Spartacus retreated with his army through Lucania toward the southern coast of Italy. Here, he planned to make an escape to Sicily on board the Cilician pirate ships he had hired. In Sicily Spartacus planned to form a great slave army capable of taking on Rome. But he was double crossed by the Cilicians, and left stranded at the bottom of the Italian peninsula.

Fearing the rebels would turn and march on Rome, Crassus commanded his army to dig a ditch that would cut off Spartacus and stop him moving north. But the general must have been rattled, as he had asked the senate to call back both general Pompey from his campaign in Spain, and general Lucullus from Thrace. Spartacus dealt with the ditch by simply filling in a section with trees and leading his army north. But the tide had turned and Spartacus' men demanded they march to meet Crassus' army head on. The scene is described by Plutarch:

> *Spartacus, seeing there was no avoiding it, set all his army in array, and when his horse was brought him, he drew out his sword and killed him, saying, if he got the day, he should have a great many better horses of the enemies, and if he lost it, he should have no need of this. And so making directly towards Crassus himself, through the midst of arms and wounds, he missed him, but slew two centurions that fell upon him together. At last being deserted by those that were about him, he himself stood his ground, and, surrounded by the enemy, bravely defending himself, was cut in pieces.*

> Plutarch, *Life of Crassus*, translated by John Dryden

Unluckily for Crassus, Pompey arrived just in time to pick off many of the stragglers from Spartacus' army, and then took full credit for suppressing the rebellion. He was awarded a full triumph in Rome for his successes in Spain, whereas Crassus only received a simple ovation. Crassus showed no mercy to the six thousand prisoners of war captured from Spartacus' army. Every one of them was crucified along the Appian Way, the first ever Roman road originally built in 312 BC to suppress a uprising of the Samnite people.

Spartacus was a lowly gladiator who had shaken the very foundations of Rome, but his legacy was a dazzling one-off. True to its pragmatic nature, Rome learned a valuable lesson from the gladiator uprising and ensured that it never happened again. It did this by changing the systems in the *ludi* – gladiators were put in chains or locked in a cell when not in training, and their weapons were carefully stowed away in an armoury at the end of every day.

The Movies

SPARTACUS

Spartacus was the subject of one of the famous 1960s 'sword and sandal' films made on the Roman Republic, alongside *I, Claudius* and *Cleopatra*. The 1960 *Spartacus* blockbuster was made with an enormous budget ($12 million), a then almost entirely unknown director (Stanley Kubrick), ten thousand extras, and a celebrity cast which included Kirk Douglas, Laurence Olivier, Tony Curtis and Peter Ustinov (who won an Oscar for his role as *lanista* Lentulus Batiatus).

The movie, complete with the tagline – It roars with fierce excitement! – certainly caused a stir when it was released. Some scenes were too much for the censor, such as the homosexual innuendo from Crassus ('do you like oysters, or snails?') directed towards his boy slave Antoninus, who is consequently compelled to escape and join Spartacus.

Kubrick filmed the movie mostly on a sound stage (so the actors could 'fully concentrate') except for the battle sequences which were shot outside Madrid using eight thousand Spanish soldiers as extras. Many of the battle scenes had to be dropped from the movie as they were considered too gory by test audiences and Kirk Douglas himself. After the movie's release Kubrick distanced himself from it, saying:

> *In* Spartacus *I tried with only limited success to make the film as [historically] real as possible but I was up against a pretty dumb script which was rarely faithful to what is known about Spartacus.*

It is hard to overlook the many features of this film which certainly date it to the time – the wooden sets and painted backgrounds, the bunsen-burner camp fires, the overblown 'epic' score, Kirk Douglas' perfectly manicured crew cut. What remains less forgivable than the special effects are the historical inaccuracies, of which there are plenty.

There is only scene in which we are shown Spartacus' prowess in the arena – at the beginning in the Capua arena. Thracian by nationality, Spartacus is neither equipped like a Thracian gladiator, nor any other gladiator in Roman history. Instead he carries a miniature shield, with which he fends off attacks from a retarius, a type of gladiator that did not come into being until the imperial age. A retarius was a net fighter usually paired against the more heavily armed *murmillo* or *secutor* (see page 76) so combat against the very lightly armed Spartacus makes for an unlikely duel.

It is also odd that Glabus is called the commander of the garrison of Rome. No such garrison existed, which is why a rebel army such as Spartacus' actually presented a real threat to Rome. Instead wealthy Romans had small, private armies hired to protect them and their families. In the imperial age the praetorian guard acted as the emperor's bodyguard, although occasionally it would assassinate them (such as Caligula) and proclaim a new one (Claudius).

It is curious that in the film Spartacus does not die on the battlefield, but on the cross among the six thousand of his followers who were actually crucified. Many believe this to be a political statement on the part of the screenwriter Dalton Trumbo, who was blacklisted during the McCarthy Era. This is represented in the scene where slaves from Spartacus' army shout out 'I am Spartacus' to the searching Romans, thus protecting their leader and suggesting solidarity against the communist witch hunts of the time. The symbolic nature of this scene was probably lost on Hollywood reviewer Hedda Hopper, who wrote of *Spartacus*: 'The story was sold to Universal from a book written by a commie and the screen script was written by a commie, so don't go to see it.'

Political connotations aside, the line gave the movie the required moment of memorable sentimentality that the epic of one hundred and eighty-four minutes screamed out for. It has also provided material for many years of spoofs and send-ups that have ensured *Spartacus* remains in hearts and minds today.

GLADIATOR

Gladiator is a 2000 movie that set off a raft of new millennium historical epics, including *Troy, 300* and *Kingdom of Heaven*. *Gladiator* cost $103 million to make and was directed by Ridley Scott.

The story follows Maximus (Russell Crowe), a fictional Roman general who is favoured by Emperor Marcus Aurelius (Richard Harris) over his son Commodus. While on campaign Aurelius tells Maximus it is his wish to make him heir so he can restore the Roman Republic. He then invites Commodus (Joaquin Phoenix) into his tent to tell him he will not become emperor. Commodus then strangles his father and orders Maximus killed. Maximus escapes and tries to get home to his wife and child, but they have been murdered by Commodus' men. The film then flashes forward to a point in the future when Maximus has become a gladiator. Despite his disinterest in his new occupation, Maximus turns out to be the greatest gladiator of all time and is soon fighting in the Colosseum. Events quickly unfold and soon Maximus is involved in a plot to topple Commodus. In a final showdown in the Colosseum Maximus kills Commodus, but then dies himself.

Gladiator had many script revisions, including several made by Crowe himself at the time of shooting. It was said Crowe took some convincing to say the climatic line to Commodus before killing him in the arena:

> *My name is Maximus Decimus Meridius. Commander of the Armies of the North. General of the Felix Legions. Loyal servant to the true Emperor, Marcus Aurelius. Father to a murdered son, husband to a murdered wife – and I will have my vengeance, in this life or the next.*

It is perhaps the number of revisions and the different input of so many, that has left the movie with so many glaring inaccuracies. Ridley Scott did hire historical advisors to make the film 'as accurate as possible' although many of them asked to have their names removed upon seeing it. Scott also said that many of the historical facts were 'too unbelievable' to include. It is a pity the facts were considered such a minor part of a recreation of history, especially considering the time and attention spent on CGI sets to rebuild large parts of Rome and the Colosseum.

It is also a shame that a fictional character needed to be introduced to carry the story of one of Rome's greatest tyrants, Commodus. Commodus did not murder his father Marcus Aurelius, nor would any emperor of that time have considered going back to the republican age. In *Gladiator*, Commodus was only emperor for few years before being killed in the Colosseum. In reality Commodus reigned for twelve years before he was finally assassinated by being strangled to death in his own bath.

In *Gladiator* Commodus was a simpering, weaselly figure with dark hair. In reality Commodus cut a strapping figure – he was tall and athletic with light curly hair and a beard. While comparing himself to Hercules and describing his mighty gladiatorial deeds on statue inscriptions, Commodus was not known to fight actual gladiators with real weapons. He was happy to use steel on animals and those who could not defend themselves, but at all other times he used a wooden sword. It is highly improbable, therefore, that he would have fought Maximus with a real *gladius* in the film's climatic last scene. It is also unthinkable that the praetorian guard would not have stepped in to save Commodus from being slain by a gladiator.

As with *Spartacus*, the weapons, armour and types of Gladiator depicted in *Gladiator* bear no resemblance to those of the time. It makes the further mistake of placing a tiger in the arena with Maximus, which clearly goes against the sequence of events performed at nearly all gladiator games in the imperial age. The animals were only ever used during the morning *venatio* and never in conjunction with the gladiator fights of the afternoon. While such points can be easily dismissed, there are equally no valid reasons for continually rejecting factual evidence to justify creative licence.

The Decline of the Games

By the end of third century AD a frayed Roman Empire was beginning to become undone. Its frontiers were under increasing attack by Barbarians, Goths and a rejuvenated Persian Empire. As a result the Roman army became more important than ever before, and used its power to supplant any emperor it did not like. Between AD 239 and 285 Rome went through no less than forty-nine emperors. But the army's increased role put a heavy drain on the imperial wallet. Emperors tried devaluing the currency, but this only served to increase inflation over the long term.

The Empire's outer reaches felt the pinch most acutely. There was certainly not enough money in the provincial coffers to organise gladiatorial games in dedication of the emperor cult, which was becoming more and more irrelevant. For centuries the emperors of Rome had provided its many territories with peace, prosperity and the protection of Rome. But word of the emperors' antics also spread far and wide. To far away Roman provinces, distant from the toxic centre of Rome, these tales must have acted as ancient soap operas, and with emperors such as Caligula and Commodus playing the starring roles, a new scandalous episode would always be forthcoming.

It was obvious to all that there was something rotten at the heart of Rome. While it provided wealth and material comforts it gave nothing in the way of spiritual guidance. Ironically a new cult from the east began to fill this spiritual void. Christianity had crept up slowly from the time of Tiberius and caught like wildfire from the middle part of the imperial age. Then, in AD 312 the Roman Emperor Constantine, converted to it.

The Christian view was that battles to the death and executions for public entertainment were not only morally corrupt but that they went against the doctrine of Christianity. Besides which, many Christians had been persecuted across the empire and had ended up dying a martyr's death in the amphitheatre. Nero, in particular, had blamed Christians for the burning of Rome and had thousands of Christians executed in the Colosseum. The effect of this was not just to alienate Christians from the Roman Empire, but also to strengthen the Christian cause, through their martyrdom.

It is perhaps not surprising, considering the fate of many of his Christian brothers and sisters that Constantine issued an edict banning the gladiatorial games:

In times in which peace and peace relating to domestic affairsprevail bloody demonstrations displease us. Therefore, we order that there may be no more gladiator combats. Those who were condemned to become gladiators for their crimes are to work from now on in the mines. Thus they pay for their crimes without having to pour their blood.

But despite Constantine's ban the games continued throughout the first half of the fourth century, especially in Italy. A further series of bans, restrictions and regulations by different emperors failed to quell the numbers of games being held – instead they continued for several decades more.

In AD 365 Emperor Valentinian made the execution of Christians in the arena illegal (although this did not apply to non-Christians) and restricted the amount that was allowed to be spent on the gladiator games. In AD 393, Emperor Theodosius made Christianity the state religion, although there is evidence of games being held in the same year. Theodosius' son, Emperor Honorius, banned gladiator games in AD 399, and closed down the *ludi* in Rome in AD 400.

In AD 404, Honorius again banned the games following the martyrdom of St Telemachus. Telemachus was a monk who had entered the arena in an eastern Roman province (it is not known exactly where) to intervene in a gladiator fight. Instead of heeding the monk's calls the gladiators were ordered to tear the old man limb from limb. Although horrifying Honorius into issuing his AD 404 edict, gladiator games continued to take place until the 440s, after which there are no further records of any fights.

Chariot racing, animal hunts and fights between animals and men continued in the Roman city of Constantinople. The city of Rome had by this time been overrun and now belonged to the Kingdom of the Goths. The Colosseum fell into disrepair over the following centuries, its purpose all but forgotten until its rediscovery in the modern age. In the beginning of the sixth century fights between men and animals were finally banned in the eastern Roman Empire, and a few decades later the animal hunts followed suit.

THE CORRUPTING CONTESTS

The Christian position was that encouraging the enjoyment of the gladiator fights and public executions turned otherwise moral men into savages. This sentiment is described by Saint Augustine, who tells the story of his friend Alypius, who were reluctantly taken to the games:

> *He had gone on to Rome…and there he was carried away again with an incredible passion for the*

gladiatorial shows. For, although he had been utterly opposed to such spectacles and detested them, one day he met by chance a company of his acquaintances and fellow students returning from dinner; and, with a friendly violence, they drew him, resisting and objecting vehemently, into the amphitheatre, on a day of those cruel and murderous shows.

He protested to them: 'Though you drag my body to that place and set me down there, you cannot force me to give my mind or lend my eyes to these shows. Thus I will be absent while present, and so overcome both you and them.' When they heard this, they dragged him on in…But Alypius kept his eyes closed and forbade his mind to roam abroad after such wickedness. Would that he had shut his ears also! For when one of the combatants fell in the fight, a mighty cry from the whole audience stirred him so strongly that, overcome by curiosity and still prepared (as he thought) to despise and rise superior to it no matter what it was, he opened his eyes and was struck with a deeper wound in his soul than the victim whom he desired to see had been in his body.

Thus he fell more miserably than the one whose fall had raised that mighty clamor which had entered through his ears and unlocked his eyes to make way for the wounding and beating down of his soul…For, as soon as he saw the blood, he drank in with it a savage temper, and he did not turn away, but fixed his eyes on the bloody pastime, unwittingly drinking in the madness — delighted with the wicked contest and drunk with blood lust. He was now no longer the same man who came in, but was one of the mob he came into, a true companion of those who had brought him thither. Why need I say more? He looked, he shouted, he was excited, and he took away with him the madness that would stimulate him to come again: not only with those who first enticed him, but even without them; indeed, dragging in others besides.

Saint Aurelius Augustine, *The Confessions Of St. Augustine*, translated by Albert C. Outler

But there was a further point about the gladiator fights in particular, which did not fit with Christian ideals. In a sense the fights gave the *infamis*, the disgraced, a chance to redeem himself. A gladiator could win his salvation by displaying Roman *virtus* — bravery, courage, contempt for death — and be granted his life back by the people and emperor. But in the Christian world only God could offer this salvation, and it certainly was not granted as a reward for prowess with a sword. Nor was God's love only on offer for a select few, born into positions of wealth and privilege, but open to everyone — slaves, foreigners, and gladiators alike.

In the end Christianity simply filled the hole that

Rome had dug itself to fall into. The gladiator fights did not end with a bang or exit with a final flourish. Instead the spectacles ebbed away slowly, as the glory of Rome faded, and its ideals became obsolete.

SAMURAI

Introduction

Perhaps the greatest samurai who ever lived was Miyamoto Musashi. He was something of an eccentric – he paid little attention to his appearance, was often described as 'unwashed', and was frequently late to his duelling bouts. Musashi was cultivated and accomplished in calligraphy, painting and sculpture, and had killed many men before he left his teens. He was a swordplay strategist and dispatched more warriors in duels than any other known samurai. Musashi often fought with sticks, branches and even the oar from a boat. However, his skill with a samurai blade was such that he could split a grain of rice on a man's forehead without drawing blood.

Musashi recorded his accomplishments in *Go Rin No Sho* (*The Book of Five Rings*), a manual of sword fighting strategy:

> *I went from province to province duelling with strategists of various schools, and not once failed to win, even though I had as many as sixty encounters. This was between the ages of thirteen and twenty-eight or twenty-nine.*

Shinmen Musashi No Kami Fujiwara No Genshin was

born in 1584, although he became known as Miyamoto Musashi after his mother's clan. By the time he was seven both of his parents had died and Musashi went to live with his uncle Dorin, who raised and educated him. Musashi's first duel was against a travelling samurai called Arima Kihei, who had posted a public notice asking for opponents. Musashi wrote down his name, and the challenge was accepted. When the news reached Dorin he was horrified and tried to call off the duel by explaining to Kihei that his nephew was only thirteen. But Kihei insisted that for his honour to remain intact the duel would have to proceed – unless Musashi showed up at the scheduled time to offer his profuse apologies. Instead, on the morning of the duel Dorin arrived on Musashi's behalf and began apologising. As this was happening Musashi himself strode into the hall, grabbed a quarterstaff and charged at Kihei, killing him instantly.

Two years later, after defeating another samurai master, the fifteen-year-old Musashi embarked on a warrior pilgrimage of the country. It did not take long for Musashi's reputation to reach mythological proportions and with good reason – the young samurai had won more duels than anyone in the history of Japan. Musashi also seemed able to turn virtually any object into a lethal weapon, and often chose to fight with the wooden *bokken* instead of a steel sword.

At the age of twenty-one Musashi arrived in Kyoto, where he set about challenging the masters of the nearby Yoshioka school. He had soon killed every one of them, leaving only twelve-year-old Matashichiro as head of the Yoshioka family. Despite the school's dwindling numbers, a challenge was issued to Musashi to fight a final duel at the Ichijoji temple on Kyoto's outskirts. But it was a trap. Instead of meeting another samurai master, Musashi was to be ambushed by a small army of the remaining Yoshioka clan, armed with bows and arrows, swords and arquebuses.

Up until that point Musashi had been late for every one of the Yoshioka duels, much to the disgust of his opponents. But on the day of the final duel he arrived some hours early, suspecting he had pushed the Yoshioka family into an act of retribution.

Musashi hid himself and lay in wait. Sure enough, a number of armed warriors soon arrived to make preparations for their ambush. Musashi then leapt from his hiding place and wasted no time in slaughtering his way through the Yoshioka army to Matashichiro, who he killed before escaping unharmed. The battle left the Yoshioka school without a leader or many students, and certainly without a reputation.

OARS AND SWALLOW CUTS

Miyamoto Musashi was twenty-eight at the time of his most legendary duel. It took place against his most deadly and dangerous opponent yet – samurai master Sasaki Kojirō.

Kojirō was known for his skill with a long straight sword, or *nodachi*, which he called 'the laundry drying pole.' Kojirō's style of swordplay was so popular he had set up a school to teach it. As part of their training students would learn Kojirō's signature stroke – the 'swallow cut'. This consisted of a horizontal slashing movement that was so fast and precise it looked like swallow's tail in flight. Kojirō was said to have ended the lives of many foes with this stroke.

The duel had been scheduled for the morning of 3 April 1612, on the Island of Funajima. However, as usual Musashi was running late, and there was no sign of him or his boat as Kojirō paced the island's shore. Musashi had simply slept in, and upon waking had no choice but to rush to the dinghy waiting to row him to the island. But as soon as the boat set off Musushi realised that he was only carrying his short *wakizashi* sword and had left his main sword, his *katana*, behind. Instead of turning back, the samurai set about carving himself a *bokken* from a spare oar as the dinghy continued across the water.

Kojirō's fury at his opponent's late arrival quickly

119

turned to mirth when he saw Musasahi's crudely fashioned weapon. But Musashi did not appear ruffled by Kojirō's taunts and simply held his weapon forward to let battle commence. The bout was as short as it was decisive. Kojirō made the first move, charging at Musashi and unleashing his swallow cut, which came so close to Musashi's head that it sliced off his topknot. But at the same moment Musashi had delivered a fatal blow with his oar. Kojirō fell forward onto his knees and then slumped backwards, his skull cracked open.

There are many different versions of this duel and much debate about the apparently improvised nature of Musashi's approach. Some argue that it was a pointed decision rather than coincidence that made Musashi choose an oar, which is far longer than the average *bokken* or sword. It was well known that Kojirō favoured the longer *nodachi*, making a duel hard work for an opponent with a shorter sword. Others suggest that Musashi showed up late deliberately, choosing the exact time when the tide turned so he could make a quick getaway should Kojirō's entourage turn on him. Others believe Musashi's lateness was an intentional ploy to upset and unnerve his opponents.

Mushashi gave up duelling in his early thirties. He fought in the war between the Toyotomi and Tokugawa clans in 1615 and helped the emperor quell the Christian uprising in 1637. But then Musashi began a quieter life of reflection:

When I reached thirty I looked back on my past. The previous victories were not due to my having mastered strategy. Perhaps it was natural ability, or the order of heaven, or that other schools' strategy was inferior. After that I studied morning and evening searching for the principle, and came to realise the 'Way of Strategy' when I was fifty.

Mushashi retired to a life in a cave at sixty to write his *Go Rin No Sho*. It was in this cave that Mushashi died in 1645; his body was found sitting bolt upright with his *wakizashi* in his belt. Mushashi has been the subject of many movies and books, not just because of his duelling prowess, but because he represented the ideal of the samurai warrior. In *Go Rin No Sho* Musashi often emphasised the importance of mastering many art forms on the path to becoming a true samurai strategist. His many books on strategy and the philosophy of swordplay are still studied in *Kendo* schools today.

CODES OF HONOUR

Samurai were the ancient fighting class of Japan who lived by a strict honour code, *bushido*, or 'the way of the warrior'. A samurai would showcase his *bushido* virtues on the battlefield, where he would seek out an enemy warrior of equal rank and social standing to engage in single combat. He would find a suitable candidate by issuing a challenge at the edge of battle and waiting for a response.

When this came, the warrior, adorned with flags and family crests, would proudly yell out his name and charge into the fray. Early samurai first engaged each other in a mounted archery duel. This required a huge amount of skill and training, as a rider had to release the reins to shoot his bow while maintaining control of his horse. If neither party was victorious in the archery bout, both would dismount and continue fighting on the ground with swords, daggers and even bare hands if necessary. Sometimes a contest between two famous samurai would create a pause in the fighting so soldiers from both sides could watch.

The victorious samurai was duty-bound to chop off his opponent's head, which he would later submit to his lord or emperor for inspection. Samurai would rather die than be defeated, and those captured, or not finished off on the battlefield, were expected to perform *seppuku*, or disembowelment, more commonly known today as *harikiri* (belly-slitting). *Seppuku* made up an important part of *bushido*, and it was under this code that the samurai dominated Japan for over seven hundred years.

History

The samurai and their fighting techniques – developed for close-quarter, one-on-one combat – arose from Japan's landscape and geographical location. Japan is an archipelago along the eastern side of mainland Asia, and separated from it by the Sea of Japan. This treacherous stretch of water is subject to an annual monsoon which brings typhoons and storms that ravage the Japanese coastline. This made a sea voyage to Japan a hazardous and potentially fatal endeavour, and ensured the country was left in seclusion for many centuries. Japan's history, therefore, is one of long periods of isolation broken by occasional incursions from outside.

But geography and weather patterns were not the only cause of this isolation. Japan often repelled visiting outsiders, and in the seventeenth century went so far as to close its borders altogether. But inside, the country was far from inert. Instead, for many centuries regional conflicts raged and samurai warlords fought for power. Japan's mountainous, forested landscape, however, did not always provide a flat plain where two large armies could engage. Japanese warfare took place at close quarters, with polearms, lances, bows and arrows and swords. The nature of this fighting favoured the rise of a warrior who spent his life training exclusively for one-on-one combat – the samurai.

The samurai first appeared around AD 8 during Japan's Heian Period. Emperor Kammu, dissatisfied with his own army's ineffectiveness, began to commission powerful clans to quash rebellions and uprisings. The fighting elite within each clan was the samurai, which translates as 'retainer' and 'to serve'. In the beginning the samurai were individual warriors, mercenaries from the country who fought for a fee. But by the eleventh century they became a warrior order and pledged allegiance to a particular clan chief. As this order became established, the samurai grew into a formidable fighting force.

By the end of the Heian Period in the late twelfth century, two clans had emerged, the Minamoto and the Taira. At the head of each clan was a *shogun*, a supreme military general charged with protecting the emperor and suppressing unrest. In 1185, the Minamoto defeated the Taira and a new military government began.

Minamoto Yoritomo became Japan's first *shogun* ruler, ushering in a new feudal age that was controlled exclusively by the samurai. For the next seven hundred and fifty years Japan's emperors would have only theoretical authority, and instead play puppet to the real ruler, the *shogun*. As such, wars between regional samurai warlords (*daimyos*) vying for supremacy blazed for over four centuries.

It was not all turmoil and national unrest. In the thirteenth century an unexpected event forced the warring clans to unite together against a common enemy – Kublai Khan's Mongol army. In 1274, 10,000 samurai came together to face a 40,000 strong Mongol force, which had sailed from China and brought with it poison-tipped arrows and exploding iron bombs. Bad weather, however, was to be the Mongols' undoing. Heavy thunderstorms lashed the landing boats and the samurai were able to slaughter the Mongols in shallow water. Anticipating another attack, the samurai constructed a 20 kilometre (12 mile) wall around Hakata Bay, on the island of Kyushu. The Mongols themselves spent four years trying to settle matters diplomatically. But every time they sent an envoy for talks the samurai simply executed him.

Finally, in 1281, 5,000 ships carrying 140,000 Mongol warriors set sail for Japan. The samurai were ready – 40,000 warriors prepared to board the Mongol fleet on small boats and stop them reaching the shore. Then, in a seemingly providential moment, a typhoon swept across the Sea of Japan and destroyed the Mongol fleet. This, the Japanese felt, was divine intervention, and they called the wind *kamikaze* – 'wind of the gods'.

MUSKETS AND MISSIONARIES

The samurai would not stay united for long. The Era of the Warring States' from 1333 to 1573 produced dozens of inter-regional clashes, which in turn put the services of the samurai in high demand. Then, in 1543 a chance shipwreck changed the face of Japanese warfare and would later inform its policy on foreign influence. A small fleet of Portuguese merchants was washed up on the rocky Japanese coastline. When the merchants appeared before *daimyo* Oda Nobunaga they presented something of great interest – the arquebus musket. Realising the musket's potential, Nobunaga made a deal with the Portuguese: if they brought him supplies of this new weapon he would let their missionaries preach in his territories.

It was a smart move, one which saw Oda Nobunaga gain supremacy over the other states and in 1573 become *shogun* of all Japan. Although he was assassinated ten years later, Nobunaga is considered Japan's great unifier, who consolidated the different factions of the Warring Era under his rule. Nobunaga's successor Toyotomi Hideyoshi would set about increasing the samurai's powers with his 'sword hunt' edict. This aimed to disarm private armies by making it illegal for anyone except samurai to carry weapons. Hideyoshi also buoyed the numbers of his samurai army by recruiting lower-class samurai foot soldiers armed with spears, firearms and bows and arrows.

Hideyoshi placed so much confidence in his new army that in 1592 he even tried to invade China. The invasion failed when Hideyoshi's forces were repelled at sea by the heavily armoured Korean 'turtle' ships, a type of enclosed, floating tank armed with a single cannon.

Hideyoshi died in 1598 and once again Japan was thrown into a period of bloody civil war. This ended in 1600 at the Battle of Sekigahara, fought between 85,000 of *daimyo* Tokugawa Ieyasu's samurai and 130,000 enemy samurai from the west. Ieyasu won the battle and began two hundred and fifty years' of *shogun* rule under the Tokugawa family. He established his government at Edo (modern-day Tokyo) and set about creating an official hierarchy of social castes, with the samurai at the top, followed by farmers, artisans and merchants.

With Japan united under *Shogun* Ieyasu, there was very little for the samurai to do except hope for an uprising so their services would be required. Such an event did occur in 1638, when a group of Christian peasants and lordless samurai rose up in what is known as the Shimabara Rebellion. The *shogun* sent a force of 125,000 samurai to crush the rebellion and remove the heads of 37,000 prisoners – a clear message to any likeminded insurgents. The outside influence of foreign Christians was blamed for the uprising, and in response Japan closed its borders to all outsiders.

For the next two hundred and fifty years Japan was a

closed society that had no contact with the outside world. This was called the Edo Period, a time of peace, with no need for armies of samurai. The *shogun* ordered these armies be disbanded and tens of thousands of samurai became unemployed. Out-of-work samurai without a master to serve were called *ronin*, or 'wave men'; destined to wander aimlessly, like the waves in the sea. *Ronin* usually drifted from town to town, visiting martial art schools and challenging its masters to duels.

In an attempt to busy the samurai they were encouraged to learn arts such as calligraphy and poetry and follow the teachings of Buddhism. Many samurai gave up their swords to become bureaucrats, farmers and teachers; professions that would have been unthinkable to samurai before them. The beginning of the end for samurai came in 1854, when American gunboats forced Japan to reopen its doors to foreigners. The country's feudal system was quickly phased out and in 1868 the samurai class was abolished.

The Way of the Warrior

Bushido or 'the way of the warrior' included the virtues of loyalty, honour, rectitude, respect, courage, benevolence, obedience, honesty, duty, filial piety (duty to one's family and ancestors) and self-sacrifice. *Bushido* was influenced by Buddhism, Zen, Confucianism and Shintoism. Buddhism taught a warrior not to fear death, as he would be reincarnated in the next life. Zen helped a warrior 'empty his mind' and maintain clarity in battle. Confucianism encouraged morality and self-sacrifice. Shintoism advocated loyalty, patriotism and ancestor worship.

While *bushido* was an unwritten code with many variations, some *daimyo* made sure their samurai were given a strict list of regulations to live by. The following is a list of 'House Codes' by *daimyo* Kiyomasa Katō (1562–1611).

Codes which all samurai should follow, regardless of rank:

1. One should not be negligent in the way of the retainer. One should rise at four in the morning, practise sword technique, eat one's meal, and train with the bow, the

gun, and the horse. A well-developed retainer should become even more so.

2. If one should want diversions, he should make them outdoor pastimes such as falconry, deer-hunting and wrestling.

3. For clothing, anything between cotton and natural silk will do. A man who squanders money for clothing and brings his household finances into disorder is fit for punishment. Generally one should concern himself with armour appropriate for his social position and use his money for martial affairs.

4. When associating with one's ordinary companions, one should limit the meeting to one guest and one host, and the meal should consist of plain brown rice. When practising the martial arts, however, one may meet with many people.

5. As for decorum at the time of a campaign, one must be mindful that he is a samurai. A person who loves beautification where it is unnecessary is fit for punishment.

6. The practice of *Noh Drama* is absolutely forbidden. When one unsheathes his sword, he has cutting a person down on his mind. Thus, as all things are born from being placed in one's heart, a samurai who practises dancing, which is outside of the martial arts, should be ordered to commit seppuku.

7. One should put forth great effort in matters of learning.

One should read books concerning military matters, and direct his attention exclusively to the virtues of loyalty and filial piety. Reading Chinese poetry, linked verse, and waka is forbidden. One will surely become womanised if he gives his heart knowledge of such elegant and delicate refinements. Having been born into the house of a warrior, one's intentions should be to grasp the long and the short swords and to die.

8. If a man does not investigate into the matter of *Bushido* daily, it will be difficult for him to die a brave and manly death. Thus it is essential to engrave this business of the warrior into one's mind well.

9. The above conditions should be adhered to night and day. If there is anyone who finds these conditions difficult to fulfill, he should be dismissed, an investigation should be quickly carried out, it should be signed and sealed that he was unable to mature in the Way of Manhood, and he should be driven out. On this, there can be no doubt.

Of the *bushido* virtues, loyalty to one's master and self-sacrifice were arguably the most important. A famous example can be found in the story of samurai Kusunoki Masashige. In 1331, Emperor Go-Daigo was trying to reclaim power by staging a revolt against the *shogun*. Many samurai joined the emperor, including Masashige, who became his champion and won many victories on his behalf. But then the emperor ordered Masashige to attack the *shogun*'s army in a battle both knew he could not possibly win. Instead of refusing the request, Masashige said he wished he had seven more lives to lay down for the emperor and then rode away to his death.

WEAPONS OF WAR

To reach Masashige's level of *bushido* a lifetime of training was required. A boy born into the samurai class began his training at the age of five. He was taught archery, horsemanship, wrestling, spear fighting, and, from the sixteenth century onwards, how to handle firearms. These firearms were the heavy and clumsy Portuguese arquebuses that employed the matchlock system. This required the user to light a long fuse which ran into the touch hole to spark the charge. This gave the rifleman time to take aim before the weapon fired, as opposed to earlier versions, which required a live match to be dropped into the touch hole.

The arquebuses were not welcomed by the samurai. It was considered offensive and dishonourable that such a clumsy weapon could anonymously kill a samurai warrior. A samurai, after all, devoted his life to the ritual of warfare and training in the weaponry of one-on-one combat. Samurai were as accomplished with the sword as they were with the spear, lance and bow.

The samurai bow was specially designed to shoot an arrow from one third of the way up its shaft, which made it easier to fire while on horseback. The bows were made from bamboo strips, glued together and wrapped with rattan. This made the bow strong, rigid and tremendously hard to pull back. Arrows were also made from bamboo, covered with lacquer and tipped with steel arrowheads. There were many different types of arrowheads, including those that whistled as they flew. These arrows were let loose over the battlefield, with each whistle signalling a different battleground command. Another arrowhead constructed in a 'V' shape was specifically designed to cut the cords that held a warrior's armour in place, thus disrobing him.

The most important weapons training for a young samurai was in *kendo*, 'the way of the sword'. Like *bushido*, *kendo* was a belief system that encouraged self-sacrifice and discipline. The samurai sword, or *katana*, was a warrior's most prized possession. Swords were curved and perfectly balanced to enable a precise cutting action. The forging of a new sword was considered a sacred art, and would take expert swordsmiths weeks to complete.

The sword would begin as a lump of iron, which was repeatedly beaten, fired and folded until it became a steel blade. The genius of the samurai blade was that it contained two different types of steel – a soft, inner layer wrapped in a hard outer layer. The result was a razor-sharp cutting edge that could also absorb shock. This reduced the chances of the blade bending or snapping in combat, and also enabled it to be used as a shield, which samurai did not carry.

The technique of sword-fighting was called *kenjutsu*, 'the art of the sword.' A samurai would grasp the handle of his sword with both hands and train in the sixteen varieties of cutting, most of which used a downwards stroke. Young samurai practised their cuts on the bodies of executed criminals, so they could experience slicing human flesh. Hours were devoted to learning a single move, such as the *laido*. This was a single movement that pulled the sword from its scabbard, struck down the opponent, wiped the blade clean of blood, and returned the sword to its sheath.

When a boy turned thirteen he was initiated into the samurai fold in a ceremony called *genpuku*. He was given an adult name, a sword and samurai armour. Samurai armour consisted of steel or leather plates, laced together, and backed with cotton or silk cloth. An outfit often included a breastplate and large shoulder plates. A helmet was made from iron or steel, which later the samurai wore in conjunction with a metal mask. The masks featured sinister grinning mouths to intimidate opponents. Unlike the heavy armour suits of medieval Europe, samurai armour was designed to be lightweight enough to fire a bow and wield a sword, while giving the maximum possible protection. Every samurai carried two swords, one long (*katana*) and one short (*wakizashi*), which he would wear at all times and keep underneath his pillow while he slept. The *wakizashi* was not used for fighting, but instead to chop the heads off of defeated warriors, and to commit *seppuku*.

SUICIDE BY SEPPUKU

Seppuku was invented partly to provide a way out for trapped samurai who faced certain capture. By performing *seppuku* these warriors could die with honour and avoid execution by crucifixion or being burned alive. *Seppuku* was also performed by a warrior who had brought shame upon himself, his household, or his master. A *daimyo* or emperor could order a warrior to carry out *seppuku* as a punishment for criminal offences or even disgraceful behaviour.

Seppuku is thought to be one of the most painful ways to die, and as such it allowed a warrior to restore some of his honour, or avoid being labelled a coward. If he was trapped or cornered, a warrior could commit *seppuku* with any knife, sword or implement to hand. At all other times *seppuku* would be committed as part of a ceremony performed in front of spectators.

The ceremony began with the samurai bathing and dressing in a white kimono. He then ate his favourite meal and wrote a death poem. The warrior then took up his blade, plunged it into his abdomen and made a deep slice from left to right, with a final pull upwards. It was considered the height of bravery to leave entrails hanging from the open wound.

It took an agonisingly long time for a samurai to die from *seppuku*, so a second was on hand to help. He did this by cradling the samurai's head and cutting it off at the neck. This was a difficult and thankless task – the second gained no acknowledgment or credit for helping the samurai, but instead faced disgrace if the job was bungled. After instances of heads flying off and hitting officials or rolling away, the second was advised to leave a flap of skin on the neck, so the severed head remained attached to the body.

Another form of *seppuku* called *jumonji giri* was performed without a second and used a vertical instead of a horizontal cut. The samurai was then expected to hold his hands over his face while he bled to death.

One legendary story concerning *seppuku* is called *The 47 Ronin*, which remains a proud example of samurai devotion to the *bushido* code. In 1701 Asano Naganori, *daimyo* of the Ako clan, was visiting Edo Castle with some other dignitaries. But Naganori had not brought an expensive enough present for Kira Yoshinaka, the Master of Ceremonies who, if properly bribed, would ensure proceedings in the castle went smoothly. Offended by Naganori's small gift, Yoshinaka began insulting him by making faces and mocking the way he spoke. After a while Naganori could bear it no more and attacked Yoshinaka with a dagger. Although Yoshinaka came away with only a small injury to his face, the *shogun* ruled that court officials should not be harmed in the castle, and commanded Naganori to commit *seppuku*.

This left forty-seven of Naganori's men without a master, which made all of them *ronin* and honour bound to avenge their *daimyo*'s death. But anticipating a reprisal, Yoshinaka had his spies put the *ronin* under surveillance. The *ronin* leader Oishi Yoshio disbanded the group and moved to Kyoto, where he started drinking, visiting geisha houses and generally behaving unlike a samurai. At one point Yoshio passed out drunk in a gutter and was spat on by a passer-by, disgusted that a samurai would act in such a way.

After a year, Yoshinaka's spies brought him news of Yoshio's drunken and debauched behaviour. Yoshinaka considered himself safe and called off his men. Then, one snowy night a year and a half after the death of Naganori, the forty-seven *ronin* made their attack on Yoshinaka's mansion. They broke into two groups, crept quietly inside, killed all who opposed them and found Yoshinaka, identifying him by the scar Naganori had given him with his dagger. Yoshio gave Yoshinaka the chance to commit *seppuku*, and even offered to be his second, but Yoshinaka could not go through with it. So Yoshio beheaded him and placed his bloody head on Naganori's grave. All of the *ronin* handed themselves over to the *shogun*.

This presented the *shogun* with a quandary: On one hand the *ronin* had acted honourably according to the *bushido* code; on the other they had defied the *shogun*'s order that there was to be no retaliation for Naganori's death. He therefore decided all of the *ronin* responsible should be put to death, but they would be allowed to carry it out themselves by committing *seppuku*. The *ronin* committed group suicide by Naganori's grave and were subsequently buried around him. The site became a shrine for pilgrims to visit and celebrate the honourable *ronin*. Legend has it that one such pilgrim was the man who had spat on Yoshio in the street. After crying by Yoshio's grave and begging for forgiveness the man committed *seppuku*.

Some accounts of the forty-seven *ronin* report many of the *ronin*'s wives also committed *seppuku* in honour of their dead husbands. This female equivalent of *seppuku* was called *jigai*, and was carried out by first tying the legs together so as to die in a dignified pose, before cutting open the jugular.

Women Samurai

Samurai were allowed to marry and also take a mistress of samurai rank, subject to checks by the *daimyo*'s officials. The role of a samurai's wife was to raise the family and manage the household. A wife was expected to follow Confucian law, which required her to be subservient to her husband, treat older family members with filial piety and treat her children with care. Samurai women were trained to fight with a polearm, called a *naginata*, so they could defend the family home if it came under attack.

Female samurai were rare, but they did exist. One such warrior was Tomoe Gozen, whose story is told in the *Tale of the Heike*, an account of the war between the Taira and Minamoto clans at the end of the twelfth century:

> *Tomoe was beautiful, with white skin, long hair, and attractive features. She was as strong with a bow as a sword, fit to confront a demon or a god, mounted or on foot, and worth one thousand warriors. She could handle unbroken horses with superb skill, and was fearless in perilous descents. Whenever a battle began, Yoshinaka sent her as his first captain, in heavy armour, a great sword, and a mighty bow; and she won more glory than any of his other warriors.*

At the 1184 battle of Awazu, *daimyo* Minamoto Yoshinaka knew the day was lost and ordered Gozen, one of his last seven riders, to leave him. Gozen was not prepared to break the *bushido* code and abandon her master, so instead went in search of the enemy. Before long she encountered thirty enemy warriors, and, surprising one of them, she 'twisted off his head' as a trophy and galloped away. Unfortunately, by this time Yoshinaka was dead and so did not see Gozen's valiant last efforts to please him. Upon hearing of Yoshinaka's death, Gozen was thought either to have committed suicide by throwing herself into the sea or to have given up the warrior life to become a nun.

Wandering Swordsmen

The accounts of Tomoe Gozen and *The 47 Ronin* are among the great legends of the Japanese samurai. Both describe the tireless loyalty and devotion a samurai was expected to show their master, even after his death. So to lose a master was to become lost and without purpose. This was the legacy facing thousands of samurai during the Edo Period, when the disbanding of the provincial armies left them not only masterless but also unemployed. These samurai had little choice but to join the ranks of the *ronin* and wander the country looking for people to fight.

The Edo Period ushered in a new era of Japanese duelling courtesy of the *ronin*, who would travel anywhere they could show off their talents and training. Some of these *ronin* became famous and earned the same notorious reputation as the gunmen of the Wild West. A *ronin*'s first port of call upon entering a new town was its sword fighting school, many of which sprang up around Japan during the Edo Period. Samurai warriors were handsomely paid to teach at the schools, although it was a risky vocation. If the master of a school lost a duel with a travelling *ronin*, he would certainly be obliged to resign – that is, if he were still alive.

Samurai duels were not like their European counterparts, which were designed to settle a point of honour. Samurai duels were intended to display a warrior's skill and dominance, and were frequently fought to the death. While these duels were supposed to follow the *bushido* code, many of them were anything but honourable; it was common for a group to lie in wait to ambush a single swordsman. By the start of the seventeenth century duelling had become so popular that *shogun* Tokugawa Ieyasu had no choice but to make it legal, though he did so begrudgingly.

To try and limit the rising numbers of fatalities, Ieyasu introduced two less harmful duelling swords. One was the *bokken*, made from solid wood, and the other was the *shinai*, made from bamboo slats. The *shinai* is still used today in the modern martial art of *Kendo*.

The First Samurai

One of the first samurai to gain lasting fame and notoriety was Minamoto Yoshiie (1039–1106). Yoshiie was the first son of Minamoto Yoriyoshi, the emperor's commander charged with suppressing a rebellion among the Abe clan of northern Honshu. The war against the Abe lasted for nine years and Yoshiie followed his father into every battle. His accuracy with a bow from horseback was legendary, and Yoshiie became known as *Hachimantaro*, 'the God of War'. The young man soon began to exhibit the dignity and honour expected of a samurai warrior.

These virtues would be displayed during a Minamoto attack on Koromo Castle, forcing Abe leader Sadato and his bodyguard to flee on horseback. Yoshiie galloped after Sadato, who became separated from his men and took refuge in a nearby forest. Sadato was wounded and tried to escape his pursuer, but Yoshiie called out – wasn't he ashamed to turn his back on an enemy who had a message for him? Sadato turned to face Yoshiie, who instead of attacking recited a verse from a poem: 'The wraps of your robe have come undone', meaning that Koromo Castle had been destroyed. To this Sadato called back another verse from the same poem: 'Over

the years its threads became tangled, and this pains me.'
At this Yoshiie turned around and let the enemy leader
go, deeming this the honourable thing to do.

Around twenty years later Yoshiie was made
governor of the north and was charged with sorting
out a disturbance there. This involved infighting among
clans of the Kiyowara family who had helped the
Minamoto defeat the Abe. After an initial investigation,
Yoshiie decided to settle the matter through force and
attacked the rogue Kiyowara clans. This led to a three-
year war that had not been sanctioned by the imperial
court. Nevertheless, the war created another legendary
Yoshiie story.

In keeping with the *bushido* code, Yoshiie had educated
himself in the philosophy and craft of warfare. One day
as he rode at the head of his army, Yoshiie noticed a
flock of birds rise suddenly from a field in front of him.
Remembering a Chinese book on strategy, Yoshiie
realised the birds may have exposed an ambush. Yoshiie
ordered his men to surround the field and create an
ambush of their own. Sure enough, a group of enemy
soldiers were found lying in wait and quickly executed.

By the end of the war Yoshiie had defeated the
rogue Kiyowara clans and strengthened the Minamoto
powerbase in the north. Although Yoshiie had the love
and devotion of his men, the imperial court was not
similarly enamoured. It disapproved of Yoshiie's gung-

ho approach to subduing the rebellion and refused his request to execute the rebel leaders. It also refused to pay Yoshiie's men, because the war had not been commissioned by the emperor.

Disgusted, Yoshiie killed the enemy leaders anyway and discarded their heads in a ditch. He then paid his men from his own pocket and left the capital for the safety of his castle. The imperial court was furious and immediately removed his governorship. But Yoshiie must have expected this retaliation, and did not seem to care. He had secured further wealth and power for the Minamoto family and enhanced his reputation as a samurai.

The power and popularity of Yoshiie and samurai leaders like him, posed a great threat to the court. The following period in Japanese history saw the court removing itself from the activities of the provincial clans, which enabled the rise of powerful samurai armies. This in turn created the *shogun* era of the twelfth century. The legend of Minamoto Yoshiie would act as a benchmark for the later *shogun* – he had shown that the might of the samurai was greater than that of the emperor.

The Last Samurai

While Minamoto Yoshiie was known as the first great samurai, Saigo Takamori was considered the last. His valour, bravery and honour not only marked the end of the samurai's power in Japan, but a new era for the country. This would become the modern age of Japan, dominated by advances in technology and armaments, changing the country from an archaic curiosity into a global military power.

Saigo Takamori was born into the lower ranks of the Satsuma clan in 1828. He grew into a physically striking man with piercing eyes and a strong sense of the samurai *bushido*, especially the virtues of bravery and honour. An excellent swordsman, Takamori moved quickly through the ranks of his Satsuma clan, winning friends and influence along the way.

In 1867 Takamori and a number of other samurai dissatisfied with the *shogun* forced his resignation and put a new emperor on the throne. The return to Japan of imperial rule is known to historians as the Meji Restoration. In 1871 Takamori was eventually convinced to play a part in the emperor's new government and took command of the imperial guard. Takamori then helped disband the last provincial armies to open the way for a new national force. While Takamori did not support conscription, which he felt diminished the samurai's power, he did call for modernisation of the military.

He also demanded Japan attack Korea, as that country had not recognised Meji as the new emperor of Japan. Takamori wanted to visit Korea as an envoy so he could provoke its government into killing him, thus giving Japan the excuse it needed to attack. But, while popular at the time, Takamori's plan was eventually rejected. This led him and one hundred of his loyal officers from the Imperial Guard to resign.

After returning to his native Kagoshima Prefecture, Takamori set up several sword fighting academies and over twenty thousand disaffected samurai from all over Japan flocked to join. Takamori was not planning anything other than preparing men for military service, but the government at Tokyo was worried. It sent several warships to empty the Kagoshima arsenals in case of a rebellion. A group of Takamori's samurai reacted angrily to this news, and on 29 January 1877 they took over the arsenals and began making weapons for themselves. Takamori was finally convinced to lead this new rebel army, but he did so with a heavy heart.

What occurred over the next six months was full-scale warfare, with both sides relying heavily on the modern weapons of rifles and cannons to fight with. From the beginning, Takamori's army suffered disastrous defeats, and between February and September his numbers fell from twenty thousand to just four hundred.

The final Battle of Shiroyama took place on 24 September 1877. Takamori's rebels had been forced back to the Shiroyama Hill where they had run out of ammunition and were reduced to using bows and arrows and swords. Over thirty thousand government troops began a short siege of the hill, digging trenches and using cannon and battleship artillery to bomb Takamori's position. Eventually, the imperial soldiers stormed the hill. This battle was perhaps the last hurrah of the samurai, who took down large numbers of the imperial troops, untrained for close-quarter combat.

After one more retreat there were only forty samurai left and they made a last charge on horseback, but were mown down by the newest military technology to enter Japan – the American Gatling gun. Caught between the modernisation of his country and its inevitable eradication of the samurai, Takamori behaved as honourably as he could according to the *bushido* code. He went down in a blaze of glory and took his own life in the face of defeat.

The Last Samurai Movie

The heroes of the samurai age have been immortalised in hundreds of TV shows, cartoons, books and movies and continue to be so today. Usually these are stylised attempts to convey samurai warriors acting in accordance with the *bushido* code. The image of the stoic, meditative, self-sacrificing samurai was especially notable in the 2003 movie *The Last Samurai*, starring Tom Cruise.

The Last Samurai sets the scene with a piece of narration as its shows aerial shots of Japan (which is actually New Zealand, where it was filmed):

> *They say Japan was made by a sword…I say, Japan was made by a handful of brave men, warriors, willing to give their lives for what seems to have become a forgotten word: honour.*

The action starts with Nathan Algren (Tom Cruise), a jaded American ex-army officer who is recruited by the Meji government to train the new modernised Japanese army. It is needed, in particular, to put down a samurai rebellion led by Samurai leader Moritsugu Katsumoto

(Ken Watanabe). But Algren swaps sides, becomes a samurai and goes onto fight in the last ever samurai battle which is won by the Japanese army. In the end Algren presents the emperor with Katsumoto's sword, who suddenly realises the importance of Japan's samurai traditions.

The movie is roughly based on Saigo Takamori (see page 146) who has become Katsumoto in the film. The time frames have been changed to fit the story, and the American characters replace the French Military Mission, which helped the Japanese train their new army in the 1870s. As the movie is not claiming to be based on fact, it is arguably unfair to pull it up for inaccuracies in the storyline, which follows the standard Hollywood format. This makes the movie wholly predictable and, at times, implausible.

Algren lives in Katsumoto's village for one winter, but in that time has achieved levels of samurai swordsmanship that allow him to take on several foes at once. He has also become fluent in the language, and has mastered the complicated *bushido* code. Algren is then left as the most honourable man standing, who by the end of the movie is able to teach the emperor a thing or two about his country's *bushido* past. As if underlining this sentiment, Cruise himself even appears to look slightly Japanese on the promotional posters.

American critics panned the movie as being a Japanese

Dances with Wolves. The Japanese were more forgiving and *The Last Samurai* did better box office business there. One Japanese critic's complaint about the movie was the depiction of the Katsumoto character, who was considered too pious and one-dimensional.

The movie's strength lies in its battle scenes. These provide a reminder of the very real history that was happening in Japan at the time. The old guard, the samurai, were being made obsolete by the country's modernisation and new weaponry. Years of training under the *bushido* code to live and die honourably by the sword became antiquated and useless in the face of a machine gun. The viewer is shown in graphic terms that there is no place for the samurai in modern warfare, which Japan itself had realised when it abolished the samurai class in 1878.

The Last Samurai was one of several western samurai movies which gave the genre a rebirth in America. But this revival, which included *Kill Bill*, was only ever made possible by the original Japanese samurai movies themselves.

Samurai in Japanese Popular Culture

Japan's long history of TV, movies and theatre about the samurai is called *jidaigeki*. *Jidaigeki* is a costume drama set during Japan's Edo Period, and features the lives of various recurring characters including samurai, villains, government officials, merchants, farmers and craftsmen. *Jidaigeki* is instantly recognisable by its characters, who follow set conventions: they wear heavy make-up, speak formal Japanese with an old-fashioned dialect, use catchphrases (such as 'it is a terrible world'), and can be easily identified by their appearance (villains are unshaven, unkempt and messy while the heroes are neat and clean-cut).

The most famous *jidaigeki* character is Zoitochi who has been the subject of innumerable TV series and movies since 1962. Zoitochi is a blind masseur and gambler who travels the country giving massages, singing, performing music and playing dice. Zoitochi gambles by listening to whether the dice have fallen on an even or odd number, and he often extinguishes the candles in a room before uttering his catchphrase: 'Darkness is my advantage.' But unbeknown to those who meet Zoitochi, he is actually a master swordsman who fights injustice and protects the innocent wherever he goes.

Zoitochi belongs to a sub group of *jidaigeki* called *chanbara*, which is made up of Japanese sword fighting movies created in a swashbuckling vein. The *chanbara* genre began with the film *The Fight at Honno Temple*, made in 1908 by Shozo Makino, often considered the father of Japanese cinema. *Chanbara* usually follows the life of a disillusioned *ronin* who is committed to spending the rest of his life travelling and fighting. Characters often experience a moral quandary about what is right versus what is required by the *bushido* code, leading invariably to a series of sword fighting duels. Even when a *chanbara* character is ambushed by multiple foes, only one or two attack at a time, the others standing politely back waiting for their turn. The genre hit its heyday in the 1960s and 1970s when the movies became increasingly violent and explicit, such as Masaki Kobayashi's *Seppuku* (1962).

SEVEN SAMURAI

The most famous director of *chanbara* films is Akira Kurosawa. Kurosawa directed *Rashomon, Throne of Blood, Yojimbo, The Hidden Fortress*, and perhaps most famously *Seven Samurai. Seven Samurai* (1954) has often been praised by Western directors and inspired an American remake, *The Magnificent Seven*, a gunfighter movie set in the Wild West.

Seven Samurai begins in a small Japanese village which is being ransacked by marauding bandits. A village elder suggests hiring a group of samurai to protect them, but the villagers worry that they cannot afford it and their daughters would be at risk from the samurai's sexual advances. But realising they have no choice, a young villager travels to the city to recruit some warriors. As the village has nothing with which to pay except food, the elder suggests looking for 'hungry samurai.' In the city, the young villager stumbles across one seemingly honourable samurai who is rescuing a child from a kidnapper. On the way to the village, the samurai Kambei Shimada (Takashi Shimura), meets six other companions who agree to join him. After some initial reservations the villagers warm to the samurai, although it is revealed they have been responsible for killing travelling samurai in the past. A heated discussion among the seven follows this revelation, but the leader Shimada argues that for many years farmers were victimised by the samurai class and so their actions are understandable. As time goes on bonds between the farmers and samurai strengthen, including a romance between one warrior and a farmer's daughter.

The samurai go about defending the village – creating fortifications around it and even launching a pre-emptive strike on the bandits' hideout. The movie culminates in a final battle in the village. The samurai seem to be winning the battle, but the bandit's leader takes refuge in a hut and shoots two of the warriors in the back. In the end the bandits are all killed and the samurai are victorious, but only three of them are left standing. In the last scene the villagers happily go to work in the rice fields, seemingly indifferent to the samurai standing at the graves of their four dead. The love interest turns her back on her warrior and runs off to join in with the singing. Shimada sums up the situation: 'Again we are defeated. The farmers have won, not us.'

Seven Samurai raises an important point about the relationship between the samurai and those beneath them. The villagers have killed samurai in the past after being abused by them and trampled under foot. And yet, they have no choice but to turn to the warrior class for protection. In turn, the samurai according to their years of training under the *bushido* code are honour bound to do the right thing, and help the weak and oppressed. And yet when this task has been completed the villagers, who are not educated or bound by the *bushido* code, simply turn their backs on the samurai to get on with their farming. The samurai who are *ronin* are simply left to go on their way, condemned to aimlessly wander like so many others of the Edo Period.

Seven Samurai was Kurosawa's first samurai movie and set the benchmark for all others that followed. It took the director a year to film and cost over $500,000 – a huge amount then and four times over the original budget. As such, the production company shut down the film three times, during which Kurosawa went fishing and reasoned that too much had been invested already for the movie to be cancelled. *Seven Samurai* went on to be Japan's highest-grossing movie of all time and Kurosawa's filmmaking has influenced the craft of many Western directors, including George Lucas, Robert Altman, Francis Ford Coppola, Steven Spielberg and Martin Scorsese.

HIDEO GOSHA

Hideo Gosha is a lesser known director in the West, but his samurai films are often credited with being just as important as Kurosawa's for their contribution to the genre. Gosha explores the darker nature of samurai, who are often plagued with the moral consequences of their actions, usually performed out of loyalty to their master or clan.

In *Goyokin*, samurai Magobei Wakizaka's (Tatsuya Nakadai) leader Rokugo Tatewaki (Tetsurô Tamba) slaughters a group of innocent farmers to steal the gold they are transporting for the Tokugawa clan. Wakizaka agrees to keep his silence as long as Tatewaki promises never to repeat his actions. But Tatewaki sends a *ronin* after Wakizaka to assassinate him, although in the end he is talked out of it. In the final scene a showdown takes place between Wakizaka and Tatewaki, who is continuing to kill innocents and take more gold. As with *Seven Samurai*, *Goyokin* questions the morality of the all-powerful samurai class and its hierarchical structure.

While the samurai are at the top of the Japanese class system, those inside the caste itself have to proffer blind devotion to the *daimyo* and *shogun* above them. This point is made at the end of movie after both samurai struggle to pick up their swords to fight in a freezing blizzard. One says: 'We sit here and die in the cold, and what does the Shogun do? He gets fatter in the heat.' It is this sentiment that has led many to call *Goyokin* an anti-samurai movie, and it certainly does not disguise its criticism of the concept of a warrior class. But the movie also presents a carefully thought out study of the plight of the samurai coming to the end of their legacy. They are left with the echoes of the *bushido* code but without the context of warfare within which to use it.

MEDIEVAL
TOURNAMENTS

Introduction

The medieval tournament is best-known for the pomp and pageantry of the jousts where chivalric knights unhorsed each other with lances for glory, valour and a lady's honour. But the first tournaments were in reality bloody free-for-all brawls. Two army-sized teams of knights met each other for a mock battle fought out over large swaths of European countryside. Knights captured in the fray were ransomed off, and savvy tourneyers became rich from the proceeds.

A famous example is William Marshal, who came from a background of humble obscurity, but through his tourneying prowess became known as the 'greatest knight who ever lived'.

William was born in 1146 to John Marshal, who fought against King Stephen during the English civil war known as 'The Anarchy.' Stephen was laying siege to Marshal's Newbury Castle when the knight sent out six-year-old William as a hostage. To Stephen's surprise, Marshal did not go on to surrender, but instead used the respite to bring in supplies and reinforce his castle. Stephen shouted out that he would hang William in front of the castle walls if Marshal didn't give himself up.

Marshal told him to go ahead, saying: 'I have a hammer and anvil to make more and better sons.'

William Marshal was not sacrificed, but instead sent to William de Tancarville's Normandy court to be trained as a squire. After being knighted in 1166 Marshal followed de Tancarville to war in upper Normandy. But eager to prove his quality, Marshal charged onto the battlefield prematurely and was quickly unhorsed. De Tancarville was furious and refused to give Marshal another mount. So it was on a borrowed steed that Marshal followed de Tancarville to his first tournament at Le Mans. It was here that the legend of William Marshal really began. The young knight displayed an uncanny ability for the tournament.

Shortly after battle commenced Marshal apprehended his first knight for ransom. He then charged back into the fracas to capture three more, and shared a fifth prisoner with another knight. By the end of the day Marshal had a tally of four and a half horses, plus equipment and ransoms.

It was not long before Marshal became friends with King Henry II's son, Henry the Younger, and the pair set about becoming rich on the French tournament circuit. Over the next ten months Marshal and Henry won one hundred and three horses and ransoms, and became the popular subjects of news and gossip at the courts of Europe.

RIVALS AND RANSOMS

Their arch rival was Philip of Flanders, who employed the dubious tactic of not entering the tournament until it was nearly over. This enabled Flanders and his entourage to make easy pickings of the exhausted competitors and earn some easy money. Marshal convinced Henry to give Philip a taste of his own medicine by joining the tournament late, thus capturing Philip and several other hapless knights in the process.

Marshal himself was also not above playing dirty when it suited his purposes. While he was taking a break at an inn, a knight outside fell off his horse and broke his leg. Marshal promptly captured the knight for ransom even though he was not participating in the tournament. On another occasion, Marshal was leading a captured horse and knight to claim his winnings, when the knight grabbed onto a drainpipe and pulled himself from his saddle. By the time Marshal turned around to check on his prize he was surprised to find the knight had vanished into thin air. Another time, two knights searching for Marshal eventually found him at a blacksmith's, where his badly battered helmet was being removed with a hammer and anvil.

But it was not all games and good fortune. In 1168 Marshal was captured while fighting in a real battle alongside his uncle, the Earl of Salisbury. Salisbury was killed and Marshal imprisoned by his uncle's enemy, Guy de Lusignan. Luckily Marshal's reputation aided his release. Henry II's queen Eleanor of Aquitaine paid Marshal's ransom, apparently impressed by his bravery at the tournaments.

After returning to England in 1170 Marshal was appointed tutor-in-arms to Henry the Younger. The two once again joined the tournament circuit, with Marshal taking on the role of team manager. It was Marshal's job to mind the young royal and ensure he was not publicly humiliated. However, it seems that Marshal was quick to abandon his post and gallop after his own quarry. Back at court Marshal became the subject of criticism among his rivals, who maintained the knight was more interested in his tournament winnings than his young charge and master. Malicious rumours and slander followed, which eventually caused Henry and Marshal to fall out. The final straw came when Marshal was accused of seducing Henry's wife, although it is uncertain whether this was true or not. Fed up, Marshal left the court to join up with a new tournament partner, none other than his old rival, Philip of Flanders.

In the end Marshal and Henry would meet once more, for a tearful reconciliation at Henry's deathbed. Henry, who was dying of dysentery and had taken his last vows, asked that Marshal take his cloak to Jerusalem. Marshal vowed to carry out Henry's last instruction and travelled to the Holy Land as a crusader. On his return, Marshal served with Henry II and fought against his son Richard, who had joined forces with Phillip of France. William once had the chance of killing Richard after ambushing and unhorsing him; the only man ever to do so. But he refrained from killing Richard and instead slayed his horse, just to make his point.

Richard did not forget this mercy and upon becoming King Richard I honoured Marshal by arranging for him to marry Isabel de Clare, heiress to the Earl of Pembroke. This made Marshal the future Earl of Pembroke and one of the wealthiest men in the country. Marshal was also named 'Protector of the Realm', and went on to serve John when he became king in 1199. Despite hostilities between Marshal and the king, Marshal served John loyally and helped his heir, Henry III, take the throne after his death.

Marshal was one of the Barons who signed the Magna Carta in 1215, and was given full burial rights as a Knight Templar when he died in 1219. He lies buried in the Temple Church in London. The thirteenth century Archbishop of Canterbury, Stephen Langton, described Marshal as 'the greatest knight who ever lived.'

CHIVALRIC CODES

Loyalty and a sense of duty were two of the chivalric virtues that greatly influenced the culture of medieval Europe. Chivalry, an ideal founded in romantic literature, would also serve as a set of rules and protocol for the tournament battlefield. The chivalric code even outlasted the tournament's demise in the seventeenth century, and went on to create the foundations of the duel of honour that followed it.

During its early years the tournament was organised mass violence, under the guise of mock warfare. Two teams would crash into each other on horseback and use swords, maces, axes, daggers and clubs to disarm and capture each other. Killing another knight was not permitted, but it frequently happened, and many combatants suffered serious injuries.

As time went on and chivalric codes took over, violence was replaced with new rules and safety features. Specially-designed tournament weapons were created, and the introduction of plate armour reduced the number of wounds. The sharpened lance was replaced by one with a non-lethal end that would easily shatter on impact. In the end the tournament was supplemented by non-violent military exhibitions which were pre-rehearsed to ensure nobody got hurt.

History

The origins of the medieval tournament stretch back to the days of the Roman Republic. Then, groups of noblemen too young to join the military were able to show off their horsemanship skills in a mock-battle demonstration called the *ludus Troaie*, or 'Troy Game'. During the *ludus* three teams of twelve men performed drills on horseback as a display of co-operation rather than actual combat.

A similar event was held in AD 842 in Strasbourg to celebrate the alliance of Holy Roman Emperor-to-be, Charles the Bald, with his brother Louis the German. As with the *ludus Troaie* the game was an exhibition that featured two groups of cavalrymen charging at each other and withdrawing before impact. While the event was noteworthy enough to be recorded, there was no real combat involved.

The eleventh century marked the appearance of tournaments that featured real fighting. These mostly took place on mainland Europe and consisted of the *melee* – a dangerous free-for-all between two teams: the visitors, or 'attackers', and the hosts, 'the defenders'. Each team was made up of dozens, or even hundreds, of knights, usually grouped together by country or province.

Melees in France, for example, often featured a French team against visiting knights from England, Germany, Italy or Spain.

The battlefield itself was an area between two towns, including the open countryside, villages, woods and any other natural features that happened to be in the way. The purpose of the *melee* was to capture knights of the opposing team, confiscate their equipment and horses and hold them to ransom. The ransomed knight was only released upon promise of future payment. The team that captured the most knights was the winner, and captors could earn themselves a tidy sum in the process.

There were only two rules – knights were not supposed to injure or kill each other; and nobody could be attacked if they were taking shelter in one of the fenced off *recets*, or rest areas. There were, however, no officials at the *melees* to enforce the rules, and so there were often serious injuries and fatalities. Villagers and other bystanders caught up in the action suffered injuries of their own, often under the hooves of galloping horses.

WEAPONS OF WAR

In the early *melees* knights used the same armour and weapons they used in real battles. These included bows and arrows, lances, swords, daggers, battle-axes and maces. Many of these weapons were dropped from the tournament repertoire as time went on. A knight's sword also grew in length from around 80 cm (31 in) long to 1.8 metres (70 in) by the fourteenth century, so it had more reach from horseback.

Later tournaments specified the use of blunted weapons and specially designed lances, although these were only used for the peaceful jousts *à plaisance*, or 'for pleasure'. On the other side were jousts *à outrance*, 'a joust to the limits', fought with sharpened points and blades. These tournaments often took place between two enemy sides as a respite during actual warfare. In 1341 during an ongoing border dispute between Scotland and England, two jousts *à outrance* were held at Roxburgh and Berwick. During the tournaments twenty knights jousted, three were killed and many more injured. Prizes were given out to the best knights at the tournament's conclusion.

Lances were an essential piece of equipment used in the jousts – a mounted duel between two knights where each would try to unhorse the other. The development of the lance went together with the evolution of the tournament. The lance had been the mainstay of European cavalries for hundreds of years, but it wasn't until the mid-eleventh century that the 'couched lance' began appearing in northern France. Before then the lance had been used either as a spear for thrusting and jabbing, or for throwing, which made it usable only once. The couched lance was a heavier, longer spear that could be held tightly under an arm and used repeatedly to charge at an opponent. Groups of French knights wielding lances were used to devastating effect in the First Crusade, and during the Norman invasion of England in 1066.

The tournament *melee* was the perfect training ground for knights to practise their battlefield charges with couched lances. However a knight would need a certain amount of skill before entering a *melee*. Knights practised their craft against a *quintain*, a revolving target attached to a pole in the ground. On top of the pole was a revolving arm with a shield at one end and sand bag at the other. The knight had to strike the shield cleanly with his lance and gallop quickly past to avoid the bag swinging round and hitting him.

CONDEMNED BY THE CHURCH

By the twelfth century the tournament craze had caught on, and they were regularly held in France, Germany, Italy, England and the Low Countries. The tournaments' rising popularity had not passed unnoticed by the Church, which set about condemning them. In 1130 Pope Innocent II issued an edict that any knight killed at a tournament would be denied his funeral rights. The papal view was enforced by those on the ground. At a 1241 tournament in Nuess, Cologne, a priest ran into a *melee* to halt proceedings in the name of God. It didn't work, but his protests were oddly providential – sixty combatants were killed in the ensuing violence, most of them suffocating in the heat and dust. Rumours quickly spread that demons, in the form of crows and vultures, circled the field as the knights perished.

The Church's line was that tournaments not only promoted violence but encouraged vice. In fact, all seven deadly sins could be experienced within one tournament, according to the Bishop of Acre, Jacques de Vitry. In 1240 de Vitry wrote that pride led the knight's need for praise on the battleground; envy caused a knight to resent those who won; anger made a knight fight back bitterly against those who attacked him; greed enticed a knight to capture others for ransom; gluttony took hold of a knight at the evening feast; sloth was displayed in defeat; and lust led a knight to show off for the attending ladies.

The Church's other issue was that tournaments created grudges among participants that were carried over to the next event. This was true – knights often sought out a foe from a previous tournament with retribution in mind. A young William Marshal was once beaten at a tournament by a knight named Matthew de Walincourt. Meeting Walincourt at another tournament years later, Marshal could not resist the opportunity to humiliate the older man in combat. Whole groups could also hold grudges. At a 1251 tournament in Rochester a group of aggrieved English knights sought revenge against all foreigners who they felt had mistreated them abroad. The tournament erupted into a serious battle where the visitors were badly injured.

Bad treatment or not, English knights seeking a tournament often had no choice but to travel abroad. King Stephen and Henry II both banned tournaments in England during the twelfth century. While Henry II policed his ban, the weak King Stephen did little to stop tournaments being held; in fact, they flourished during his reign. Tournaments at this time were subversive by definition – they gave the proverbial finger to the reigning monarch and created a recruitment ground for like-minded knights who harboured rebellious intentions.

The tournament's potential as a recruiting ground was a point not lost on Richard I, who took the throne in 1189, and was always looking for skilled knights to join his foreign conflicts. Richard had also heard a rumour that English knights were thought clumsy and badly trained compared to the dexterous, graceful French knights. Richard realised that if this theory held weight it was only because the French knights were getting more practice at the tournaments. Richard was also said to dislike the damage large *melees* were doing to the villages and countryside.

With all of these factors in mind, the king legalised the tournaments under royal licence. This meant organisers could buy a licence to hold a tournament in one of five designated places – Warwickshire, Suffolk, Northamptonshire, Nottinghamshire or Wiltshire. The tournaments had to abide by a set of regulations, which among other things clearly stated that no foreign knights were allowed to attend. The Church relaxed its attitudes to the tournaments over time, and in 1316 Pope John XXII lifted the papal ban. Like Richard I, the pope could see the advantage of tournaments as a recruiting station. The tournament provided soldiers for the Church's crusades.

A NEW ERA

By the end of the twelfth century the brutal, brawling *melee* was gradually replaced by the sophisticated refinement of the joust. Now, a tournament's *melee* was merely a prelude to the joust, and took place within a smaller, easily visible area. This enabled the introduction of stands and an influx of spectators, which importantly included women. This was the new age of the tournament led by a new code of virtues which would guide Europe through the medieval era – chivalry. Chivalry in its simplest term referred to the honourable and courteous conduct expected of a knight, an idea that formed the basis of chivalric literature and romances of the time. Chrétien de Troyes was the best-known author in this genre. He described the chivalric attributes of tourneying knights in depth in his Arthurian romance, *Erec Et Enide, completed around 1170*. From this point on the tournaments were bound up in stories of honour, loyalty and courtly love, where gallant knights fought for a lady's good name and won her heart through bravery on the field. An example of the chivalric tournament is described in *Erec Et Enide*:

> *A month after Pentecost the tournament assembled, and the jousting began in the plain below Tenebroc. Many an ensign of red, blue, and white, many a veil and many a sleeve were bestowed as tokens of love. Many a lance was carried there, flying the colours argent and green, or gold and azure blue. There were many, too, with different devices, some with stripes and some with dots. That day one saw laced on many a helmet of gold or steel, some green, some yellow, and others red, all aglowing in the sun; so many scutcheons and white hauberks; so many swords girt on the left side; so many good shields, fresh and new, some resplendent in silver and green, others of azure with buckles of gold; so many good steeds marked with white, or sorrel, tawny, white, black, and bay: all gather hastily.*
>
> *And now the field is quite covered with arms. On either side the ranks tremble, and a roar rises from the fight. The shock of the lances is very great. Lances break and shields are riddled, the hauberks receive*

bumps and are torn asunder, saddles go empty and horsemen ramble, while the horses sweat and foam. Swords are quickly drawn on those who tumble noisily, and some run to receive the promise of a ransom, others to stave off this disgrace.

Erec rode a white horse, and came forth alone at the head of the line to joust, if he may find an opponent. From the opposite side there rides out to meet him Orguelleus de la Lande, mounted on an Irish steed which bears him along with marvellous speed. On the shield before his breast Erec strikes him with such force that he knocks him from his horse: he leaves him prone and passes on...While riding back he met the King of the Red City, who was very valiant and bold. They grasp their reins by the knots and their shields by the inner straps. They both had fine arms, and strong swift horses, and good shields, fresh and new.

With such fury they strike each other that both their lances fly in splinters. Never was there seen such a blow. They rush together with shields, arms, and horses. But neither girth nor rein nor breast-strap could prevent the king from coming to earth. So he flew from his steed, carrying with him saddle and stirrup, and even the reins of his bridle in his hand. All those who witnessed the jousting were filled with amazement, and said it cost him dear to joust with such a goodly knight.

> *Erec did not wish to stop to capture either horse or rider, but rather to joust and distinguish himself in order that his prowess might appear...But on the morrow he did much better yet: for he took so many knights and left so many saddles empty that none could believe it except those who had seen it. Every one on both sides said that with his lance and shield he had won the honours of the tournament.*
>
> *Erec et Enide* by Chrétien De Troyes, translated by
> W. W. Comfort

REGULATION AND REFINEMENT

By the fourteenth century the tournaments had become altogether highbrow. The *melees* had fallen out of fashion and the tournaments centered solely on the jousts. As the event had become more refined and dignified it was considered necessary to keep out 'undesirables'. Knights in England, Italy and Spain had to prove their noble ancestry before entering a joust, or face being turned away. In Germany the regulations were even stricter – a knight would have to prove his family had been fighting in tournaments for three generations to participate.

If the knight did not provide the necessary documentation he was subject to a sound beating and expulsion. Knights could also be excluded if they had committed such offences as adultery, money lending or robbery.

Those knights guilty of such crimes who still had the gall to show up at certain tournaments were duly punished. The knight was beaten, had his horse confiscated and was then forced to sit astride a saddle on the tournament boundary fence for the duration of the event.

Regulations were not only set up to police participation, they also made the events safer. Weapons had to be blunted and the sharp end of a lance was replaced with a three-pronged coronel end, which could not pierce armour or skin. The coronel end also pushed the force of the impact back into the lance, thus encouraging it to splinter more easily. By the fourteenth century, lances were typically around 3 metres (9.8 feet) long and painted bright colours to go with the pageantry of the later tournaments. It was assumed that most tournaments were now fought *à plaisance*, although a joust *à outrance* was sometimes requested, for which a sharp-ended lance was re-employed. By the seventeenth century the chivalric tournament had hit its peak and the tradition began to peter out. The tournaments were replaced with events that had nothing to do with violence, or indeed combat, except for that of make-believe. In this way, the tournaments reverted back to the harmless fun of the *ludus Troaie* or the Strasbourg war games of 842.

In France a type of mock battle called a *carousel* began to emerge, which was pre-rehearsed warfare with very little danger involved. The tournament as a practice ground for battle training began gradually to be taken over by the aristocratic pursuit of fencing. The heavy bladed swords used on the battlefield gave way to thinner Italian models suitable for thrusting and fighting at close quarters, which eventually gave rise to the duel. By the end of the seventeenth century plate armour had all but disappeared and the day of the knight was over. But the ideals of chivalry reflected in the duels between knights at the medieval tournament would live on into the Age of Enlightenment.

TRAVELLING TO TOURNAMENTS

The purpose of a tournament was to put a knight's prowess on display within the confines of a mock battle. They were also greatly enjoyed. A tournament would be held at most events – knightings, coronations, a campaign end, or most commonly, a wedding. Disaster sometimes struck during these entertainments. At the 1315 double wedding of Frederick of Austria and his brother, a local count was killed, several ladies died when the stands collapsed, and a number of jewels were stolen.

From the eleventh to the fourteenth century, companies of knights would travel great distances to join the great sporting festivals of the medieval age. Tales of the errant knight filled the annals of romances and chivalric literature, and many adventures were encountered. Some travelling knights were boisterous and full of good cheer, while others were surly, arrogant and apt to commit highway robbery.

This caused Richard I to issue a charter for knights on the road. Tourneying knights were not to take food without permission, nor allow any person to be harassed by his men; they should keep the king's peace especially in the woods and markets; and they were responsible for punishing any criminal met along the way. William Marshal once took matters into his own hands when a passing couple woke him as he slept by the side of the road. Sword drawn, Marshal interrogated the travellers, who turned out to be two runaway lovers. The woman was already married and Marshal threatened to take her back to her husband but after she protested he let the matter drop. What he did do, however, was to relieve them of every penny they had for their future together, which he then divided up between his friends.

Knights travelled to tournaments accompanied by at least one squire, usually the son of a knight or nobleman sent to train with a friend or relative. While even the lowliest of knights travelled with at least one squire, prestigious knights of wealth and standing would take whole caravans on the road with them. One of the most famous tourneying knights, Austrian Ulrich Von Liechtenstein was recorded as travelling with two stewards, twelve mounted squires, three pack horses, three war horses and a band of musicians.

These travelling retinues were seen as a tremendous nuisance, not only by other travellers using the roads but the towns at which the tournaments were being staged. Small local communities groaned under the weight of visiting tourneying numbers. Hundreds, if not thousands, attended any given tournament. One large event was held in Angouleme by Edward of Woodstock (also known as the Black Prince) to celebrate his son's birth. It was recorded that 706 knights, 154 lords and 18,000 horses attended the tournament.

For this reason the site for any *melee* had to be large enough for two opposing armies to face each other – in other words, the size of a battlefield. The largest sites were found in northern France and often lay between two towns, so that each side had a base to lodge in and prepare. Anything within the designated area could be used for battle. Often groups of knights formed small bands of ambushers who used the cover of a barn or wooded area to wait for a lone horseman to defeat.

A Day at the Melee

In early times tournaments were a one-day event, but by the thirteenth century they stretched over several days. At the tournaments of the eleventh and twelfth centuries knights could not sustain the fighting for more than a day. Many reported taking weeks to recover from injuries and bruising. Preparations for the tournament began before dawn. Heralds and servants were the first ones awake, preparing breakfast and setting out the armour and weaponry. After rising, the knights visited church to pray for luck, or alternatively, safe passage to heaven. The participating knights then converged at a central point and made sure both sides had equal numbers. If they did not, heralds balanced out the teams, switching knights as needed. Each side carried a distinctive team banner.

With the preliminaries out of the way, the proceedings began. First there was a long procession of participants – minstrels, squires, foot soldiers, archers, spearmen and the knights themselves, who announced themselves with their particular war cry. Often a bout of jousting acted as a prelude to the *melee*. This was designed to symbolise a duel between two champions before the opposing armies attacked. These jousts also gave younger, inexperienced knights a chance to spar before the main event.

The *melee* began with trumpet blasts and drums, and two lines of mounted horsemen would form up and face one another. Then, with a great roar, they would charge – weapons pointed forward, banners flapping, and clouds of dust kicked up under thundering hooves. An ear-splitting clash followed as lance, shield, sword, man and horse collided. The strategy was then to turn (the word 'tournament' is thought to have derived from this action) and attack those still mounted.

The aim of the *melee* was to unhorse another knight and capture him. There were three broad strategies to achieve this. The simplest was to knock an opponent off his horse with a lance, as knights would do in the individual jousts. There were risks involved in this, as the attacking knight had to make sure to stay seated himself, and both had to avoid the splinters from the shattering lance. If a lance did break, spares could be taken from attending squires (some tournaments allowed only three spares), or a sword or mace could be drawn.

Another method of capture was to grab hold of the opponent's reins and seize his horse, a particular favourite of William Marshal and one that never failed to win applause. Reins gone, the captured knight would then have no control of his horse and no way to escape except jumping off – a dangerous action in full armour. A third tactic was to jump at a mounted opponent and try and pull him off his horse. In a 1274 tournament the

Count of Chalons tried this manouevre against Edward I of England, when he grabbed him around the neck. Edward, in return, pulled the count off his horse with his free hand. The French knights were so outraged by the sight that they began fighting for real, and an all-out brawl developed, joined by nearby foot soldiers, squires, heralds and even spectators.

OVER THE HILLS AND FAR AWAY

After the main clash of the *melee* several smaller battles took place. Many knights chased each other across distant hills and fields, to carry on their contests and avoid being taken captive. The aim was to capture rivals for ransom, and clever competitors such as William Marshal (see page 160) made their fortunes this way. Once a knight was captured he was escorted to a fenced off rest area, called the *recets*. Here the knight would give his word to pay the necessary ransom, and was then free to rejoin the *melee*. Of course, this was only possible if the captured knight had an alternative steed, as a captured horse often served as the main part of a ransom. While knights such as William Marshal won their fortunes through ransoms and horses, others similarly used the tournaments to profit from horseflesh.

During an 1179 tournament in Epernon, Marshal left his horse with a boy on the street while he visited an inn.

But as soon as Marshal had disappeared inside a thief pulled the boy down from the horse by his hair and rode off. On hearing the boy's cries, Marshal dashed out from the inn and cornered the thief in a side street. Here he clobbered the thief so hard that he lost an eye. Marshal had to stop his friends from lynching the thief, saying he had been punished enough.

While many participants enjoyed the day at the tournament, others did not make it to nightfall. While the purpose of the tournament was to win ransoms, there is no doubt many 'accidental deaths' were actually murders. Even in later tournaments, where chivalry and honour were supposed to inform all encounters, there are reports of knights using sharpened swords instead of their blunted tournament versions.

Other deaths were of course accidental and the rather obvious outcome of two lines of knights charging at one another. Among the list of high profile casualties was Leopold, Duke of Austria, who in 1194 was squashed under his own horse.

By dusk the tournament began to wind down. Knights found their way back to the inns and lodgings to celebrate their winnings or bind their wounds. The side that had won the most captives, horses and ransoms was the winner of the day.

Bohort

The Bohort was a less formal tournament which was often thrown together in an impromptu manner. Bohorts used either blunted weapons, mock weapons, or no weapons at all, and as such were safe enough to have the sanction of the Church. The Knights Templar obeyed the papal ban on the tournament, but did allow its members to take part in the Bohort, provided that no spears were thrown. The Bohort was often the domain of squires and younger knights not yet of tournament age, but eager to try out their burgeoning skills. Entire practice tournaments for these young knights called the *tirocinium* were also held in Germany.

Of course Bohorts would sometimes get out of hand, and the wearing of bells in some countries was hoped to limit potential fatalities. In Aragon, Spain any man participating in a bohort who did not wear bells and killed a man was guilty of homicide. If he had been wearing bells he would be acquitted. As the tournament became more regulated and focused on the joust, the bohort died out in most European countries. In Italy, however, it continued and in France it formed the basis for the *carousel*, a non-violent tournament that emerged in the seventeenth century.

Pas d'armes

The *pas d'armes* evolved from early romances and chivalric literature, and involved a knight defending a piece of ground against any who tried to pass. A challenging knight who won such a duel would then have to take the place of his predecessor. A *pas d'armes* would typically involve a group of knights defending a bridge, gate, or lane.

One famous *pas d'armes* was the 1434 Passo Honroso in Spain. Here, a knight called Suero de Quinones and ten of his companions proclaimed they would defend the Orbigo Bridge until 300 lances had been broken. After about three weeks, 166 lances had been broken against 69 challenging knights, and de Quinones concluded the *pas d'armes*.

At other *pas d'armes* a 'Tree of Chivalry' was adorned with shields or a horn, which would have to be struck or blown to issue a challenge to the defenders. In 1443 the Duke of Burgundy, Philip the Good, held a *pas d'armes* next to the 'Tree of Charlemagne', which featured two hanging shields. Thirteen of Philip's knights defended the road next to the tree for forty days. According to the fifteenth century chronicles of Enguerrand de Monstrelet there were some specific rules for challengers:

In the first place, two shields shall be suspended on the tree of the Hermit, and all those who shall by a king at arms or pursuivant touch the first shield, shall be bounden to perform twelve courses on horseback with me, or with one of my aforesaid knights or esquires, with blunted lances...if either of the champions, during their twelve courses, be unhorsed by a direct blow with the lance on his armour, such person, thus unhorsed, shall present to his adversary a diamond of whatever value he please.

The Chronicles of Enguerrand de Monstrelet, translated by Thomas Johnes

The Jousts

By 1340 the *melee* tournament had all but died out, replaced by the safer tournament based on jousting and inspired by chivalry and chivalric literature. The legend of King Arthur was responsible for what became known in the thirteenth century as the Round Table – a brotherly order of knights with the highest chivalric virtues. The Round Table would also become an event, a tournament created in imitation of Arthur's court. The earliest of these was held in 1223 in Cyprus to celebrate a knighting. In 1446 Rene of Anjou built an entire castle to host a Round Table.

The Round Table itself was represented by a pavilion, on which the members of the order hung their shields. Those wishing to challenge a knight inside would do so by striking his shield. A joust between the knights would follow, watched by judges, ladies and other spectators from the nearby stands. The knight who out-jousted all challengers was given their horses and a gold crown to present to his lady.

It was this interaction between the spectators and the knights which made the jousts more popular than the *melee*. Now a knight was able to showcase his individual talents and fight for a lady's honour as spectators urged him on. A *melee*, by contrast, came to be seen as a rather base and unnecessary event with limited spectator participation. Often *melee* spectators had to stand and watch helplessly as the knights chased each other off into the far distance. Now the lists, or boundary lines, were defined by a much smaller area, thus allowing the building of wooden stands for spectating. Although these stands were often constructed from cheap wood they were covered in plush cloth and rich tapestries.

The lists themselves were decorated with brightly coloured flags, banners and knights' coats of arms. Early coats of arms were simple lines or crosses, but with time became more elaborate, such as King Richard I's three golden lions. Marriages between two houses required a new coat of arms to be created, borrowing features from either side of the family.

The system of heraldry, or displaying one's colours or coats of arms, became complicated by the fifteenth century, because there were so many in circulation. It fell to the tournament heralds to identify the different coats of arms and explain to the spectators who they were. Heralds, who had previously just acted as commentators at the tournament, were now expected to be well educated in knightly family histories as well as the colours they flew. Heralds were certainly useful to have around for spectating ladies who had their eye on a particular jouster. Ladies were central to the idea of the latter day tournaments, which were often held in their honour. They would also serve as inspiration for the jousting knights, who would wear their scarf into the fray. A lady would also present the prizes, or if she was sponsoring a particular knight, present him with his lance before he began his joust.

The rise of the jousts required knights to develop new techniques for handling their couched lances. This was in part due to the introduction of a central 1.8 metre (6 foot) high barrier called a tilt, designed to separate the charging knights and stop head-on collisions. The tilt also meant knights had to hold their lance at a 25-degree angle, which encouraged it to break up on impact, making the joust safer.

Tips and Techniques

Duarte King of Portugal was such a devoted tourneyer that he wrote a manual of jousting techniques in 1434. In *The Art of Good Horsemanship* Duarte discusses everything from how to hold a lance to why a jouster may fall from his horse:

> *This is what you should teach; if the lance is being rested on the leg, which is what most people do, hold it with your hand supporting it from below. If you rest it on your chest, put your arm as you can and bend it in such a fashion that it can be used as a rest for your lance...And when you want to place the lance under your arm, lift it in such a fashion that the shaft is free from your arm.*

Duarte then goes on to explain where jousters can go wrong:

> *Men often fail to score a hit for lack of sight, poor control of their lances or horses or lack of determination. As for sight, some close their eyes when they are about to hit and yet they do not realise because they are concentrating so much. Others realise that they*

close their eyes but cannot stop themselves from doing so. Others lose sight of their target because they are wearing a helmet or carrying their shields incorrectly. Others cannot see because at the point of meeting the other knight they only turn their eyes or heads, but continue in the same straight posture.

Most of all Duarte recommends going into a joust without fear or a strong desire to win, to avoid having a fall:

Owing to a lack of confidence, those who joust can fail in four different ways: firstly, because they want to avoid the encounter; secondly, because they veer away, fearing the moment of encounter; thirdly, by failing to keep their body and lance steady because of the effort required; fourthly, they are so anxious to gain an advantage over their adversary that they end up by failing.

Duarte King of Portugal, *The Art of Good Swordsmanship*, translated by Antonio Franco Preto

Rules and Regulations

Rules for early tournaments in the eleventh and twelfth centuries were very basic. Knights were simply required not to injure or kill each other and not to attack anyone taking refuge in the *recets*. Captured knights had to agree to forfeit their horse and pay a ransom, but could be released upon promise of payment.

By the time of the Round Tables, knights had to swear an oath to abide by the rules of the tournament. Judges were on hand to enforce the rules and a knight found breaking them would be expelled. Rules varied between tournaments, but would typically cover the required bluntness of the weapons and length of the lances; the boundaries of the field of play; disqualifications for cheating; the number of squires and lances each knight should be allowed; the prizes awarded; and the method of scoring. In 1466 Sir John Tipoft detailed a list of rules:

How many ways the prize is won:

✧ Who so breaketh most spears as they ought to be broken, shall have the prize.

✧ Who so hitteth three times, in the sight of the helm, shall have the prize.

✧ Who so meeteth two times, coronel to coronel, shall have the prize.

✧ Who so beareth a man down with stroke of a spear, shall have the prize.

How many ways the prize shall be lost:

✧ Who so striketh a horse shall have no prize.

✧ Who so striketh a man, his back turned, or disgarnished of his spear, shall have no prize.

✧ Who so hitteth the toyle (or tilt) three times shall have no prize.

✧ Who so unhelmeth himself two times shall have no prize, unless his horse do fail him.

In addition, a knight would be immediately disqualified for: striking below the belt; dropping his sword; fastening his sword to his hand; failing to show his sword to the judges; and resting on a barrier during combat. Prizes awarded would vary from gold chains to gold bars and jewels. Roger de Mortimer put up a golden lion as the prize for the 1279 Round Table tournament at Kenilworth Castle, England. De Mortimer himself won the prize.

Armour

Knights entering the tournaments of the eleventh and twelfth centuries used the same armour and equipment as they would take to war. The conditions of the *melee* were practically the same as on a real battlefield, so no special alterations were needed. The armour consisted of a chainmail hauberk with a hood, spurs and a body-length shield. Hauberks were often knee-length, but with a split in the front and back to allow for riding. Short sleeves were gradually extended to cover the wrists and hands, although the palm was always left exposed to better grasp the weapon.

Custom-made armour was specially designed for the jousting tournaments of the thirteenth century. Helmets of the twelfth century typically covered only the top of the head with a nose guard at the front. In the thirteenth century the helmet was extended to cover the whole head. These 'great helms' were cylindrical with a flat top, small slits for the eyes, and breathing holes around the mouth. This made it as hard to breathe as it was to see, but the helmet did protect the wearer from any sharp points. The problem with the 'great helm' was that it made it impossible to distinguish one knight from the other. To solve this problem, knights wore a crest on top of the helmet. Crests were often feathers, horns, or some type of creature, such as a dragon or lion. Individual coats of arms also decorated a knight's shield, horse, banner or surcoat covering his chainmail armour.

Chainmail protected the wearer from gashes, but not bruising. From the thirteenth century, knights started to wear padded linen armour, whalebone armour and leather armour as an alternative to chainmail. Leather armour was called *cuir bouilli* and boiled in hot wax for several hours to make it light and malleable, but tough enough to withstand a sword blow. The new technology of plate armour also had an impact on tourneying wear. Steel plates were custom-made into gauntlets for the hands and wrists; *sabatons* for the feet; *greaves* for the legs; *bracers* for the arms; a *gorget* for the neck and chin; and a breastplate for the torso. By the end of the fifteenth century plate armour had evolved into a full, joined-up suit of armour. The helmet also developed into the 'frog mouthed' helmet, which was smaller, rounder and provided less of a target for a lance.

The size of the shield changed from the full-length version used by a foot soldier in battle to a smaller triangular shield that better suited a mounted knight. The shield would further develop into a more oval shape specifically for jousts *à plaisance*. By the sixteenth century, the tournaments were designed to be as safe as possible while still creating an entertaining spectacle for the audience. A mechanical shield was built for just this purpose. It was put together with a series of springs which caused it to shatter into pieces when it was struck by a lance.

Medieval Tournament Movies

IVANHOE

Until the invention of moving pictures, the medieval tapestries, etchings, paintings and weapons left behind were the only visual accompaniments to stories about the tournaments. Since the early days of film, studios have tried to capture the sights and sounds of a day at the tournament, especially of knights jousting. The three movies featured over the next few pages were chosen not just for their attempts to feature the jousts, but their portrayal of the middle ages and chivalric values as well.

Ivanhoe is a 1952 adaptation of Walter Scott's classic tale, with all the Hollywood flourish expected of an MGM movie of this time. The acting is lofty, the armour new and sparkling, and the score dramatically overblown. Nevertheless, the movie remains one of the first to feature a convincing medieval tournament within the context of themes of the day.

The movie opens on Ivanhoe (Robert Taylor, who called *Ivanhoe* 'one of my iron jockstrap movies'), searching frantically for Richard I, who has disappeared en route from the third crusade. Ivanhoe tracks Richard down to the castle of Leopold of Austria, and spends the rest of the movie trying to raise the 150,000 marks needed for his release. His plan is to win the purse of a local tournament, but Prince John and his evil Norman knights get in the way. By the end of the movie, Robin Hood (Harold Warrender) and Elizabeth Taylor's character have both made an appearance and Richard I (Norman Wooland) is restored to his throne.

Ivanhoe was nominated for three Academy Awards and set a box office record, taking $1,310,590 in just over a month. This success spilled into two sequels – *Knights of the Round Table* (1953) and *The Adventures of Quentin Durward* (1954), both starring Robert Taylor. The film's scriptwriter did not fare so well. Marguerite Roberts was brought before the House on Un-American Activities Committee (HUAC) for belonging to the American Communist Party. She was blacklisted for not supplying the names of other party members and was consequently removed from the movie's credits.

Although the sword fighting is unconvincing, the tournament scene does much to evoke the atmosphere and excitement of the event. The pageantry and fanfare of the joust is successfully offset against the violence of the jousting knights. This scene and the climatic duel at the end of the film make it worthwhile viewing for enthusiasts of medieval war craft.

EXCALIBUR

The 1981 *Excalibur* is based on the 15th century romance *Le Morte D'Arthur* by Sir Thomas Malory. The movie was produced, directed and written by John Boorman, and features several members of his family. *Excalibur* earned a reputation as being a highly stylised, visually entertaining movie with a confused plot, wooden dialogue and little real substance.

The action begins with Arthur's father Uther Pendragon (Gabriel Byrne) and details Arthur's conception. Then attending a joust in the forest as a boy, Arthur pulls Excalibur from a stone and becomes king. Arthur (Nigel Terry) then meets and fights Lancelot (Nicholas Clay) who is holding a *pas d'armes* by a bridge. The meeting leads to Lancelot's affair with Queen Guinevere, the search for the Holy Grail, a climatic battle against the evil Morgana (Helen Mirren), and the dying Arthur being shipped away to Avalon.

John Boorman admitted he wanted *Excalibur* to emphasise the mythology of Arthur rather than focus on historical accuracy, and the movie achieves this aim. Boorman had tried to sell the concept of *Excalibur* to the

United Artists studio, who rejected it but instead offered him J.R.R Tolkien's *Lord of the Rings*. But the studio turned down Boorman's *Lord of the Rings* script, which they said was too long at three hours and would cost too much to make. Boorman was not able to sell *Lord of the Rings* elsewhere, but did sell his *Excalibur* script.

It is perhaps Boorman's work on *Lord of the Rings* that adds to the fantasy feel of *Excalibur*. It is full of striking visual imagery, which looks like brightly coloured filters interacting garishly with dry ice, but at other times brings out the rich colours of pageantry among the lush, earthly hues of the forest. The fantasy element is in further evidence with the armour, which is bright, silver plate metal. This armour only existed from the fifteenth century onwards, so contradicts the movie's timeline. The lists, stands, clothes and colours also belong to the late middle ages, as do the concepts of chivalry, which the movie focuses on. Courtly love, honour, and knightly conduct form the basis of Malory's *Le Morte D'Arthur*, but again did not exist in the dark ages.

As with *Ivanhoe* the movie's strength lies in its battle sequences. There is a reasonably convincing joust between Lancelot and Gawain, after which both knights are dismounted. The fighting continues on the ground with maces. This accurately portrays two cumbersome knights swinging at each other with heavy weapons, an ungraceful, clumsy and exhausting contest. But the armour becomes notably lighter during Lancelot's *pas d'armes* scene, and both Lancelot and Arthur can easily scramble down a bank. They also wield a weapon in each hand, which is unlikely, but the movie keeps to Malory's script by featuring the *pas d'armes*, an important part of the chivalric age of tournaments.

A KNIGHT'S TALE

A Knight's Tale is a 2001 Brian Helgeland movie that features jousting and the tournament circuit in the 1370s. Helgeland wrote, produced and directed the movie, which combines music and conventions from the twentieth century within the context of the primitive Middle Ages.

The movie centres on William (Heath Ledger) and his fellow squires Roland (Mark Addy) and Wat (Alan Tudyk) who have just discovered their master Sir Ector has died of dysentery between jousting bouts at a tournament. William decides to pose as Ector and when he wins the trio decide to continue the farce full time.

En route to their first tournament the group are joined by Geoffrey Chaucer (Paul Bettany) and many tournaments and hijinks ensue. After a final climactic joust, the heroes win, and Chaucer wonders whether he shouldn't write the whole story down.

A Knight's Tale is the first medieval movie to open with a tournament crowd chanting 'We Will Rock You' and the movie continues down this path for its duration. Classic rock tunes, modern day parlances 'hellooo', 'foxy lady') and sports logos are used throughout. In this sense Helgeland's deliberate anachronisms act like a get-out-of-jail-free card that made sure he wouldn't be judged for historical inaccuracy. Despite this, many audiences did not favour his approach, and critics panned the movie for being generally bland and uninspired.

As with the other two examples in this chapter, the movie retains the watcher's interest because of the jousting scenes. Helgeland spent time finding the right combination of materials to best splinter a lance on impact. The final result was an end made of balsa wood and dried pasta, which looks impressive in slow motion as it explodes on breast plate armour. Helgeland also had his front tooth knocked out by Ledger wielding a broomstick when the two were discussing jousting moves, which could possibly be considered suffering for one's art.

It is hard to know whether Chaucer would have approved of Helgeland's use of modern conventions in *A Knight's Tale*, but it is fairly certain the master satirist would have found a smarter mechanism to make the Middle Ages appeal to a modern audience.

DUELLING

Introduction

One of the most famous duels ever fought was also one of the most savage and deranged. The 1712 fight between James Douglas, Duke of Hamilton, and Lord Charles, Baron Mohun, was so appalling that it shocked many of the English gentry into rethinking the whole notion of duelling. The two aristocrats abandoned all the elaborate codes and rules of the duel and instead hacked, slashed and tore at each other like demented thugs. It was difficult to see how the contest of the duel could be defined as gentlemanly and honourable, when such acts of extreme barbarism were taking place in its name. In fact, this dreadful bout of butchery became instantly notorious throughout England and marked a turning point in the history of this form of one-on-one combat. It sowed the seed that eventually led to the death of the duel.

The pair were bluebloods long inculcated in the honour code of duelling. Hamilton was fifty-four and a Jacobite, one of the followers of James II after he was forced from the throne in the Glorious Revolution of 1688. His affiliations saw Hamilton in and out of favour with the royal court, and at one stage had him imprisoned in the Tower of London on charges of treason. These were later dropped and Hamilton changed his political persuasion, becoming a Tory and winning the favour of Queen Anne. By 1712 Hamilton had been awarded the Order of the Garter and the Order of the Thistle, the only non-Royal to be a knight of both orders. Hamilton did not have a reputation as a dueller, although he had once seen off a group of five swordsmen who were hired to kill him.

Charles Mohun's upbringing was in stark contrast. He was born into the world of the duel. When Charles was born in April 1675, Mohun's father was on his deathbed after being wounded in a duel. The estate was left heavily in debt and the child Mohun was not able to afford a formal education. But he was a chip off the old block. Even as a teenager he gambled to support his hedonistic lifestyle and at sixteen years old entered his first duel with Lord Kennedy in London. Both men received only light wounds during the bout, but the scene was already set for the more lurid incident that followed.

This time the fight was about a woman. Mohun had been keeping the company of Captain Richard Hill, by all accounts a dangerous degenerate who had become fixated on an actress called Anne Bracegirdle. Hill's plan was to abduct Bracegirdle after she had finished her performance at a West End theatre, and he recruited Mohun to help. Bracegirdle did not appear but her fellow actor William Mountford did, a man Hill was convinced stood in the way of his future relations with Bracegirdle. Mohun approached Mountford on the pretext of being drunk and caught him in an embrace, as Hill ran up behind the two and stabbed Mountford through the chest. Hill promptly fled to the continent and Mohun was tried for murder in the House of Lords. The trial was the talk of the town and Mohun became a celebrity defendant, although appeared to have no remorse about his deed. In the end he was acquitted on the grounds that Mountford had drawn first.

Mohun decided to move abroad where he served in the army before returning to London in 1697. Soon after his arrival Mohun killed another man in a duel and was once again acquitted of the crime. Soon after he took his place in the House of Lords and killed yet another man in a duel. This time Mohun did not need to stand trial but was instead given a royal pardon by King William III, who saw his Whig support as valuable. In 1701 the Earl of Macclesfield died, leaving Mohun, whom he had taken under his wing, most of his estate. But there was another claimant to the estate – James Douglas, Duke of Hamilton.

Hamilton and Mohun would wrangle over the estate through the courts until 1712. Mohun needed to win the estate to pay off his debts, but feared that Hamilton, the darling of the royal court, had the upper hand. In a hearing on 13 November, Hamilton made it known that he considered Mohun's main witness to be of untruthful character. Mohun took this as a personal affront and challenged Hamilton to a duel to take place two days later at the Ring in Hyde Park.

SEEDY SETTINGS

Hyde Park, situated in a slightly seedy area on the outskirts of the city proper, was a popular location for duels in the early eighteenth century. At 6 a.m. on the morning of 15 November, a coachman called John Pennington picked up Mohun and his second General George MacCartney from a brothel and drove them to the park. MacCartney was an unsavory character who had been convicted of rape and was thought to live off handouts from Mohun. MacCartney was also said to have his own personal issues with Hamilton's second, Colonel John Hamilton. Upon arriving at Hyde Park Mohun ordered Pennington to bring him some ale, which he attempted to do by waking up a local inn keeper. The inn keeper, rightly thinking the request was to do with an imminent duel, followed Pennington back to the park.

By this stage Hamilton and the Colonel had arrived and preparations were being made to begin duelling. Pennington and the inn keeper were just two witnesses who watched the duel, and a conversation regarding the use of seconds was overheard. Mohun suggested the quarrel was between the principals and that the seconds should not play a part. But MacCartney had come for the fighting and made a comment about 'taking his share.' Hamilton reciprocated this sentiment and indicated the Colonel felt the same way. Both of the principals then drew their swords.

What followed was a brutal bloodbath with no holds barred. Eyewitness accounts as well as the testimonies of MacCartney and Hamilton recorded the event, although the various versions contradict each other at times. What is clear is that Mohun and Hamilton both lunged abruptly and abandoned all pretence of sword-play to instead set about slashing, hacking and grabbing at each other like unhinged animals.

Hamilton drew first blood when he rushed at Mohun and sliced open a 15 cm (6 in) deep gash on his left side. He then ran Mohun through below his lower right rib, with the sword re-emerging by his left hip. Mohun slashed back wildly at Hamilton cutting a wound 18 cm (7 in) deep in his right leg. Mohun then attacked again, this time cutting through Hamilton's elbow and slicing the main artery in two. Mohun lashed out as he staggered backwards, making a downwards cut into Hamilton's chest between his second and third ribs – a fatal wound. But Hamilton fought back at the fallen Mohun and thrust his sword through the man's groin, the point exiting through his left buttock, which sliced through the main artery in the leg. It was this wound which killed Mohun, although the surgeon who examined the body said he would not have survived the first cut through his chest. In addition to the other injuries, three of Mohun's fingers had been all but severed as he tried to grab at Hamilton's blade. Hamilton's left foot had been cut open.

Hamilton staggered to the nearest tree and collapsed. His second, the Colonel, called for his coach, but by the time Hamilton reached home he had bled to death.

The Colonel and MacCartney would have played out their own bloody contest had their drawn swords not been confiscated and bent in two by the bystanders. Both seconds went into hiding after the duel, news of which had reached the ears of every Londoner by lunchtime that day.

When the Colonel re-emerged it was to deliver news that would shock the public – already outraged by brutal details of the duel – into disbelief. The Colonel reported that it was actually MacCartney who had delivered the fatal thrust to Hamilton's chest, creeping up behind the man as he stood over Mohun. This news spread like wildfire, sparking a raft of conspiracy theories, gossip and documents that outlined the innocence of both men. *A True and Impartial Account of the Murder of his Grace the Duke of Hamilton and Brandon* was a righteous defence of Hamilton, which was counterbuffed by *A Letter from Mr MacCartney to a Friend of his in London* which did the same for MacCartney.

Within one month Hamilton had been cleared for his part in the duel. It took a further four years for MacCartney to be acquitted of Hamilton's murder.

Queen Anne and the Church laid bare their outrage and disgust at the Hamilton-Mohun duel; the English public concurred. There was no disguising this duel behind a veneer of honour and gentlemanly conduct, and England began a slow withdrawal away from the contest. Instead boxing began to emerge as an acceptable way for gentlemen to carry out their grievances, which, unlike the duel, would be fought out in public.

A GENTLEMAN'S CONTEST

Duelling was always an act of violence, but it was an act of violence between gentlemen. It was therefore surrounded by ritual, etiquette and an elaborate set of rules to make it fair and above board. Throughout the whole business a gentleman's honour was at stake, and the battle would have to proceed in accordance with the duelling code. Whole manuals were published on the mechanics and protocol of a duel. Seconds – the gentlemen's gentlemen – were brought on board to organise, oversee and even join the fight if necessary. Gentleman from Russia to Ireland were brought up to fight with sword and pistol, and could expect to use them in their lifetimes.

A gentleman's honour was considered his greatest

asset and he would willingly die defending it. Gentlemen, therefore, were often ready to take offence at any slight, affront or insult. Some 'offences' could be as trivial as one gentleman's dog attacking another. Others were more intimate and unforgivable – in other words, they were about women. Russia's greatest poet, Alexander Pushkin, died in a duel over the honour of his wife.

Duelling practice varied from place to place and from time to time. Sometimes the duellists lunged with sabres, sometimes they stood and shot. Many fired into the air or the ground, although duelling code forbade this. The duel was against the law and banned by the church, but for 400 years it flourished. Duels were still being fought in France, Italy, Hungary and the Americas until the middle of the last century.

History

The duel was born in the dark ages, developed throughout the age of chivalry, and reached its peak during the age of enlightenment. As the duel was a prearranged fight between two gentlemen to settle a dispute or point of honour, it was called the duel of honour. A duel started with an insult, real or imagined. If the offending gentleman could not, or would not, rectify the situation, the offended party issued a challenge.

The challenge was a formal, written piece of correspondence outlining the grievance and the time, place and weaponry to be used to settle it. Further correspondence between the two parties could discuss the terms until consensus had been reached.

The duel was a bout of violence governed by elaborate ritual and protocol. The terms of the duel determined, for example, if it was to be fought with swords or pistols, or where the duellists should stand in relation to each other. All the arrangements would be made by the gentleman's second, who would also step in to fight his opposite number if required. The aim of the duel was to give the insulted party 'satisfaction', in the manner he saw fit – whether it be by drawing his opponent's blood or by killing him.

In most countries the duel of honour was banned by

the State and the Church, and as such usually took place in remote, secret locations. The Church's condemnation of peacetime combat was nothing new; medieval tournaments of the eleventh and twelfth centuries had suffered similar treatment (see page 180). These were the free-for-all brawls called *melees*, which were gradually replaced with jousting tournaments fought according to a chivalric code. This code also underpinned the duel of chivalry, which emerged in Europe in the late thirteenth century.

The duel of chivalry was much like the duel of honour – it was used by two quarrelling knights to settle a dispute. The chivalric behaviour expected of all jousting knights formed the basis of the duel of honour. Duelling gentlemen, just like jousting knights, were expected to conduct themselves in a fair, honest and honourable way. But the duel of honour also had its roots in a much older and stranger tradition – trial by combat, also known as the judicial duel.

The Judicial Duel

The judicial duel was a dark age custom used among small Germanic tribes to decide a person's guilt or innocence of a crime. If the accused was unable to produce evidence of his innocence, his accuser could challenge him to a duel. It was thought that God would protect the innocent and allow him to defeat either the guilty party or the false accuser.

The judicial duel was first made law in 501 by Gundebald of Burgundy, who had taken the throne by killing or scaring off the other heirs, his brothers. He then converted to Catholicism. It was Gundebald's view that if God chose the rightful winner in battles between warring countries, then he would do the same for disputes between individuals. The judgment of God therefore became the rationale for the judicial duel, which quickly spread across the continent.

The judgment of God was also used in a more disturbing trial of this period, created by the Church – trial by ordeal. Trial by ordeal first appeared in parts of Europe in the sixth century and continued until the fifteenth century, when it was largely replaced with confession by torture. A trial by ordeal used fire or water to determine whether a person was guilty or innocent.

In an ordeal by fire, the accused was forced to walk across a long line of red-hot plow blades. Afterwards, the person's feet would be bandaged for three days and then inspected. If the wounds had healed the accused was considered innocent, but if they were raw and festering, then he was guilty. It was believed that God would protect the innocent by intervening with a healing miracle if needed.

Ordeal by hot water forced the accused to reach into a cauldron of boiling hot water, lead or oil and pull out a stone or similar object. The person's arm, which would usually lose most of its skin, was again wrapped in a bandage and inspected three days later. In trial by cold water the accused was thrown into a stream. Those who sank were deemed guilty, even if a millstone or rock had been attached to them, which it often had. If, during any of the ordeals, the accused died it was considered divine intervention, and the fate of their soul then lay in the hands of God.

While trial by ordeal had the full sanction of the Church, its less bloody companion, the judicial duel, was not held in the same regard. Although the judicial duel called upon God to expose guilt or innocence, the Church's stance on the matter was mixed. It was banned by the pope in 855, given papal blessing in 858, and condemned again from the tenth century. In the fifteenth century Pope Julius II, otherwise known as

'The Fearsome Pope', threatened to excommunicate any monarch who allowed the judicial duel.

These threats did nothing to abate the popularity of the judicial duel, which flourished across Europe in the middle ages, often with the knowledge of the reigning monarch. In 982, Holy Roman Emperor Otto the Great defied the Church and allowed the judicial duel. In France the judicial duel spread like wildfire and a ban in the twelfth century did little to reduce its occurrence. Its use only slowed down in 1566, when Charles IX decreed that anyone involved in one would be executed. The French brought the judicial duel with them to England in 1066, where it was in use until the sixteenth century and not banned completely until the nineteenth century.

As the judicial duel developed, procedures and rules of conduct were formed. The duel was open to everyone except women, priests, the sick and men under twenty or over sixty. Commoners usually fought with wooden quarterstaffs and leather shields, while gentlemen were allowed to fight on horseback. A gentleman could also appoint a champion to fight in his place. Champions were typically professional fighters or hardened soldiers, but the practice was still a risky one. If the champion lost he would lose his arm as punishment and the accused was hanged.

The duel itself began when the challenger threw down his gauntlet, which, if accepted, was picked up by the accused. Both men then had to swear their testimony had been true, that they were not carrying magical amulets and were only fighting with the prearranged weapons. The spectators had to remain quiet for the duration or risk having a limb amputated as punishment. The duel ended when one combatant was too badly wounded to fight on. His opponent then finished him off with well-placed dagger thrust.

FRENCH FARCE

Although the judicial duel thrived for several centuries, its fallibility was often clear. A good example was the duel between Frenchmen Jacques de Gris and Jean de Carrouges in 1386. The two noblemen were, at one time, friends, but they became rivals and then bitter enemies after de Gris was accused of raping de Carrouges' wife, Marguerite. A court trial ran for some months and when no satisfactory verdict could be found, the King of France Charles VI ordered a judicial duel.

The duel took place at a Parisian monastery in front of Charles, his court, a crowd of thousands and Marguerite, who faced execution if de Gris was found innocent. After a long contest de Carrouges had de Gris on the ground, and finished him off by stabbing him through his throat. However, a few weeks later another man was arrested and confessed to the rape of Marguerite. Rumours then spread that de Carrouges had falsely pinned the crime on de Gris to begin with.

Other judicial duels were even more bizarre. In 1371 Richard Macaire murdered his friend and fellow knight Aubrey de Montdidier and buried him in a forest in Bondy, near Paris. De Montdidier's dog ran to the house of a nearby friend and dragged him to the grave, whereupon de Montdidier's body was dug up. From that point on every time the dog saw Macaire he would attack him, leading to many raised eyebrows and suspicion. King Charles V caught wind of the story and ordered a judicial duel between Macaire and the dog in Notre Dame square. To even up the odds between man and beast, Macaire was required to fight buried up to his waist. Minutes after the trial began the dog took Macaire by the throat, compelling him to confess his guilt. He was hanged by the neck that afternoon.

ENGLISH EXPIRATION

Across the Channel the judicial duel had also taken hold. In 1095, Count William d'Eu was planning to overthrow King William II, but news of the plot reached Baron Geoffrey Baynard who tipped William off. William sent an army to attack the rebels at their castle at Bamburgh and three months later they were defeated. William then ordered a judicial duel to be fought between d'Eu and

Baynard, which Baynard won. As punishment d'Eu was castrated and blinded, and died from his wounds.

The judicial duel in England continued throughout the Middle Ages and into the reign of Elizabeth I, although by then it was not a regular occurrence. The law courts were therefore caught unawares when in 1571, a man called Paramour demanded a judicial duel over a land dispute with a man called Lowe. Both men chose champions to represent them.

The duel was supposed to be fought at 10 a.m., on 18 June at Tothill Fields, London. The trial had gained much publicity and over three thousand spectators gathered to watch Lowe's champion, a fencing teacher called Henry Nailer, as he warmed up. But Paramour and his champion failed to make an appearance and the crowd were left disappointed. Some speculated Elizabeth herself had intervened to put a stop to the spectacle.

There was one more attempt to hold a judicial duel in England, nearly three centuries later. In 1817 Abraham Thorton was charged with the murder of Mary Ashford. But then to the court's bewilderment he threw down a glove and demanded the right to fight the charges with a judicial duel. After a heated discussion between the lawyers, Judge Ellenborough ruled that a judicial duel was Thorton's right by law. He ordered a judicial duel between Thorton and Mary Ashford's brother. As the brother refused to participate Thorton was found innocent and acquitted of all charges. The English Parliament made sure such a case would never occur again by abolishing the judicial duel in 1819.

The Duel of Honour

By the middle of the sixteenth century the judicial duel was on the wane in Europe. It would be supplanted by a closely-related successor – the duel of honour. The first recorded duel of honour was the 1528 challenge made by the King of France Francis I to Holy Roman Emperor Charles V.

Most of Charles' reign was taken up warring with his nemesis Francis, so he was enraged in 1527 to find the French king had broken a carefully negotiated peace deal by attacking him. Charles sent word to Francis that he considered him a dishonourable man without integrity. In response Francis challenged Charles to a duel, which Charles duly accepted. The duel would set a benchmark in modern history; never had two such powerful leaders met to duke out their problems in person. Nor would they now. Francis did not think that Charles would accept his challenge and set about wriggling his way out of it, thus further confirming Charles' insult. Through his backtracking Francis had unwittingly created one of the most important rules of the duel of honour. Any man challenging another to a duel would have to make good his intentions or suffer public disgrace. The duel of honour was fought in private but it didn't take long for everyone to hear about its outcome. The secretive nature of the duel of honour was also the biggest difference between it and its closest relatives – the duel of chivalry and the judicial duel, both of which were held in front of a crowd.

In the sixteenth century, the duel of honour became so popular that manuals and rule books were being written about it. Some of the first manuals were the Italian *code duello*, which were published in the hope that regulating the duel would cut down on the numbers killed through vendettas. The *code duello* advised the duel should take place as a last resort, and even then only if the rules were strictly observed. It further advised having medical care and witnesses on hand in case one party fell foul of the other and the authorities become involved.

It is no coincidence that the rise of the duel of honour across Europe in the sixteenth century occurred around the same time as the Italian Wars. French troops stationed in Italy not only became familiar with the duel; they often found themselves involved in them. Soldiers returning to France brought with them copies of the *code duello* and first hand experience of preserving one's honour with a blade.

The French took to the duels of honour with a vigour that far surpassed their Italian counterparts. In 1559 the French parliament banned duelling but this did nothing

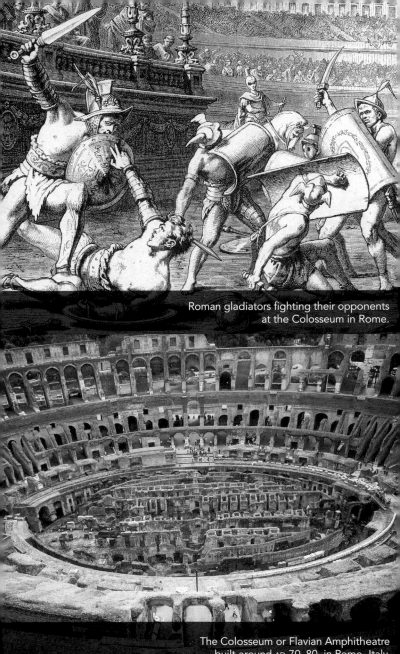

Roman gladiators fighting their opponents
at the Colosseum in Rome.

The Colosseum or Flavian Amphitheatre
built around AD 70–80, in Rome, Italy.

Samurai warriors fight to the death. Every samurai would carry two swords, one long (*katana*) and one short (*wakizashi*). The *wakizashi* was not used for fighting, but to decapitate defeated warriors.

Noblemen watch on as a jousting competition takes place. Jousting was an opportunity to settle disputes, showcase talent and fight for a lady's honour.

In 1804, American politicians Aaron Burr and Alexander Hamilton engaged in a pistol duel. The wave of public outrage that followed began its subsequent demise in popularity.

Despite Billy the Kid's reputation as a murderous outlaw, he was described as having a cheerful disposition and a way with the ladies.

Notorious gunslinger John Wesley Hardin was known as 'the meanest man in Texas', and once shot a man dead for snoring.

Jack Dempsey's savage fighting style combined with his rugged, frontier-town image made him one of the most popular boxers in modern history.

Fighter pilot legend The Red Baron enjoyed his victories so much that he would collect trophies from the planes he shot down

In a 1966 fight against Cleveland Williams, Muhammad Ali landed over one hundred punches on his opponent and won in three rounds.

to stem its popularity, and between 1589 and 1607 over four thousand French men were killed in duels. As with the judicial duel, the duel of honour soon found its way across the Channel to England.

By the end of the sixteenth century the English authorities had as much chance of containing the duel as those on the continent. The English duel was further influenced by Italian literature, such as Baldassare Castiglione's *Libro del Cortegiano*, a treatise on Renaissance manners, etiquette and honour. It was not long before a raft of English alternatives lined the shelves of bookstores, including G. H. Ghent's *The Private School of Defence*, a handbook of duelling advice and instruction.

CHOOSE YOUR WEAPONS

Another Italian import was the rapier, a civilian sword that replaced its heavier battlefield predecessor. Italian fencing teachers, such as Roco Bonneti, instructed the English in the rapier's use. The rapier was used to good effect – a rough estimate puts the number killed in duels during the reign of Henry IV of France (1589–1610) between five thousand and seven thousand.

By the time Charles II took the throne in 1660 the duel was not only a daily occurrence on the streets of London but had also permeated every part of English society. Newspapers were filled with duelling reports and the latest bout became the topic of conversation and gossip across the country. Even after Charles II decreed that duellists who killed would be tried for murder, new duelling clubs sprang up around the capital. Membership of clubs like the 'fire-eaters' was given only to those who had killed at least one man. In France, King Louis XIII's accession to the throne marked the beginning of a duelling fanaticism in France that would not end until the 1815 defeat of Napoleon at Waterloo.

Soon new weapons were added to the duelling arsenal – the smallsword and the duelling pistol. From the 1770s the pistol became the first choice of weapon, especially in North America, which began a duelling tradition all of its own. Duelling was finally banned in England in 1852, but continued in France, Germany, Italy, Hungary and Latin America until the mid-twentieth century. Whatever the regional or national differences, almost all duels shared three common elements – the challenge, the use of seconds and rules of engagement.

The Challenge

All duels began as a result of an affront, insult or slur made by one gentleman to another. This could be something as minor as an impolite gesture, a brushing of shoulders in the street, or a mumbled comment. Often, if offence had been taken, an explanation was demanded, and if given to the satisfaction of the aggrieved party the matter was put to rest. Insults of a more severe nature, which included name-calling and libellous insinuation, would require a full apology, explanation and retraction. Physical contact was considered the most serious misdeed and one unlikely to be glossed over. But the nature of the insult, perceived or otherwise, was almost secondary to the fact that a gentleman had been insulted to begin with.

A gentleman treasured his honour and was ready to die defending it. Honour defined a man's place in the world – his rank and position, his name and reputation, his courage and power. An insult made in front of gentleman's peers was the gravest of offences as it could affect a man's standing in society. If a gentleman did not defend his honour he would be branded a coward, resulting in a loss of face and future opportunities in his professional and personal life. To keep his honour intact, a gentleman had to be prepared to assert his dominance by resorting to combat. Combat would not be fought at the time of the insult, as this would constitute a non-gentlemanly brawl only fit for the lower classes (swords between gentlemen were of course sometimes drawn at the time; these were known as 'encounters').

It was also considered bad form to become openly upset or overly excited by an insult. Rather, an insulted gentleman was expected to show a coolness of nerve and self-control. Often he would wait before issuing a formal challenge and instead write a letter to his insulter asking for an explanation. Such a letter created the necessary time for the smoke to clear, or a chance for both parties to sober up. This point is made clear in the 1777 Irish *code duello*: 'Challenges are never to be delivered at night, unless the party to be challenged intend leaving the place of offense before morning; for it is desirable to avoid all hot-headed proceedings.'

If the insult had been made in the heat of the moment, a courteous and apologetic reply was sent back to the insulted party and the matter resolved. However, if no such letter was forthcoming or the reply considered inadequate, a formal challenge would be issued. This often took the form of another letter which would detail the dispute and the time, location and weaponry to be used in the duel. According to the 1777 *code duello*: 'The challenged chooses his ground; the challenger chooses his distance; the seconds fix the time and terms of firing.'

The terms of the duel were all-important, as they aimed to make the contest fair and above-board. If one party had an impediment of some sort, steps would be made to balance out the odds, which is why Richard Macaire fought his friend's dog with the disadvantage of being buried up to his waist (220). Once the terms had been agreed upon the duel was set and all either party could do was wait.

Seconds

The role of a second was of vital importance to the duel and a principal would name his second from the outset. Manuals and code books of the day had much to say about picking a suitable second, who had to be steadfast and reliable in character. The 1777 *code duello* says: 'Seconds to be of equal rank in society with the principals they attend, inasmuch as a second may either choose or chance to become a principal, and equality is indispensable.'

It was the second's job to watch their principal's back, make sure the duel was conducted according to the agreed rules, and if necessary fight his opposite number. But before the duel even began, it was the second's duty to act as go-between, handling all communication and correspondence between the principals and trying to find a peaceful resolution.

Even on the duelling field the seconds tried to reconcile the principals, or if this failed, to see that injuries were kept to a minimum. Some seconds even informed the authorities of the duel, which was considered very ungentlemanly. Nevertheless, many duellists met each other at dawn ready for a fight to the death, only to have the police arrive and arrest them.

If pistols were involved the seconds had to measure out the agreed distance and load the weapons. After the first shot had been fired, or a period of sword fighting passed, the seconds intervened to check if the challenger's honour had been restored, or if the challenged wished to restore it by issuing an apology. If this was not forthcoming the seconds reloaded the pistols or backed away so that the principals could begin swinging their sabres once more.

The 1777 *code duello* mentions an occasion upon which seconds may also enter the fray: 'Where seconds disagree, and resolve to exchange shots themselves, it must be at the same time and at right angles with their principals, thus: If with swords, side by side, with five paces interval.'

A duel ended whenever the challenger called out that he was 'satisfied'. This often occurred after he had drawn first blood. At that point the matter was considered resolved and both men could depart with their honour unscathed – although the same could not always be said for their bodies. Following this outcome the seconds often drew up a report and had all parties sign it. At other times there was only one principal left alive, rendering such a document unnecessary.

Women

Politics, gambling and women caused many a duel. As with the chivalrous medieval knight, it was expected of a gentleman to protect his lady's honour. This sentiment formed an important part of the 1777 *code duello*:

> *Any insult to a lady under a gentleman's care or protection to be considered as, by one degree, a greater offense than if given to the gentleman personally, and to be regulated accordingly…Offenses originating or accruing from the support of ladies' reputations, to be considered as less unjustifiable than any others of the same class, and as admitting of slighter apologies by the aggressor: this to be determined by the circumstances of the case, but always favorable to the lady.*

Duels between women were rare but did occur. Usually such events were overseen by amused men who put an end to proceedings before blood was drawn. An exception to this was Julie d'Aubigny (also known as Mademoiselle de Maupin), an opera singer and fencer. D'Aubigny was trained in the art of sword fighting as a child, and from a young age displayed a fiery temper and penchant for combat. D'Aubigny sang in inns and taverns and then changed into men's clothing to give fencing exhibitions. She was said to be so talented that on one occasion a man shouted out that she must be a male to fight so well, prompting her to stop the fight and rip open her shirt to disprove the claim.

After spending time with various lovers d'Aubigny declared she had had enough of men, cut her hair short and began dressing as a man full time. Thinking she was indeed a man, a young blonde woman displayed her affection, which d'Aubigny reciprocated and an affair ensued. The blonde was sent away to a convent in Avignon, which d'Aubigny herself joined to be closer to her lover. One day a nun died and d'Aubigny put the body in her lover's bed and set it alight, thus faking her death. The two ran away together, but after three months d'Aubigny became bored and sent her lover away. Charged with kidnapping, arson and body snatching, she fled to Paris where she became an opera singer again, now under the assumed name of Mademoiselle de Maupin.

De Maupin was loved by her audiences but hated by the other performers. She also continued fighting as a duellist, attacking three nobles at a court ball in 1693, and then fleeing to escape arrest. She returned to Paris four years later and went back to the opera. She performed for the last time in 1705 and then retired to a convent, where she died in 1707.

Sword Duels

The popularity of the duel grew along with the use of the new duelling sword from Italy, the rapier. The rapier had a thin, straight blade between 83 and 134 cm (33 and 53 in) long and a sharp end with which to thrust. The Roman soldier knew the importance of a short thrusting sword, which was far more likely to hit a major organ or artery than one that slashed and cut. The Roman gladius had been made obsolete by the large, heavy broadswords wielded during the dark ages, but now the thrusting sword for close quarter combat was back in vogue.

From the end of the sixteenth century Italian fencing teachers were setting up schools all over Europe to teach the new techniques in rapier swordplay. The duellist was also taught to fight with a dagger, which was held in the left hand mainly as a defensive weapon. Sometimes a chainmail glove was worn on the left hand to parry blows. At the end of the seventeenth century a shorter thrusting sword emerged called the smallsword. The smallsword had a blade between 79 and 89 cm (31 and 35 in) long and was small enough to be worn at all times, replacing the awkwardly long rapier for this reason.

Duelling gentlemen were expected to fight with swords of the same length and it was the job of their seconds to make sure this was so. The principals then heard the terms of the duel before taking up their position, with the ends of their swords crossed. By the time of the smallsword the daggers or gloves were disallowed and the left hand had to be left entirely out of play. The best swordsmen were often the ones who had been taught by expert fencers – they were nimble-footed enough to pull back into a defensive stance as well as to lunge forward and deliver a fatal thrust.

By the end of the nineteenth century sword duels were largely going out of fashion, and were instead being replaced by the modern sport of fencing. Fencing required the use of mesh helmets, hand guards and pointed ends to reduce the chances of injury. But by contrast, the sword, which could end a duel after first blood, was supplanted by a much clumsier alternative – the pistol.

Pistol Duels

Unlike duels with a sword, the distance over which a pistol duel was fought was determined by the severity of the insult. Short distances were chosen for extreme insults to ensure one of the principals was seriously hurt. For milder affairs where the main objective was not to kill but instead to make a point, a long distance was picked.

In England 9 metres (10 yards) was considered the minimum distance. In France it was 13.7 metres (15 yards) but this could extend to over 22.8 metres (25 yards), which was too far to hit anything accurately. At the opposite extreme, in one 1827 duel in the Bois de Boulogne, the principals were only three paces apart and, predictably, both were killed.

Distance was only one factor determining the outcome of a pistol duel. Another was the type of duel. The most common pistol duel in France and Britain was the stand and fire. For this, two opponents faced each other at an agreed distance and fired at the same time. A variation gave the challenged man the first shot. Another method saw the two duellists standing back to back, walking in a straight line, and at the agreed signal turning and firing.

In Russia the barrier duel was favoured. Both men started 27.4 metres (30 yards) apart and walked slowly towards each other and a central barrier – a buffer zone which neither could cross. Once one man had fired he had to stand still, allowing his opponent to walk to the edge of the buffer zone to take his shot.

The pistols themselves played a vital part in the conflict, but it was not until the later years of the duel of honour that a matched pair was made a requirement. The seconds would load and cock the pistols, and prepare a back-up in the same way. The seconds would then stand away with their own loaded pistol in case any of the rules needed enforcing.

The duelling pistols developed for the duels of the late eighteenth century were built with a wooden handle and a barrel around 25 cm (10 in) long. Pistols often came in a case containing various implements to load the pistol, including a powder flask and a ramrod. To load the pistol, powder was poured down the barrel and a round lead bullet dropped into the muzzle, which was packed down tightly with the ramrod. Pulling the trigger detonated the charge and fired the shot.

Clothes were also important as a bullet could take piece of cloth with it into the wound, sometimes causing infection and a long agonising death. Many men wore silk, which was considered a purer material, while others stripped to the waist. Some wore several layers of thick cloth, paper and metal sheeting, to lessen a bullet's impact. It was the job of the seconds to check over a principal's attire to make sure fob watches, hipflasks and coins had been removed.

For the classic duel it was customary for the men to stand side on to each other to make themselves a smaller target. They would then raise their pistols to eye level and shoot on a count of three. It was not uncommon for at least one of the duellists to lose their nerve and shoot wide. Others, not intending to injure or kill, fired their shot into the air. Both of these actions were expressly forbidden in the 1777 *code duello*:

> *No dumb shooting or firing in the air is admissible in any case. The challenger ought not to have challenged without receiving offense; and the challenged ought, if he gave offense, to have made an apology before he came on the ground; therefore, children's play must be dishonorable on one side or the other, and is accordingly prohibited.*

All agreed that the rules and etiquette of a duel had to be observed at all times. The duellists were expected to behave as gentlemen, with the same self-control they had displayed on being insulted in the first place – even if they had been shot. In this instance it was recommended the duellist retain a calm decorum, forgive his opponent, and die with the grace befitting a gentleman.

Duellists and Duels

SHERIDAN-MATHEWS

British playwright Richard Brinsley Sheridan and Captain Thomas Mathews met each other for two bouts of combat. Their story had all of the classic duelling elements and more – unrequited love, defamation, cowardice and bloodshed. Richard Brinsley Sheridan was born on 30 October 1751 to theatre manager, Thomas Sheridan. Thomas Sheridan often hired a musician, Thomas Linley, whose daughter Elizabeth was said to catch the eye of every man who passed her. Richard Sheridan fell hard for Elizabeth and the two became lovers. But Elizabeth's father did not see the union as favourable and the door was left open for other suitors.

One such man was Captain Thomas Mathews, a married man, who threatened to take Elizabeth by force if she did not sleep with him. Instead Elizabeth fled to France with Sheridan in tow. The couple eloped to Lille and Sheridan wrote a letter to Thomas Linley explaining what had happened. But Thomas Mathews caught wind of the news and set about blackening Sheridan's name. Mathews arranged for an article calling Sheridan a 'liar' and 'scoundrel' to appear in the *Bath Chronicle*.

When Sheridan heard about this scurrilous attack he had no alternative but to sail back to England and defend his honour. On arrival Sheridan went straight to Mathews' lodgings and, despite it being past midnight, banged on the door until Mathews let him in. Mathews quickly realised Sheridan had not yet read the article and managed to convince him that its contents had been greatly exaggerated. But the next day Sheridan was enraged to find the article was just as libellous as he had been led to believe and challenged Mathews to a duel. The date was set for Hyde Park on 4 May at 6 p.m.

Mathews had studied fencing in France and was said to be something of a swordsman. But Sheridan had been schooled by an Italian fencer and was confident in his abilities. Sheridan was the first in Hyde Park, where he and his second Simon Ewart waited for Mathews. Eventually Mathews appeared with his second Captain Knight in tow, although he instantly dismissed the surroundings as being too public and asked for a change of location. After moving to another part of the park Mathews claimed to have seen a policeman, and both parties left the park.

In the end the duellists and their seconds ended up in a back room of the Castle Tavern in Covent Garden. The seconds went about lighting extra candles and making the room suitable, but they needn't have bothered as the fight was over as quickly as it began. Within seconds of raising their swords Sheridan had disarmed Mathews, who began apologising profusely and begging for his life. Sheridan demanded his opponent give up his sword or continue to fight to which Mathews demurred. Furious, Sheridan grabbed Mathews' sword from him, broke it and flung the hilt across the room. After a further exchange of words Sheridan dictated an apology on Mathews' behalf to be sent to the *Bath Chronicle*. Reluctantly Mathews signed the document and travelled back to Bath with his tail between his legs.

News of Mathews' conduct at the duel followed the Captain home, and he soon found his reputation to be in tatters. He tried to sway accusations of cowardice by telling people he had only apologised out of generosity and the breaking of his sword had been an unprovoked action. Once again Sheridan caught wind of Mathews' retelling of the duel, and decided to pen his own account, which not only made Mathews out to be the loser but also a liar.

PISTOLS AT DAWN

Sheridan must have been expecting Mathews' response to such provocation. Sure enough, a challenge was issued to Sheridan, this time to be held in Bath with pistols. Sheridan was under no obligation to accept the challenge – after all, he had settled the matter by winning the last bout. But nor did Sheridan want to be accused of cowardice, especially by a mudslinger like Thomas Mathews. So he agreed to the challenge and travelled to Bath to meet Mathews in combat.

Sheridan and his second stopped at the White Hart Inn on the night of 31 July 1772 and drank heavily until around 3 a.m. Then they set out by coach to Kingsdown Common, where the duel was to be held. The contest started out with pistols – both fired without finding purchase and swords were drawn. Mathews ran at Sheridan and broke his sword on him, leaving some jagged ends poking out from the hilt. But Mathews was not to be undone again and jumped on Sheridan and set about punching and stabbing at the man with his broken sword hilt. Mathews stabbed Sheridan over thirty times, as Sheridan in vain tried to hack back at him with his own weapon. Fearing the worst Sheridan's second shouted out to him: 'My dear Sheridan, beg for your life,' to which Sheridan yelled back 'No by God, I won't.'

After he deemed Sheridan sufficiently injured, Mathews rolled off him and stumbled off to his coach for London. Sheridan was helped into his coach and taken back to the White Hart Inn, where his wounds were tended to. It took Sheridan just over a week to recover, whereupon he learned Mathews had fled to the continent. This was considered the action of a coward who had fought unfairly, and although Sheridan for all intents and purposes had lost the second bout, he emerged the winner of the conflict.

He went on to officially marry Elizabeth and became a well-known playwright, writing *The Rivals, The School for Scandal* and *A Trip to Scarborough*, among others. But the marriage was not similarly successful, despite its romantic beginnings, and both spouses soon began affairs with other people. Elizabeth died in 1792. Between 1780 and 1812 Sheridan was a member of parliament, but also ran up such large debts that he spent his last years warding off creditors. In 1815 Sheridan died without a penny to his name. He was buried in Poets Corner at Westminster Abbey.

JARNAC-CHÂTAIGNERAIE

The sixteenth century duel between Guy de Chabot Baron de Jarnac and Francois de Vivonne seigneur de La Châtaigneraie was made famous for two reasons – it introduced a phrase for 'low blow' into duelling lexicon, and also marked the last judicial duel in France. But despite being a judicial duel, the duel between Jarnac and Châtaigneraie had all the hallmarks of the duel of honour that was to follow, as pride, reputation and a gentleman's honour were all at stake.

Châtaigneraie was the darling of the French court and a master swordsman. He had studied fencing in Italy, which he used in combination with his skills as a wrestler to devastating effect. He would first disarm his opponent and then tackle him to the ground so he could cut his throat with his dagger. Châtaigneraie was a handsome man, with a muscular build and an ego to match.

Jarnac stood a couple of inches taller than Châtaigneraie and was considered a reasonable soldier, but he did not have Châtaigneraie's athletic physique or bravado. Instead, Jarnac was a thoughtful and pious man who came from reasonably modest means. After the death of Jarnac's mother his father had married a rich noblewoman, who paid Jarnac a monthly allowance. It was this matter that was at the heart of the dispute.

One day at court Dauphin Henri asked Jarnac how he could afford to buy himself such nice fineries. When Jarnac explained that he was paid an allowance by his stepmother, Henri pondered whether Jarnac was 'a kept man'. This was a thinly veiled accusation that Jarnac was indulging in incestuous relations, which was delivered in front of a full court. Jarnac was outraged, but could not challenge the heir to the throne. Instead Châtaigneraie took it upon himself to become involved, and told the court Jarnac had confessed to sexual relations with his stepmother. In response Jarnac accused Châtaigneraie of being a liar. Now the gloves were off. With both men aggrieved, they visited Francois I to ask permission to hold a judicial duel. Francois liked both men and didn't desire either one of them dead, so their request was refused. The matter divided the Royal court and festered for over a year. It was still a pressing enough issue that only weeks after Francois' death both men went to Henri II to once again request a judicial duel. Henri gave his approval for a duel to take place a month later.

The two men spent this time quite differently. Châtaigneraie strutted around the court like the cat that got the cream, and behaved as if he had already won the contest. He even arranged for a magnificent banquet to be held in his honour following the duel, sparing no expense to source the finest ingredients and silverware.

Jarnac, by contrast, attended church services and asked people to pray for him. He also sought out the services of Italian fencing master Captain Caizo. Caizo probably weighed up Jarnac's chances carefully – he was taller but lighter than Châtaigneraie and almost completely inexperienced in duelling. The longer the two were in the ring together the less likely it was that Jarnac would win. He needed what is known in fencing terms as a *botta segreta*, or a 'secret thrust' that ensures victory. Whether a *botta segreta* really existed is a contentious matter, but Caizo said he had one, and set about training Jarnac how to use it. Caizo did not bother training Jarnac with any other fencing moves. This was all or nothing; if the move didn't work Jarnac had little chance of surviving.

Jarnac also set out to delay the duel. As the challenged party it was his right to choose the weapons, and he made sure they were expensive and difficult to obtain. At one point Jarnac put forward a list of specific horses, saddles and thirty different types of weapons to be used. On seeing the long list of requests Châtaigneraie said: 'This man wants to fight my valour and my purse.' In the end Jarnac chose to fight on foot, with swords, daggers, shields and helmets. The duellists would be further protected with a brassard – a piece of plate metal armour for the arm, which stopped the wearer from bending it. The brassard was to stop Châtaigneraie from wrestling Jarnac to the ground, where he would be defenceless.

THE BOTTA SEGRETA

On the morning of 10 July 1547, a large crowd gathered in a field by the Chateau Saint-Germain-en-Laye. A square piece of ground had been prepared and spectators gathered eagerly behind the barricades. Both Châtaigneraie and Jarnac had a pavilion at either end of the battlefield. The opponents used the period before the duel in typical fashion. Châtaigneraie paraded around the ground with his retinue, full of pomp and confidence. Jarnac prayed. Then there was a delay of some hours while seconds went between the two pavilions to approve the weapons. Châtaigneraie did not want to use the brassard, but he was overruled. Finally both men, now dressed for battle, went before the king. They both had to swear that they did not have any secret weapons, magical aids or potions. The crowd were then warned they were not to make any noise or distract Châtaigneraie or Jarnac in any way. The herald then announced that battle could commence.

Châtaigneraie was full of self assurance and made straight for Jarnac in an attempt to finish him off quickly. Jarnac crouched down and lifted his shield to block Châtaigneraie's first blow. At the same time as this strike, Jarnac delivered his *botta segreta* – Caizo's secret move that he had been practising for the last month. The move was as simple as it was effective. Jarnac simply reached around Châtaigneraie and cut the tendons behind his knee. It worked. Châtaigneraie fell onto one leg, with a look of shock and amazement. He then tried to pull himself up and thrust at Jarnac. Jarnac simply reached behind his other leg and sliced open his other hamstring. Not completely crippled, Châtaigneraie fell into a heap as surprised gasps went up among the crowd.

With his opponent defeated Jarnac now had three options according to the rules of a judicial duel. He could either kill Châtaigneraie; let him live in return for a retraction of the original insult and an admission it was a lie; or present him to the king, who could restore Jarnac's honour and decide on Châtaigneraie's fate. First Jarnac lent over Châtaigneraie and asked him to admit that he had lied about his stepmother, but there was no answer. Then Jarnac approached King Henri and said:

'Sire, I give you La Châtaigneraie; take him, Sire, and may my honor be given back to me.'

But Henri sat silent in his chair apparently as dumfounded as the other onlookers. Jarnac then knelt in prayer and went back to Châtaigneraie who had managed to pull himself onto one knee and was making ready to strike at Jarnac. Jarnac simply stepped out of Châtaigneraie's reach and said: 'Do not move, or I will kill you,' to which Châtaigneraie cried back 'kill me then!' Jarnac moved Châtaigneraie's weapons out of reach and presented them to the king. Henri finally seemed to respond, perhaps sensing he needed to intervene before Jarnac became obliged to kill Châtaigneraie. He rose, embraced Jarnac, and said: 'You have done your duty and your honour is restored.'

At this Châtaigneraie was carried off the field to his tent where he was tended to by a priest and surgeons, and his wounds bandaged. But Châtaigneraie did not want to recover, he tore off his dressings and let himself bleed to death. The duel shocked all who had seen it, especially the king, who banned the judicial duel from the kingdom.

Jarnac himself had managed to avert his own demise through his swift *botta segreta*, a move that would from that point on be known as the *coup de Jarnac*. At first a *coup de Jarnac* was attached to a 'clever and unexpected thrust.' But over time this changed, as history looked upon Jarnac less favourably. Instead it began to mean 'low blow', or 'stab in the back.' Perhaps this meant Châtaigneraie's honour was restored and his defeat in the duel forgiven, albeit posthumously.

HAMILTON-BURR

The 1804 duel between politicians Aaron Burr and Alexander Hamilton is the most famous in America's history. It is also the most controversial. Although there is no doubt about the outcome of the meeting, the events on the day are still hotly contested. The wave of public consternation and outrage that followed the duel began its subsequent demise in popularity.

Alexander Hamilton was born on 11 January 1755. He grew up to fight in the American Revolution and become one of the United States' founding fathers. Hamilton was the first Secretary to the Treasury and leader of the Federalist Party. While thought of as an upstanding citizen whose character was above question, Hamilton had mud on his boots. In 1791 he had an affair with Maria Reynolds and was then blackmailed by her husband. Hamilton responded by writing an open letter of confession to the public, his wife and family. This was the first sex scandal in the history of the American government and Hamilton was obliged to resign from office. But he still had backroom sway. In the 1800 presidential election, Hamilton's influence helped win Thomas Jefferson the White House. Hamilton had vehemently opposed the democratic-republican candidate Aaron Burr, and the incumbent John Adams, even though he was from Hamilton's own party. Although this action once again damaged Hamilton's reputation, he had supported the candidate most likely to defeat his sworn enemy Aaron Burr.

Aaron Burr was born 6 February 1756, and like Hamilton was considered one of the founding fathers. He was elected twice to the New York Assembly, was New York State Attorney General, US senator and Vice President under Jefferson. Burr was the son of a Presbyterian minister and was known to have progressive views on equal rights for women and slavery.

At one time Hamilton and Burr had been friends who occasionally met to dine. But in 1791 Burr ran against Hamilton's father-in-law for the New York seat of the US Senate, which Hamilton took as a personal affront. This animus continued into Burr's 1804 campaign for Governor of New York, when Hamilton did all he could to discredit Burr. Hamilton said Burr was 'dangerous' and should not be trusted with government offices. At a dinner party Hamilton went a step further, saying that he had a 'despicable opinion' of Burr, words which subsequently appeared in the newspapers. This was a defamation of character that Burr could not allow. He wrote to Hamilton asking him to make a public apology and retraction. Several letters passed between the two, in one of which Hamilton said he could not recollect any such comment. This was not good enough for Burr who challenged Hamilton to a pistol duel.

Burr had fought in two pistol duels, neither of which ended in death. Hamilton had been challenged to ten duels, all of which were settled peacefully. But Hamilton also had a much larger duelling skeleton in his closet, which involved the death of his son. Philip Hamilton had argued with a Burr supporter in New York, challenged him to a duel and was mortally wounded in the subsequent exchange. Hamilton struggled over whether to call the duel off, but decided to go ahead rather than risk public humiliation. He penned a letter explaining his predicament and the reasons for his decision. In part of the letter Hamilton wondered whether he might shoot wide, therefore maintaining his honour by not committing a violent act.

Nathaniel Pendleton, Hamilton's second, sent the duellists a letter outlining the regulations for the day. Both parties were to be taken by boat at 5 a.m, on the 10 July, to a strip of land in New Jersey. They were to be accompanied by their seconds, two surgeons, and four oarsmen. The two were to stand at a distance of 9 metres

(10 yards) apart and fire at each other with pistols. If one man fired first, then the other was obligated to call out 'one, two, three, fire' before shooting. If either man was wounded he could still fire his pistol, as long he could do so unaided.

FIRING WIDE

On the morning of the 10th the two men were rowed in separate boats up the Hudson River to Weehawken, New Jersey. The seconds were waiting on a strip of land by the water's edge, which was surrounded on three sides by a steep cliff. The seconds tossed a coin to decide who would stand on which side. Hamilton lost the toss and was forced to fight facing the sun. He then asked proceedings be halted while he put on his spectacles. The order was then given to fire, which is when accounts of the events differ and the controversy surrounding the duel begin. Pendleton maintains that Burr shot first and Hamilton followed, but shot wide because he had been hit. Burr's second William Van Ness said that Hamilton fired first, his shot going wide and hitting a tree above Burr. Burr then lowered his pistol, took aim and fired back.

What is clear is that Burr's bullet entered Hamilton's body above his right hip, passed through his liver and lodged in his spine. It was a mortal wound. Hamilton's surgeon rushed over to examine him and Van Ness hurried Burr on to his boat, as duelling was an illegal act and the sooner Burr was away from the scene the better. Hamilton was also rowed away, back to Manhattan where he lay in agony at a friend's house for over thirty hours until he finally died. Burr was now wanted for murder and was forced to flee from New York.

What Burr did not realise was that Hamilton's death would make him the most hated man in America. Hamilton, on the other hand, was practically turned into a saint. Many ugly rumours were spread. One said that Burr had ambushed Hamilton and laughed after shooting him.

But what remains the real point of debate is Hamilton's wide shot. Some historians say Hamilton's letter in which he considers shooting wide, is clear proof he didn't wish to harm Burr. Others say a hair trigger caused Hamilton's wide shot, or a random muscle spasm. Many wonder why Hamilton had been so interested in wearing his glasses if he wanted to shoot wide. Whatever happened on the day did not change the outcome for Burr. He was publicly vilified and his political career destroyed. He died in 1836 in New York.

The duel also brought itself much negative criticism, and it was generally agreed that duelling had more to do with barbaric savagery than it did gentlemanly honour. As such the Hamilton—Burr duel marked the beginning of its slow decline in America.

SACKVILLE-BRUCE

The reign of James I represented a 'Golden Age' of art, literature and culture as England fell under the spell of the European Renaissance. But it was also a period of great violence and bloodshed. James was obsessed by witchcraft and had personally been involved in the torture of 'witches'; Guy Fawkes was discovered planting dynamite under the parliament buildings in a plot to blow it up; and duelling became more prevalent than ever before, despite James' attempts to ban it.

For many English duellists the simplest thing was to travel to the continent, where they were not subject to prosecution. Such was the plan hatched by Edward Bruce, 2nd Lord of Kinloss for his duel with Edward Sackville, 4th Earl of Dorset.

As with many duellists, Sackville and Bruce had once been friends but had fallen out over a woman. Bruce was the aggrieved party and had challenged Sackville to a duel, which they arranged to hold in 1613, in France. But James caught wind of the challenge and made both parties assure him they would not duel. Coincidently the two met by chance later that year in Canterbury. A bystander noted that Bruce slapped Sackville several times in the face with his glove and then the men had to pulled apart.

Bruce sailed to France, apparently to learn how to

fence, and wrote to Sackville from Paris. In his letter he asked Sackville to do him the courtesy of letting him 'right the wrong bestowed upon his honour.' He wrote he would wait for Sackville to send word on the time, place and weapons he wished to use. A period of correspondence followed until the details of the contest were at last agreed. The rules were reasonably specific – if one man fell or slipped he would be considered at the other's mercy, and the defeated party. If either man's sword broke it could be considered the consequence of bad luck, and the duel rescheduled for a different time. Bruce went so far as to send his sword to England, so Sackville could have a matching one made.

The duel was to be held near the town of Bergen-op-Zoom, located between the Spanish Netherlands and the Dutch Republic. This would give the duellists a chance to escape over a border if needed. Both men brought a second and a personal surgeon with them. After meeting, Bruce explained to Sackville that he actually wanted the duel to be to the death. He suggested that the seconds should be excluded in case they tried to interfere. Sackville was surprised by this news, but agreed to go along with it.

Both men stood facing each other in ankle-deep marshland. Sackville made the first thrust, but it was too short and Bruce countered by making a deep cut to his arm. Sackville made another lunge, but it left his body exposed, and Bruce stabbed him through his right nipple and deep into his chest. Both men then grabbed at each other swords and held onto the blades. Sackville's little finger was nearly severed and only held in place by a small flap of skin. The two stood like that panting for a moment and then Sackville wrenched his sword away and put it to Bruce's throat. He demanded that Bruce yield his sword or ask for mercy, to which Bruce replied that he would do neither.

Sackville then realised he was losing blood from his three gaping wounds and needed to act fast. He ran Bruce through with his sword, pulled it out and ran him through again. Bruce cried out 'I am slain' and collapsed on the spot.

Sackville turned Bruce onto his back and crouched over him, demanding he beg for his life, to which Bruce replied that he wouldn't. Sackville asked if he wanted his surgeon and Bruce said yes. Sackville then pulled himself off his opponent and staggered over to his own surgeon who began tending his wounds. But then something remarkable and unexpected happened. Bruce's surgeon suddenly grabbed Bruce's sword and ran at Sackville. Sackville was only saved by his own surgeon, who saw the man coming and parried his blow with Sackville's sword. Bruce was as surprised by this action as the others and shouted for him to 'hold thy hand!'

Bruce died from his wounds soon afterwards and

Sackville was taken back to England, where it took him some weeks to recover. News of the duel soon reached English shores and Sackville found himself out of favour with the royal court. This did not last forever, however, as Sackville was made Lord Chamberlain in 1642 and lived until 1652.

The Sackville–Bruce duel was the last straw for James I. The king issued his *Proclamation against Private Challenges and Combat*, which outlined new legislation to prosecute duellists. However, James was known as a soft touch and his Proclamation did little to curb duelling. Instead, English duels continued to thrive throughout James' reign.

PUSHKIN-D'ANTHÈS

Although Russia joined the duelling tradition relatively late, the subject found great appeal among its writers and poets. Many of the country's greatest authors not only featured the duel in their works but also had personal experience of it. It is no surprise then, that Russia's most notorious duel is the one fought by its most celebrated writer – Alexander Pushkin.

Duelling reached Russia in the same way it had travelled from Italy from France – by way of its military. Russian soldiers fighting in Europe often became embroiled in duels, and returning soldiers were soon issuing challenges on their own shores.

There had already been a small tradition of duelling in Russia, but those caught at it would be hung, along with their seconds. But by the eighteenth century, the rising tide of duelling could not be held back. Catherine the Great decided to address the matter head-on in her 1787 *Manifesto on Duels*. But Catherine's line was hazy – what she didn't see she didn't mind. Nicholas I was less ambiguous, and in 1828 he set down a blanket ban on all duelling. But, as with the edicts issued in France and England, Nicholas' ban did almost nothing to quell the popularity of the duel. By the end of the nineteenth century the duel had grown to such large proportions that Alexander III all but made it legal.

It hadn't taken long for the duel to appear in the literary works of Russia's finest writers. Tolstoy, Chekov, Turgenev and Dostoevsky all wrote about the duel. Tolstoy once challenged Turgenev to duel when the men fell out. Mikhail Lermontov and Pushkin were both prolific duellers. Pushkin even seemed to foretell the outcome of his most famous duel – probably the best-known in all of Russian history – in his novel in verse *Eugene Onegin*.

Alexander Sergeyevich Pushkin was born on 6 June 1799, and by fifteen had published his first poem. In 1817 Pushkin took up a government post and became a part of St Petersburg's literary and intellectual elite. Pushkin lived a flamboyant lifestyle where he socialised, womanised and duelled. His first duel came in 1821 when he accused an officer called Zubov of cheating at cards. Legend has it that Pushkin nonchalantly ate cherries while Zubov took his shot, a detail he used in his story, *The Shot*. Zubov missed and Pushkin casually asked him if he was now satisfied, and did not bother to fire back.

Pushkin's outspokenness on social reform and his alliances with various literary radicals put him out of favour with the government. Pushkin was banned from St Petersburg in 1820 and spent time travelling through the Caucasus and the Crimea. It was during this time he began writing *Eugene Onegin*. The story centres on a man of Pushkin's age, Lensky, a romantic, freedom-loving poet. Unbeknown to him at the time, Pushkin would go on to share Lensky's fate.

Meanwhile, Pushkin was transferred to an outpost called Kishinyov in modern day Moldava, where he drank and duelled. One encounter came in January 1822, when he argued with Colonel S. N. Starov at a ball over what tune the band played next. The duellists met during a snowstorm and although only twelve paces lay between them, they both missed. The matter was settled amicably that evening over dinner and drinks. Pushkin complained bitterly in letters about his continued exile, but was transferred to Odessa in 1823 and then again in 1824 to his mother's estate in the province of Pskov.

Despite his relative isolation Pushkin produced one of his best-known works, *Boris Gudunov*, which explores the relationship between the ruling class of Russia and the people. The play's revolutionary message won popular appeal but it terrified the monarchy, which was subject to the Decembrist Uprising only a year after the play's release. Despite this Nicholas I was forced to acknowledge Pushkin's popularity, and allowed him to leave exile in 1826.

In 1831 Pushkin moved to St Petersburg where he married Natalya Nikolaevna Goncharova, a woman who was considered to be the great beauty of the city. Pushkin was then awarded the title of Kammerjunker (Gentleman of the Emperor's Bedchamber), a lowly rank which Pushkin bitterly suspected was only given so the tsar could enjoy Natalya's presence at court. Pushkin was not suited to court life, whereas Natalya blossomed under the attentions of the empire's most powerful and influential men.

One such man was Frenchman George d'Anthès, adoptive heir of Dutch Baron, Jacob Van Heeckeren. D'Anthès was a dashing young diplomat who was much adored by the ladies at court. It was not long before rumours of an affair between d'Anthès and Natalya reached Pushkin's ears. In an apparent move to deflect such claims, d'Anthès married Natalya's sister Ekaterina Goncharova in 1837, although many, including Pushkin, suspected this was just a way to become closer to Natalya.

Things reached boiling point when Pushkin received a letter calling him a 'cuckold'. Furious, Pushkin wrote a letter to Baron Heeckeren slanderously insulting his heir. A series of letters were exchanged, trying to resolve the issue peacefully, but Pushkin would not back down and eventually he received a challenge from d'Anthès himself. His second was to be Vicomte d'Archiac and Pushkin's was Lt Colonel Konstantin Danzas.

D'Archiac drew up the terms for the duel, which was set for 27 January 1837 at 5 p.m. The opponents would stand twenty paces apart, with a central barrier between them measuring ten paces across. At the signal, the duellists would walk towards the barrier and fire at will. Once a man had fired he would have stop in his tracks and let his opponent shoot. If neither party had hit the other, then the pistols would be reloaded and the duel restarted.

SHOOTING IN THE SNOW

On the day of the 27th Pushkin went about his usually business and waited for Danzas to pick him up by sleigh at around 4 p.m. It was an icy day and Pushkin wrapped himself up in his large bear coat. According to Danzas, Pushkin seemed in good spirits and cheerfully greeted acquaintances who passed them by. On the outskirts of St Petersburg the sleigh pulled up next to d'Anthès and d'Archiac and the seconds went about their business of preparing the ground. The seconds trampled down a section of knee-deep snow and marked the central barrier off with their overcoats. Then they loaded the pistols and handed one to each of the duellists.

Danzas gave the signal and the Pushkin and d'Anthès started walking slowly towards each other. D'Anthès later reported that it was not his intention to kill Russia's favourite writer, as this at the very least would have meant the end of his career. Instead d'Anthès was planning to shoot Pushkin in the leg, hopefully before he was shot himself. So when Pushkin stopped and started lowering his gun to aim, d'Anthès quickly brought down his own pistol and fired. The bullet hit Pushkin at the top of his thigh, ricocheted off the bone and entered his abdomen. Pushkin dropped to the ground and did not move. D'Anthès and the seconds ran over to Pushkin, who lifted himself and said he felt strong enough to take his shot. D'Anthès then ran back to his last position and stood side on to Pushkin. Pushkin aimed and fired. The bullet passed through d'Anthès' arm and hit his chest, although not penetrating it. Pushkin called out 'bravo,' and slumped forward.

Danzas carried Pushkin back to the sleigh and drove him back into St Petersburg, during which Pushkin chatted to him about duelling. Once at home, Pushkin was taken to a day bed in his study where doctors examined him and gave the writer almost no chance of surviving. Pushkin did live through the night, and in the morning said goodbye to Natalya and his children. Outside his house a large crowd had gathered to keep a candlelit vigil. Pushkin made it through one last night, although in terrible agony, and died the next afternoon. D'Anthès managed to get off lightly – he was discharged from the army and deported, as was Baron Heeckeren.

Eugene Onegin was reprinted only days after Pushkin's death and sold in the thousands. The work retains an eerie legacy as it seems to foretell Pushkin's own end through the fate of its protagonist Lensky. Both the fictional and real duel were fought in the snow, with a central barrier and French Lepage pistols.

It is worth noting that the writer who many thought of as Pushkin's successor would also die in a duel using Lepage pistols. Mikhail Lermontov was so upset by the death of Pushkin that he wrote a elegy renouncing the royal court. As a result he was exiled to the Caucasus, just as Pushkin had been. But like Pushkin, Lermontov was prolific during his period in exile, and produced *A Hero In Our Time* – an account of a duel much like the one which would claim his life.

In 1841 Lermontov made a joke about a fellow officer Nikolai Martynov, who had taken offence and issued a challenge. In the duel, held at the foot of Mashuk Mountain, Lermotov was killed instantly by Martynov's first shot. In the end the writer tipped to take the great Pushkin's throne would succumb to the same fate.

FIGHTING FITZGERALD

Duelling in Ireland is remarkable for its short, ferocious lifespan, which began in 1760 and peaked forty years later. The duels of this time largely came about because of the death of George III, which created a surge in politically-motivated violence. Irish parliamentary elections were only held when an English monarch died, so George II's 1760 demise ushered in a once-in-a-lifetime chance to change the political landscape. This happened to coincide with another phenomenon coming from England – the duel.

Newspaper reports about English gentlemen duelling on the streets of London had found their way across the Irish sea, and it wasn't long before the first duels were fought in Dublin. Many more followed – by 1780 the number of duels in Ireland had reached such high numbers that a set of regulations was published. In 1777 an Irish *code duello*, otherwise known as 'the Clonmel Rules' was drawn up. The *code duello* stated it was:

> *Adopted at the Clonmel Summer Assizes, 1777, for the government of duellists, by the gentlemen of Tipperary, Galway, Mayo, Sligo and Roscommon, and prescribed for general adoption throughout Ireland.*

It was hoped that by following the rules that duellists might be spared from the legal punishment of hanging, although the *code duello* provided no official protection by law. The law seemed of little consequence to Ireland's most notorious dueller, George Robert Fitzgerald, aka 'Fighting Fitzgerald.'

Fitzgerald was born in Turlough, Castlebar, County Mayo in 1748 to an aristocratic family. He was educated at Eton, joined the army at seventeen and was stationed at Galway. It was here he fell into a dispute with another officer called Thompson and the two scheduled a pistol duel for the following morning. Fitzgerald's aim was off – he only managed to hit Thompson's hand – but his luck was extraordinary, as he survived Thompson's shot which hit him square in the forehead. The bullet was removed from Fitzgerald's skull, which was trepanned and had a silver plate inserted. It was this plate which many believe was the cause of his increasingly eccentric and outlandish behaviour.

In 1772 Fitzgerald married the rich and beautiful heiress Jane Connelly and the newlyweds spent time at the French royal court. Fitzgerald was in favour for a time, but soon ran low on funds and had to return to Ireland with recorded debts of well over £100,000. One of his creditors, Major Baggs, made it known that Fitzgerald was not honouring his debts, which caused Fitzgerald to challenge him to a duel.

The duel was held in Valenciennes, which was part of Austria at the time. The duellists stood twelve paces apart and were ready to commence firing when the major called a halt to the proceedings. Baggs called out that he believed Fitzgerald to be wearing a steel plate under his shirt. Fitzgerald answered simply by stripping to the waist, and then demanded that Baggs do the same. The major said it was too cold for him and asked if he could remain dressed, to which Fitzgerald assented. The major then crouched on his haunches like a cat and Fitzgerald moved into a lunging position. Both men fired at the signal, and as Fitzgerald was raising his second pistol Baggs slumped over, calling out that he was wounded. 'But you're not dead,' Fitzgerald answered and shot Baggs again, this time hitting him in the leg. At this Baggs summoned the strength to run at Fitzgerald and discharge his second pistol into Fitzgerald's thigh. Both men were then helped to their respective carriages and driven away.

Fitzgerald moved to London and was involved in several more duels, but his next encounter of note was fought in 1775 against an officer called Thomas Walker. Fitzgerald had lent money to Walker after he had lost heavily on the horses, but after paying the money back Fitzgerald said he owed him more in interest. Walker responded by challenging Fitzgerald to a duel in Cavendish Square in London. The men stood twelve paces apart, which Fitzgerald remarked was too far for him to shoot safely. Accounts on the duel differ but agree that Fitzgerald shot first. He then somehow evaded Walker's bullet, either by ducking or stepping sideways. He then ran up to Walker and apologised for hurting him. Walker decided to put the matter to rest and told Fitzgerald he was satisfied with the outcome. Upon hearing this Fitzgerald, once again, demanded the money he said Walker owed him.

Fitzgerald then returned to Ireland, where his behaviour became increasingly unpredictable. His wife passed away and he moved back to the family estate at Castlebar. Here, he began keeping wild animals as pets, including a bear, and encouraged his friends to participate in hunting games by torchlight. He also won legal custody of his father, who he imprisoned in his room and once tied to his pet bear.

BARKS AND BULLETS

Fitzgerald's behaviour was publically condemned by the High Sheriff of County Mayo, Denis Browne. Browne was a hard-nosed and opinionated man who had sent over two hundred men to the gallows. Fitzgerald caught wind of Browne's disapproval and decided to teach him a lesson by riding to his house and shooting his wolfhound. Following this action, Browne called out a challenge from his front doorstep, but ran inside after Fitzgerald shot at him, saying he would not fight such a manic. Instead his neighbour Richard Martin challenged Fitzgerald, after catching sight of the dead wolfhound. The two would not actually duel until some months later. Martin had sent his second to issue the terms to Fitzgerald, who had responded by beating him senseless. The duel was set for 14 July 1784 at Castlebar. Fitzgerald spent the morning waiting for Martin's carriage by walking up and down the streets and boasting about Martin's impending death. When Martin arrived he walked up to Fitzgerald and demanded he draw his sword at once. Fitzgerald said that the ground was too uneven on the street. Martin said he would therefore wait for him in the barrack yard. Martin, Fitzgerald, their seconds and a crowd then walked to the yard where the seconds declared a pistol duel should be held at twelve paces. But Fitzgerald demurred, accusing Martin of indulging in 'child's play' and wondering if he was worried 'he would be hurt?'

This was enough for Martin, who walked right up to Fitzgerald so their pistols were all but touching. Both men fired. Fitzgerald somehow missed completely but Martin hit his opponent and the blast threw him backwards onto the ground. Martin was about to fire his second pistol when Fitzgerald asked the duel be restarted as a matter of honour. The men then got into position twelve paces apart to restart the duel. Both fired and found purchase – Martin was hit in the chest and Fitzgerald in the neck, although this was only a flesh wound. Fitzgerald then ran up to Martin to shake hands and hoped the matter was resolved. Martin was duly tended to by a surgeon and announced the conflict resolved. What remains unclear is how Fitzgerald managed to survive Martin's first bullet. Some accounts report he was wearing plate armour under his shirt and others say it was deflected by a large coat button. The duel with Martin was to be the last of fifty duels Fitzgerald had been involved in.

His ignominious end came when he became involved in the assassination of his neighbour Patrick McDonnell. Fitzgerald was hunted down and attacked by a group of McDonnell's friends who then frog-marched him to the local jailhouse. He was tried for murder, found guilty and sentenced to be executed. A large crowd gathered for the hanging, including dozens of soldiers who were expecting a rescue attempt. Fitzgerald walked up onto the scaffold and the noose was put around his neck. But as he dropped the rope snapped and Fitzgerald fell nearly thirty feet onto the ground below. Some murmured that he should now be set free, but another rope was set and once more put around Fitzgerald's neck. The bolt was drawn, but instead of swinging in the air Fitzgerald again fell to the ground, much to the horror and disgust of the gathered crowd. The third rope held tight around Fitzgerald's neck, and he was said to turn the colour of lead before finally passing away.

MACNAMARA-MONTGOMERY

While many duels were fought over defamatory comments, insults to honour, women, politics and gambling, they also took place for far more trivial reasons. Such was the case in the 1803 duel between Colonel Robert Montgomery and Captain James Macnamara, which was fought over a dog.

An account of the dispute and the trial that followed appeared in *The Newgate Calendar*, an eighteenth and nineteenth century periodical about vices and criminal acts committed in London. The *Calendar* was cautionary in tone and hoped to dissuade its younger readers from a life of crime by describing the gruesome details of murders and court trials. The *Calendar* provides a riveting portrayal of the Macnamara–Montgomery duel, as it uses the actual court testimony of witnesses to the event.

Colonel Montgomery was riding on the afternoon of 6 April, with brothers Stephen and William Sloane, and his Newfoundland dog. By chance a different dog of the same breed was following another group of riders and at one point the two dogs began fighting. According to the testimony of William Sloane, Montgomery immediately jumped off his horse and demanded of the mounted group: 'Whose dog is this?' Captain Macnamara replied: 'It is my dog.' Montgomery said: 'If you do not call your dog off, I shall knock him down.' Macnamara replied:

'Have you the arrogance to say you will knock my dog down?' Montgomery said: 'I certainly shall if he falls on my dog.'

The two then proceeded to swap names and Montgomery repeated: 'I don't mean to quarrel with you, but if your dog falls on mine I shall knock him down.'

According to Macnamara, Montgomery left with some parting words: 'If you are offended with what has passed, you know where to find me.' This was what really riled Macnamara, who immediately made the challenge. It was agreed that both men would meet later that day for a duel with pistols. A certain Lord Buckhurst testified that he came up to Macnamara as Montgomery and the Sloanes rode away. Macnamara seemed to be shaking his stick at the party, but then Buckhurst realised the shaking came as a result of his anger. Macnamara said he would always avenge an insult and fight Montgomery or any other man that offended his honour.

The two duellists and their seconds, Captain Barry and Sir William Keir, met at Primrose Hill and walked to the top together. A case containing the pistols was brought out and examined by the principals. An eyewitness, one James Harding, Vintner of Jermyn Street, described the events in court:

> *I stood about fifty yards distant from them. I saw Sir W. Keir and Captain Barry conversing together*

and preparing the pistols; one was discharged to see whether they were in good condition. The parties separated to about six yards. Colonel Montgomery fired and Captain Macnamara fired; they stood face to face. Both fired at the same time. Colonel Montgomery fell; Captain Macnamara did not. I went up. Colonel Montgomery was extended on the ground, and, shortly after, Mr Heaviside opened his waistcoat and looked at his wound; it was on his right side. Mr Heaviside administered relief to him and then went to Captain Macnamara. I think he said he was wounded, and that he must bleed him. I assisted in carrying Colonel Montgomery; his eyes were fixed, and he was groaning. I saw the corpse afterwards on a bed in Chalk Farm.

Montgomery had sustained a mortal wound to the chest and died less than an hour later. Macnamara had been shot through his lower abdomen, but the wound had not healed. Macnamara stood trial for murder sixteen days later.

TRIALS AND TRIBULATIONS

In court the charges against Macnamara were read out by a clerk:

James Macnamara, you stand charged on the coroner's inquest for that you, on the 6th of April, did, with

> *force of arms, in the parish of St Pancras, in the*
> *county of Middlesex, on Robert Montgomery, Esq.,*
> *feloniously make an assault, and a certain pistol, of*
> *the value of ten shillings, charged and loaded with*
> *powder and a leaden bullet, which you held in your*
> *right hand, to and against the body of the said Robert*
> *Montgomery, did feloniously shoot off and discharge,*
> *and did feloniously give, with the leaden bullet so as*
> *aforesaid discharged by force of the gunpowder, in the*
> *right side of the body of the said Robert Montgomery,*
> *one mortal wound.*

Macnamara would go to the gallows if found guilty.
Despite this he pleaded not guilty. His defence was relying
on something that held far more weight in Victorian
England than the law – a gentleman's character. To prove
Macnamara's quality a few star witnesses were called in,
including three admirals and three lords. Among them
was one Horatio Nelson, who said of Macnamara:

> *I have known Captain Macnamara nine years; he*
> *has been at various times under my command. During*
> *my acquaintance with him I had not only the highest*
> *esteem and respect for him as an officer, but I always*
> *looked upon him as a gentleman, who would not take*
> *an affront from any man; yet, as I stand here before*
> *God and my country, I never knew nor heard that he*

ever gave offence to man, woman or child during my
acquaintance with him.

It is hard to imagine that a jury would have disregarded the evidence of Britain's greatest ever naval commander, but Macnamara's personal testimony certainly clinched the deal. His speech acts as an interesting historical document about the duel. Macnamara's contention was that the tone of one man's words and stance against another was enough to present a grave insult. Even though there was no slur on Macnamara's character or slanderous accusation there was a facing off that had emasculated Macnamara in front of his peers. This was Macnamara's speech to the jury:

The origin of the difference, as you see it in the
evidence, was insignificant: the heat of two persons,
each defending an animal under his protection,
was natural, and could not have led to any serious
consequences. It was not the deceased's defending his
own dog or his threatening to destroy mine that led to
the fatal catastrophe: it was the defiance alone which
most unhappily accompanied what was said; for words
receive their interpretation from the avowed intention
of the speaker. The offence was forced upon me by
the declaration that he invited me to be offended, and
challenged me to vindicate the offence by calling upon

him for satisfaction. "If you are offended with what has passed, you know where to find me." These words, unfortunately repeated and reiterated, have over and over again been considered by criminal courts of justice as sufficient to support an indictment for a challenge.

Gentlemen, I am a captain in the British Navy. My character you can hear only from others; but to maintain any character in that station I must be respected. When called upon to lead others into honourable dangers I must not be supposed to be a man who had sought safety by submitting to what custom has taught others to consider as a disgrace. I am not presuming to urge anything against the laws of God, or of this land. I know that, in the eye of religion and reason, obedience to the law, though against the general feelings of the world, is the first duty, and ought to be the rule of action; but in putting a construction upon my motives, so as to ascertain the quality of my actions, you will make allowance for my situation.

Justice Heath then told the jury they must retire from the court to deliberate on the case. On their return the foreman pronounced a verdict of not guilty.

BOUTEVILLE-BEUVRON

France during Louis XIII's reign (1603–1643) was a country obsessed by the duel. It was said the streets rang out night and day with the sound of swords clashing, many of which were impromptu battles that ignored the etiquette of a formal challenge. It was all but obligatory for seconds to join in and fight their opposite number, and on many occasions a duel featured three or four pairs of combatants.

The powerhouse behind Louis' throne was Cardinal Richelieu, the King's austere and deeply pious first minister. Richelieu not only objected to the duel on religious grounds, but had a personal vendetta against it. Years earlier the Marquis de Themines had taken issue with Richelieu but could not duel with a priest. So instead he challenged Richelieu's older brother, who he subsequently killed.

Louis gave Richelieu carte blanche to stop duelling in France using whatever method he saw fit. In 1626 Richelieu issued an edict that only those men who killed another during a duel would face execution. This amended the law that any caught duelling would suffer the death penalty – legislation which had no teeth. But Richelieu's edict caused much anger among the duelling nobility, who had traditionally been above the law and were not interested in giving up their favourite pastime.

The country's most notorious dueller was Francois de Montmorency-Bouteville, a young aristocrat who had fought in over twenty duels. In 1627 Bouteville and his friend and second Rosmadec des Chapelles had fled to Brussels to evade the French authorities. They were followed by the Marquis de Beuvron, who wanted to avenge the death of his friend killed by Bouteville in his last duel. But the regent of Brussels, Isabella, caught wind of the Frenchmen's arrival and immediately had them arrested. Bouteville convinced Isabella to write to King Louis and ask him to allow their free return. Louis, probably with Cardinal Richelieu breathing down his neck, said he could not sanction the return of Bouteville or Chapelles. This news infuriated Bouteville, who swore that he would return to Paris and fight in the Place Royale, a fashionable Parisian square where Richelieu himself lived.

True to his word, Bouteville and Chapelles snuck back into Paris where they met with the returned Beuvron to discuss the terms of the duel. It would be held, as Bouteville had threatened, in the Place Royale with swords and daggers. Chapelles would serve as Bouteville's main second and Marquis de Bussy d'Amboise as Beuvron's second. In addition, both men would take an extra second making the duel a bout between three sets of pairs. At 2 p.m. on 12 May 1627, all six duellists arrived in the Place Royale to the utter surprise and excitement of the bystanders who happened to be there. Bouteville had a high profile and his duelling history was well-known among Parisians. It was also plain that the impending duel served as an audacious finger up at King Louis, who did not even know the exiled Bouteville was back in France.

The battle had been some time coming and Bouteville and Beuvron rushed at each other with wild abandon, as did the two pairs of seconds. Many witnesses reported the bout was more like a street brawl than a contest between gentleman, with grabbing, punching and wild hacking. After around fifty minutes Bouteville had his dagger at Beuvron's throat, and for the first time that day displayed some of the honour expected of a duelling gentleman. Bouteville said that both men had fought gallantly and that they should now separate as friends. The seconds, however, had not fared as well. Chapelles had run d'Amboise through and mortally wounded him. Seeing a man was down and fearing immediate reprisals, Beuvron, Bouteville and Chapelles fled. Bouteville and Chapelles were apprehended soon afterwards when their covered coach was pulled over by the King's guard. Beuvron somehow managed to evade capture and escaped to England.

With Bouteville in custody, Louis faced an agonising decision about his fate. The French aristocracy flocked to Bouteville's aid and pressured Louis to let him live. But

Louis was also being pressured by Cardinal Richelieu, who made it clear that Louis could not let this pass. Louis reluctantly agreed, and both Bouteville and Chapelles were beheaded. If Richelieu hoped the example of Bouteville would put an end to French duelling he couldn't have been more wrong. Duelling only increased in popularity and went on to reach endemic proportions under King Louis XIV, who took the throne in 1643.

MUSSOLINI

Italy was the birthplace of the duel of honour, where it thrived from the sixteenth the twentieth century. Unlike the other European countries that had gleaned the tradition from their Italian neighbours and later adapted it for pistols, Italy clung obdurately to the sword. Of the nearly three thousand reported duels in Italy between 1880 and 1890, over ninety per cent of them were fought with swords.

There had been a backlash to guns among many European duellers. Any machine designed for the destruction of men from afar could not be considered honourable, especially when compared to the elegancy of the sword. An accomplished swordsman had some control over how badly he wounded his opponent, and by the twentieth century a fencer was considered unskilled if he actually hurt his sparring partner. Many sword duels were fought to first blood, and a few drops of blood were often enough to rectify a gentleman's wounded honour. But there was no way of regulating the wounds inflicted by gunfire; once fired it was anyone's guess whether it killed, grazed or mortally wounded the opponent, who often died slowly over several days from a festering bullethole.

In the late nineteenth century two thirds of those duelling were reported to be soldiers or journalists. Among them was a man who belonged to the ranks of both professions, Mussolini.

Benito Amilcare Andrea Mussolini was born on 29 July 1883 to a socialist blacksmith father and a schoolteacher mother. The young Mussolini was a disobedient and aggressive child who was expelled from two different schools for stabbing his classmates with a penknife. However, Mussolini was bright and easily passed his exams. He soon made a name for himself through political journalism, public speaking and trade union work. He founded a newspaper (*La Lotta di Classe*, or 'The Class Struggle) and went on to become editor of the official Socialist newspaper *Avanti!* in 1912, the editorial voice of which strongly opposed Italy's intervention in World War I.

Then Mussolini changed his mind about opposing the war. He resigned from *Avanti!*, was expelled from the Socialist party and became editor of *Il Popolo d'Italia* (The

People of Italy), which advocated Italy's involvement in the war. The paper would also support Mussolini's emerging fascist doctrine as well as publish reports of his duels. Mussolini had been duelling since he was a young man. He would use code to let his wife, Rachele, know he was duelling ('make spaghetti today') so as not to upset his children. Rachele who was not only upset by her husband's duelling but by the number of shirts he would ruin doing so. Her ultimatum was for him to give up duelling or wear the same shirt each time. Mussolini chose the latter option and on 'spaghetti' days she would dutifully go and fetch his torn, bloodstained shirt for him.

Mussolini was not considered a particularly skillful dueller, but what he lacked in ability he made up for in determination. He would smear his glove in pitch so he could not be disarmed, and would practice for hours with his personal fencing teacher Camililo Ridolfi.

Mussolini made good use of his duels and the publicity they brought. The duels served to create the myth of Mussolini as a brave, daring and courageous leader capable of immense physical feats.

In 1915 Mussolini called socialist lawyer Lino Merlino a rogue and slapped him in the face. Merlino responded by challenging Mussolini to a duel, which was arranged for 25 February. The duel was a fast and ferocious one, fought with sabres. Within minutes both men had sustained an injury to their arm, which resulted in the fight's early but satisfactory conclusion. Two months later Mussolini was at it again, this time with another former editor of *Avanti!*, Claudio Treves. Mussolini had accused Treves of being a political neutralist and hiding behind his wife's apron strings, which led Treves to issue a challenge.

The bout was fought on 29 March in Milan. An account of the duel appeared in *Il Popolo d'Italia*, where it was reported that the duellists were so eager to fight they jumped the gun and attacked before the duel had officially commenced. Leonardo Prachi ordered both men back to their positions where the duel could begin in the correct manner. After the first, short assault Mussolini had bent his sabre so badly it needed to be replaced. A break was called and two more assaults followed, during which both Mussolini and Treves both sustained arm injuries. By the eighth assault Mussolini had been badly wounded in his ear and the duel was terminated, this time without a gentlemanly reconciliation. Prachi later commented that he had never seen such a violent bout.

By 1920 Mussolini's fascist blackshirt squads were terrorising the country. All political opponents were intimidated, beaten up or murdered. By 1921 the fascists controlled most of Italy and their opposition, the Socialist Party, had all but collapsed. This was also the year of Mussolini's most famous duel against Socialist Party Deputy Francesco Ciccotti-Scozzese. Mussolini had called Ciccotti-Scozzese 'despicable' in the press and the challenge had been issued. The upcoming bout had attracted international press coverage and the Italian police were doing everything in their power to stop it from taking place.

HEARTS AND MINDS

On 27 October the police tailed Mussolini as he sped in his sports car from Milan to the appointed duelling ground. The police intervened twice before a suitable villa was found nearby which both duellists could sneak into. Mussolini started the duel with his usual energetic vim, but Ciccotti-Scozzese, who suffered from a heart condition, held a defensive position and was loathe to attack. After 14 short assaults the observing surgeons put an end to the duel, which they said was making Ciccotti-Scozzese's heart condition worse. Ciccotti-Scozzese was put straight to bed and Mussolini drove back to Milan.

The *New York Times* reported that the suspension of the combat 'was due to Ciccotti being so exhausted that his heart nearly collapsed', and 'the duel between Signor Ciccotti and Signor Mussolini will be resumed tomorrow with pistols.'

But there was to be no further contest. Ciccotti-Scozzese was not a well man, and the duel with Mussolini was to be his last. Mussolini acted as though the duel had been a great victory. He later wrote that it was not

Ciccotti-Scozzese's heart condition that made him end the duel prematurely but because 'fear had set him all aflutter.'

By 1922 Mussolini had seized power and had become the first fascist dictator of the twentieth century. Mussolini's duels received international coverage further contributing to the legend of *Il Duce* (The Leader) as an all-powerful superman. This account was reported in the *New York Times* in 1922:

> *MILAN, May 15.—Professor Benito Mussolini, leader of the Fascisti, who bears more than 100 wounds received in battle, engaged in a duel yesterday with Signor Missiroli, editor of the* Turin Secolo, *over differences arising in their respective newspapers. Professor Benito Mussolini is the editor of* Il Poplo d'Italia *of Milan. Mussolini was the victor in seven assaults lasting forty minutes. The duellists refused a reconciliation after their meeting.*

Mussolini, at his high point, would make sure more contests followed. Shortly after becoming dictator Mussolini set up the Colosseum Mussolini – a sporting academy for young athletes to dazzle the world with their fencing prowess. But the man himself was on his way down. In 1938 he adopted Hitler's doctrine of Semitic persecution and in 1940 joined the war against the allies. Mussolini was overthrown in 1943 and forced into exile. In 1945 Mussolini was caught trying to escape Italy disguised as a German soldier. Mussolini and his mistress Claretta Petacci were shot on 28 April 1945 and their bodies hung upside down in the Piazza Loreto in Milan.

Duelling Movies

SWASHBUCKLERS

Sword fighting duels have been a part of the moviemaking tradition from its earliest days. Classic tales such as *The Mask of Zorro* and *The Three Musketeers* have always made irresistible subject matter for movie producers, with *The Three Musketeers* making its debut on celluloid in 1903. It would be remade again in 1921, this time with actor Douglas Fairbanks playing the role of D'Artagnan and ushering in a new era of swashbuckling adventures. These silent films would feature the protagonist as a heroic swordsman who would dispatch a series of villains with daring and flashy displays of sword fighting prowess.

Fairbanks would follow up *The Three Musketeers* with *Don Q, Son of Zorro* (1925), *The Black Pirate* (1926), and *The Iron Mask* (1929). While the outcome of the screen duels weighed predictably in favour of Fairbanks, his sword fighting at least was made as realistic as possible under the watchful tutelage of fencing master Fred Cravens. Cravens would also go on to instruct Fairbanks' swashbuckler successor, Errol Flynn.

From the outset Flynn's movies such as *Captain Blood* (1935) and *The Adventures of Robin Hood* (1938) presented a more elaborate level of fencing than Fairbanks, with a larger and more expensive production value, and of course the addition of sound.

Swashbucklers were out of favour by the 1950s and sword fighting films were few and far between. It wasn't until the 1970s that the sword fighting hero would again revisit the big screen. But it was no longer enough for the hero to produce a series of neatly clashing strokes and parries as directors sought to achieve an accurate portrayal of a bout. Elements of the sword fighting duel, such as sweat, dirt and blood, which had never be seen before by the movie-going public were now in evidence.

An excellent example of the new realism is Ridley Scott's 1977 film *The Duellists* (see below). From the 1970s on the sword fighting duel has remained a regular feature of the top grossing blockbuster movies of all time, from *Stars Wars* (1977), *Highlander* (1986) and *Braveheart* (1995), to *Gladiator* (2000), *Lord of the Rings* (2001), and *Troy* (2004).

THE DUELLISTS

The Duellists (1977) is director Ridley Scott's first film and is based on a short story of the same name by Joseph Conrad. Conrad's tale follows the twenty-year conflict between two French captains, Dupont and Fournier.

The officers met in Strasbourg in 1794. Fournier, a fanatical dueller, had angered his commanding officer by killing a fellow soldier in a duel. Fournier was consequently banned from the wake and Captain Dupont was sent to tell him so. But Fournier became so enraged by the news that he challenged Dupont to a duel. As the challenge was a point of honour between two officers, Dupont had little choice but to accept. The two fought with swords and Fournier was wounded. They then subsequently agreed to duel whenever they came within one hundred miles of each other, and stuck to the agreement for two decades.

As time went on, both men climbed through the military ranks until in 1813 General Dupont wanted to marry. He proposed a pistol duel with General Fournier to be fought in a forest. But Dupont tricked Fournier by dressing up a branch in his coat and hat. Fournier fell for the deception and fired twice at the empty clothes. Dupont then walked up to Fournier and levelled two cocked pistols at him. He said he would spare Fournier's life, but if he ever wanted to duel again that Dupont would have two free initial shots from only a few yards difference. This was warning enough for Fournier and the two never duelled again.

Conrad found a newspaper clipping about the duel of Dupont and Fournier and used it as the basis for *The Duel*, changing the duellists' names to Feraud and d'Hubert.

In the film adaptation, *The Duellists*, Feraud is played by Harvey Keitel and d'Hubert by David Carradine.

The movie follows the two duellists through their time in Napoleon's army, as they rise through the ranks from Captain to General. As in the novel, General d'Hubert wants to marry and finish with the conflict with a final duel. In the end d'Hubert wins the day and spares Feraud, but tells him he is dead to him and can never make contact again.

Fencing teacher William Hobbs was responsible for the duelling choreography in *The Duellists*, and from the outset he and Ridley Scott agreed to make the sword fighting as realistic as possible. The movie achieves this to tremendous effect, especially in the second duel which is fought with sabres. The scene starts halfway through what has clearly been an exhausting contest. Both men have torn clothes, bloody shirts and are panting, sweating and grunting like animals. There is no delicate interplay with rapiers that appear to not weigh anything, but instead a clumsy swinging of swords that are have become almost too heavy for the duellists to lift.

It is hard to reconcile the savagery of this duel with the gentlemanly values it is supposed to represent, especially when no obvious offence has been given. Harvey Keitel does a magnificent job of portraying the obsessed duellist. Feraud appears to seethe at d'Hubert every time he is near, like his perceived insult is constantly bubbling away despite the numbers of years that have passed. He is fanatically focused on d'Hubert and will not rest until his honour is restored. D'Hubert, by comparison, would rather never see Feraud again, and visibly slumps with every encounter. However, he is honour bound to duel with Feraud and never fails to meet this duty, despite numerous opportunities to walk away from it.

This is the ethos of the duel in a nutshell, and the movie describes it beautifully. It is only at the end, when d'Hubert has everything to lose that he vocalises what he has felt from the beginning – that the duel is an utterly futile occupation that has no positive outcome for either party.

BARRY LYNDON

Barry Lyndon is a 1975 Stanley Kubrick film that features the duel as its predominant motif. The film is an adaptation of William Thackeray's *The Luck of Barry Lyndon: A Romance of the Last Century*. The story appeared as a serial in *Fraser's Magazine* in 1844, and claimed to be written by George Savage Fitz-Boodle, a pseudonym for Thackeray. The story is written in the first person by John Lyndon as he is dying in his Fleet Street jail cell. But Lyndon's narrative is skewed and unreliable, as the 'editor' Fitz-Boodle informs the reader through numerous footnotes. Lyndon is the archetypal anti-hero whose only concern is his own reputation. He connives and cons throughout his life to enhance this reputation and duels any man who impugns it. He is given his just deserts in the end as he dies in prison from an alcohol related disease.

In *Barry Lyndon* Kubrick paints a slightly more sympathetic picture of Lyndon, who at times is not without virtue and honour. The movie begins and ends with a duel, the first of which is responsible for killing Lyndon's (who is then called Redmond Barry) father. As a teenager the young Barry falls in love with his cousin Nora, but is rejected in favour of English officer John Quin. Enraged, Barry challenges Quin to a pistol duel, which he wins. He then flees to Ireland, thinking he has killed Quin, to join the English Army in the Seven Years War. An Irish officer tells Barry the duel with Quin had been staged as a ploy to get Barry out of the way, and that Quin is alive and now married to Nora.

After leaving the army Barry marries the Countess of Lyndon and changes his name to Barry Lyndon. But he mistreats his wife and so her son, Lord Bullingdon, challenges Lyndon to a duel. It is this duel, fought in a barn with pistols, that is the movie's great climax and it is played out to great effect. Diffuse blue light shines through the thin vertical windows, straw is littered on the floor, and pigeons coo and flap around the rafters. Bullingdon's second follows duelling etiquette to the latter, explaining each action clearly and asking the principals if they understand: 'Mr Lyndon these are matched pair pistols and as you can see I have loaded one and your second has loaded the other. But as they belong to Lord Bullingdon, you may have whichever one you wish.'

The duel is protracted and pace agonisingly slow, as it is explained the first shot will be determined by a coin toss. Bullingdon wins and is taken to one end of the barn. The second draws a line in front of him with his cane and then counts ten paces to the other end, and draws another line for Lyndon to stand behind. Then:

'My Lyndon are you prepared to receive Lord Bullingdon's fire?'

When Lyndon nods and turns sideways, Bullingdon is told to cock his pistol. But it misfires and Bullingdon demands another pistol as his was faulty. But the second carefully explains it is not in the rules and that, as his pistol has fired, it is now up to Mr Lyndon to have his shot. Bullingdon subsequently runs to the wall and throws up. Once returned he stands sideways to Lyndon, who after a pause shoots into the ground. Bullingdon is amazed to still be alive and Bullingdon's second asks: 'Lord Bullingdon in view of Mr Lyndon having fired into the ground, do you now consider that you have received satisfaction?'

But to everyone's surprise Bullingdon says he has not. He is subsequently given another pistol which he fires, hitting Lyndon in the lower leg. The duel is concluded.

The leg then becomes infected and has to be amputated below the knee. Bullingdon then offers

Lyndon a yearly annuity on the condition that he never sees the Countess of Lyndon again. Lyndon has no choice but to accept and the movie ends with Bullingdon and the Countess writing Lyndon a cheque.

Kubrick's asserted that he wanted to shoot a period picture without the bright studio lights commonly used. To do this he sourced the same cameras NASA used to film the moon landing, which were built with oversized apertures to film low light situations. As such, some scenes in *Barry Lyndon* were shot with only the candles for lighting, giving the movie a painterly effect. It also contributed to the reaction of some critics that the movie had a feeling of being cold and detached. Other move enlightened reviewers suggested the tone of the film was deliberate, and intended to symbolise the gap between high society and those trying unsuccessfully trying to become a part of it, such as Lyndon. This detachment is evidenced in Lyndon's duel with Quin and Bullingdon. The duel is portrayed as a stuffy, inflexible institution conceived and led by the aristocracy, but there is little life beyond its etiquette and the mechanics of engagement.

BOXING

Introduction

When boxing first became an Olympic event 1300 years ago the rules were basic – two men would stand and punch each other until one gave up or was knocked out. By the twentieth century the sport had become a regulated event, but the most popular boxers remained those who could knock a man out in the ring.

There were few that could hold a candle to Jack Dempsey when it came to pure slugging power. Dempsey's mercilessly savage fighting style combined with his rugged, frontier-town image made him one of the most popular boxers in modern history.

Dempsey was born on 25 June 1895, in Manassa, Colorado. His parents were poor Mormons who travelled from town to town to find work. After leaving home at sixteen, Dempsey lived the vagrant life of a hobo and made money by boxing in saloons. He would enter a bar and wager he could beat any man in the place for $100, a boast he would usually cash in on.

It wasn't long before Dempsey fell in with manager Jim Kearns, who promoted him as the 'Manassa Mauler': a hardworking, salt-of-the-earth slugger from America's western heartland. Kearns would cultivate this image by making sure Dempsey kept a deep tan and wore working man's clothes. He would also pit the fighter against opponents Dempsey had a good chance of beating, and made sure none of them were black. Jack Johnson had been the first black man to win the heavyweight title in 1908, to an eruption of white outrage. Fearing history would repeat itself, the championship was kept to white boxers only for another twenty years.

By the time Dempsey went up against the heavyweight champion Jess Willard, he already had a reputation and popular appeal. Willard was 'the great white hope' that had defeated Jack Johnson, but he disappointed the public with his lack of charm and personality. The public yearned for a popular new boxing hero to pick up the mantle. Not that anyone thought Dempsey could win. Most were putting their money on Willard, who at 6 foot 7 and 245 pounds was a mountain to Dempsey's 6 foot 1 and 187 pounds.

The fight, set to take place in Toledo, Ohio on 4 July 1919, would exploit the difference in size and bill it as 'David versus Goliath'. However, Willard would appear more like a lofty, cumbersome oaf than a man-slaying giant. In the opening round Dempsey came out fighting – he appeared to detonate against Willard with a brutality and power no one had expected. After three rounds Dempsey had knocked Willard down seven times, broken his jaw, ribs and cheekbone, and knocked out six of his teeth. By the fourth round, the floor of the ring was soaked with brown patches of Willard's blood. His trainers would not let Willard out of his corner and the towel was thrown in.

The severity of Willard's injuries compared to Dempsey's apparently unscathed hands led many to believe the boxer had inserted an iron bar into his gloves. Later, after being sacked by Dempsey the disgruntled Kearns confirmed this 'loaded gloves' theory by admitting he had fixed the match. He reported applying plaster of Paris to the wrappings under Dempsey's gloves and betting heavily that Willard would be knocked out in the first round. Other critics felt Dempsey had not played fair by repeatedly standing over the downed Willard and hitting him as soon as he got up. This move was actually legal in 1919, if not considered altogether sporting. Either way the outcome was the same; Dempsey had become heavyweight champion of the world and an American superstar.

Dempsey's key to success was his speed, aggression and power. He described himself as 'exploding' against his opponent, and did so with a violence that was often wholly unexpected. He could also move – bobbing and shifting from side to side continuously, almost as if boxing to some unheard music.

DRAFT-DODGING DEFENDER

Dempsey would not have to defend his title until September 1920; but the fight turned out to be something of a non-starter. Dempsey knocked out challenger Billy Miske after three rounds. He then dispatched Bill Brennan in December of that year. America went sporting mad in the 1920s and Dempsey's next title defence against Frenchman Georges Carpentier in 1921 was eagerly anticipated. The match was billed as 'The Fight of the Century' and made much of the men's differences. Carpentier was the popular World War I hero, and Dempsey a draft-dodging slacker (the slur was unfair – Dempsey was later able to prove he had tried to enlist and had been rejected).

The much-hyped fight was a historic occasion – it was the first to make sales of a million dollars and be broadcast live by radio. Black heavyweight champion of the future Joe Louis remembered listening in to the wireless ardently. Carpentier had the upper hand during the first round by landing a few well-placed blows. But then in the second round Carpentier's luck turned and he broke his thumb. Then in typical fashion Dempsey exploded and gave Carpentier such a beating in the third round that he did not return for a fourth.

Dempsey' last successful title defence was against Argentinean Luis Angel Firpo, which took place in

September 1923 at the Polo Grounds in New York. The match attracted a monumental audience across the Americas and a radio transmission was broadcast live to Buenos Aires. The arena itself reached its capacity of eighty-five thousand and three thousand more stood outside trying to get in.

On the bell Firpo charged at Dempsey and laid a punch to his jaw that sent him reeling. Dempsey came back punching and knocked Firpo down four times. The second round would continue in the same way – Dempsey knocked down Firgo another four times, and Firgo knocked down Dempsey twice. In his second knock down Dempsey was famously punched out of the ring altogether and landed on the press bench. The reporters pushed the boxer off their typewriters and Dempsey sprang back to knock Firpo out and finish the fight off.

But the win was not without controversy. The referee had failed to count down Dempsey's time outside the ring, which constituted a legal knockout. He had similarly failed to enforce a new rule which forbade fighters from standing over a downed opponent ready to punch as soon as he got up. The Firgo fight had made Dempsey rich, but his unwillingness to move away from a downed opponent would cost him the next title defence and begin the decline of his boxing career.

The next defence match was fought in Philadelphia in September 1926. Dempsey's opponent was US marine and Shakespeare reader Gene Tunney, who had only one defeat to his name. The match did not go well for the champ. Tunney managed to completely outbox Dempsey, who seemed slow and out of shape. Dempsey was so badly battered in the bout that he apologised afterwards to his aghast wife, by famously saying: 'Honey, I forgot to duck,' a phrase reused by President Ronald Regan after surviving an assassination attempt.

The rematch between Tunney and Dempsey was scheduled for 22 September 1927, and generated record breaking sales of $2 million. By the seventh round Dempsey was losing on points but managed to let fly a trademark left hook to Tunney's chin, which knocked him down. Tunney seemed down for the count, but Dempsey broke the new rule by continuing to stand over Tunney. In the end the referee led Dempsey to a neutral corner and only then began Tunney's count, which gave the boxer an extra five seconds to recover. Dempsey was not able to knock Tunney down again and the marine won the match on points. Because of the controversy the match became known as the fight of 'The Long Count.'

The match was to be Dempsey's last as a professional and the thirty-one-year-old retired. After a stint in the Coast Guard Reserve during World War II to silence any last draft-dodging quips, he opened a restaurant in Times Square, New York – Demspey's. He died in 1983 aged eighty-seven.

REGULATING THE VIOLENCE

Many believe Dempsey's title defeat was a consequence of a change in rules. When Dempsey began boxing it was legal to stand over a knocked down opponent, and he was unable to adapt when this rule was amended. Rule reform is nothing new in boxing. The early story of boxing is in many ways about attempts to civilise the sport and regulate its violence.

In the eighteenth century boxing emerged as an alternative to the much-maligned duel, and quickly became the domain of the English gentry. Gentleman would soon introduce a series of rules to keep the sport fair, above board and differentiate it from the common bar brawls and punch-ups that a lower class of man might participate in. It was to be a losing battle.

From the twentieth century America would dominate the sport, where it would become entangled with issues of race, political ideology, and the cult of celebrity. But boxing would eventually fall into a slump in the late twentieth century, as the sport became overly corporate, confused by too many governing bodies, and blighted by the violence of its boxers outside of the ring.

Whatever steps have been taken to regulate boxing and make it acceptable to society, it is difficult to dress up the sport's true nature – two men slugging it out with their fists.

History

Fighting with fists is man's most primal and primitive form of one-on-one combat. It would not have taken homo-erectus long to curl up his hands when grunting and foot stomping did not seem enough and aggression got the better of him.

It is hard to imagine our ancient ancestors had time for fist fighting purely for entertainment before the domestication of animals and the first permanent settlements. But by the time the first cities were constructed it had become a sport. Third Millennium wall reliefs from ancient Mesopotamia show early pugilists in action. Similar illustrations found in the ancient Egyptian capital of Thebes date from 1350 BC.

However, it was in ancient Greece that the organised sport of boxing first began. The contests were simple – both men would stand facing each other and punch until one was on the ground, or conceded defeat. Punches could fall anywhere on the body, but wrestling or holding one another was not allowed.

Boxing featured in many of the athletic festivals across ancient Greece and made its first appearance at the Olympic games in 688 BC. The bouts were held outside at midday, although not fought within a defined area such as a ring. Nor were there weight divisions, points, or rounds. The contestants were drawn by lots of two, with the winners of each lot meeting until there were only two fighters left.

The boxers protected their hands by wrapping them in soft ox-hide thongs, called *himantes*. The *himantes* supported the fighter's wrists and helped prevent hand fractures. Himantes are mentioned in Homer's *The Iliad*, when a boxing match is held at the funeral games for Patroclus. Nestor asks that the two best boxers step forward, the winner to claim 'the hard working-jenny' (female donkey) and the loser a two-handled goblet donated by Achilles. Immediately a young, powerful man called Epeios steps forward and claims he will win the prize, saying:

> *For I tell you this straight out, and it will be a thing accomplished. I will smash his skin apart and break his bones on each other. Let those who care for him wait nearby in a huddle about him to carry him out, after my fists have beaten him under.*

The challenge is met by the 'godlike' Euryalos and the scene is set for action:

> *First he pulled on the boxing belt about his waist, and then gave him the thongs carefully cut from the hide*

of a ranging ox. The two men, girt up, strode into the midst of the circle and faced each other, and put up their ponderous hands at the same time and closed, so that their heavy arms were crossing each other, and there was a fierce grinding of teeth, the sweat began to run everywhere from their bodies. Great Epeios came in, and hit him as he peered out from his guard, on the cheek, and he could no longer keep his feet, but where he stood the glorious limbs gave. As in the water roughened by the north wind a fish jumps in the weed of the beach-break, then the dark water closes above him, so Euryalos left the ground from the blow, but great-hearted Epeios took him in his arms and set him upright, and his true companions stood about him, and led him out of the circle, feet dragging as he spat up the thick blood and rolled his head over on one side. He was dizzy when they brought him back and set him among them. But they themselves went and carried off the two-handled goblet.

Homer, *The Iliad*, translated by Richmond Lattimore

The soft *himantes* would give way to sharp thongs in the fourth century: strips of hard leather that were designed to cut into skin and flesh. By the time boxing had been adopted by the ancient Romans, the Grecian *himantes* had been replaced by the *caestus*, a type of glove made with metal studs and plates and spikes. For the Romans, boxing made up part of the *munera* (see page 35) and the *caestus* ensured these contests were sufficiently violent, bloody and to the death. This form of the sport would only last as long as Rome itself, but as the Empire fell into decline, boxing too seemed to disappear from the annals of history. It would re-emerge over a millennia later in a world that was taking its inspiration from the classical period – the Age of Enlightenment.

BRITISH BEGINNINGS

It was late in this age that the gentlemanly pursuit of duelling began to slowly fall out of favour in England. In the eighteenth century it was largely replaced with sports, particularly fencing and boxing. Both forms of entertainment would feature on the bill of James Figg's London amphitheatre, the venue that would revive boxing and transform it into the popular modern sport of today. Figg himself was a master swordsman who was also handy with his fists. By 1719 Figg had become the first boxing champion and would remain undefeated until his retirement in 1734.

Boxers of this period fought for an agreed fee and spectators made wagers on their performances. But the bouts could be a gamble – there were no weight divisions or rules, meaning a David could easily find himself up against a Goliath. The fighters fought without gloves and the fights generally continued until one boxer was incapacitated. Wrestling was permitted, as was punching a man when he was on the ground.

Boxing would continue in this unregulated form until 1740, when new champion Jack Broughton killed his opponent in the ring. Broughton, who was a student of Figg's, set about drafting a set of rules as a result of the fatality. The Broughton Rules would govern boxing until they were replaced by the London Prize Ring rules in 1838. The Broughton Rules specified that a boxer could not hit an opponent when he was down, and that a downed man should be given thirty seconds to get up again. Wrestling was still permitted but holding or punching a man below the belt was forbidden. However, there was still no limit on how long a boxing match lasted and bouts would continue until one man was knocked out or yielded.

Broughton also introduced a new safety feature for practising, which would later revitalise the way the sport was played. His gloves, or 'mufflers', allowed greater protection for the hands as well as providing shields with which to deflect incoming blows. This created a new style of boxing, which used the block to fend off an opponent's attack. Practice gloves not only helped prevent hand fractures but also allowed more punches to be delivered to an opponent's head. Brain damage as a result of boxing therefore increased after the introduction of gloves.

Broughton used his gloves as a way of attracting gentlemen to train at his new boxing academy, as: 'Mufflers are provided that will effectively secure them for the inconveniency of black eyes, broken jaws and bloody noses.' No such assurance was given for the matches themselves, which were still held with bare knuckles. Further methods to tempt in the upper classes included comparing the modern sport to its classical origins. One advertisement provided a quote from Virgil's *Aeneid*, saying that learned men, who: 'Boast themselves inheritors of the Greek and Roman virtues should follow their example in conflicts of this kind.'

Broughton's reign as champion symbolised the first golden age of boxing but the period fell into decline shortly after Broughton was beaten by Jack Slack in 1750. After that, boxers and money men worked in cahoots to fix fights and the popularity of the sport waned. Nevertheless, towards the end of the 18th century boxing experienced a revival spearheaded by a new breed of boxer, in particular Daniel Mendoza and 'Gentleman' John Jackson. At this time there were still no weight divisions and by boxing standards Mendoza was not a heavy man, weighing only 73 kg (160 pounds). He therefore had to use speed and agility over brute force and is credited with bringing both tactics to the game.

'Gentleman' John Jackson managed to bring boxing an air of respectability by recruiting members of the aristocracy to its ranks. Jackson's behaviour in the ring, however, was often anything but gentlemanly. In the championship contest of 1795, Jackson grabbed Mendoza by the hair so he could hold his head while he punched it. While this was in flagrant disregard for the rules it did still win him the title.

No such behaviour would have been allowed in 1838, which was the year the British Pugilists' Protective Association published the London Prize Ring Rules. The rules specified the sport would be fought in a 24-foot-square ring cordoned off with rope barriers. Each round lasted until a man was knocked down, although there was no limit to the number of rounds fought. A new round would begin 30 seconds after the fighters were back in their corners and each man had only eight seconds to reach the 'scratch' line in the centre of the ring, or be declared 'not up to scratch'. Head butting, eye gouging, biting and punching below the belt were all banned under the London Prize Ring Rules.

AMERICAN ACCESSION

The middle of the nineteenth century signalled the emergence of the American boxer. From early in the century British and Irish champions had toured the USA to fight new opponents and the sport had taken root in the cities of Boston, Philadelphia and New York.

As boxing popularity rose in America it equally began to struggle in Britain. By the second half of the nineteenth century there was a blanket ban on all boxing matches. In fact, boxing was never officially made legal in Britain and today is fought under a loophole in legislation that allows 'exhibitions of skill.' But in the nineteenth century the 'sweet science' of pugilism, which had attracted England's upper class during John Jackson's day, was more commonly associated with street brawling.

To address this issue, a new set of rules was written in 1867 by Lord Lonsdale and Arthur Chambers in association with the Marquess of Queensberry. The rules revolutionised the sport and whitewashed its name with a new layer of legitimacy. The Queensberry Rules made four major improvements to boxing: all contestants would have to wear gloves; each round would consist of three minutes followed by a one minute rest period; wrestling would be illegal; and downed boxers would have ten seconds to get up, or be declared knocked out. The rules were soon revised to set the number of rounds to twenty, create a scoring system for a boxer's performance, and introduce weight divisions. The London Prize Ring Rules were still kept on for some fights, but the Queensberry Rules had soon supplanted them.

Although the Queensberry Rules had made the sport safer it would never regain its former level of respectability. England's emerging middle class affiliated boxing with the undesirable activities of drinking, gambling and brawling. It was these new values, coupled with the condemnation of the Church, which caused the sport's decline in Britain. By contrast, churches in the United States not only encouraged the activity, but set up their own gyms to support it. The 'muscular Christianity' movement saw boxing as a way of enhancing physical and moral strength, a view advocated by President Theodore Roosevelt. Roosevelt had boxed himself as a young man and had only stopped when he suffered a blow that left him blind in one eye.

British domination of the sport came to a final end in 1889 when Irish-American boxer John L. Sullivan became world champion in the last bare-knuckle fight to be held. For the next hundred years boxing champions of the world would be American.

Within America's own borders the legality on boxing varied from state to state. In those states where it was ruled illegal, matches were held on barges, out at sea, or in member's clubs which were knocked together overnight to stage a contest. But by the 1920s, boxing seemed almost unanimously loved. From its initiation into the United States boxing had often been sold to spectators as minority grudge matches. An Irishman would fight an American and violence would often erupt between the opposing supporters. American boxing in the twentieth century was also often promoted along minority lines, but this time that of race.

Jack Johnson was the first black man to win the heavyweight championship in 1908, to the jubilation of the country's black population. But many white people were not similarly enamoured, and a search began for a 'great white hope' to topple Johnson. In the end James J. Jefferies came out of retirement 'for the sole purpose of proving that a white man is better than a Negro.'

Boxing would take on international cultural significance when world champion Joe Louis met the German champion Max Schmeling, touted by Hitler as a shining example of white Aryran supremacy. The spread of radio in the 1930s gave the sport even wider appeal, which was further enhanced by proliferation of the television set. Boxing would reach a golden age in the 1970s, which featured the best-known boxers of all time – Muhammad Ali, Joe Frazier, and George Foreman.

The sport would experience a resurgence of popularity in the 1980s and 1990s with boxers such as Mike Tyson and Evander Holyfield, but the 1970s represented the sport's peak. Boxing has suffered a distinct dip in popularity in the last two decades, partly caused by the confusing number of governing bodies.

In the early twentieth century British boxing was overseen by the British Boxing Board of Control (BBBofC), and the International Boxing Union (IBU) was set up in Paris. In 1920 in the United States two bodies were established – the National Boxing

Association (NBA) and the competing New York State Athletic Commission (SAC). The situation was further complicated when the IBU became the European Boxing Union, the World Boxing Council (WBC) was established, the NBA changed its name to the World Boxing Association (WBA), and the new International Boxing Federation (IBF) was formed.

The large number of boxing organisations has stymied efforts to create one clear set of regulations for the sport. This, in turn, has caused a re-emergence of corruption, unclear safety measures and ambiguous promotion laws. At the present time, if a boxing promoter is banned by one body, or disagrees with its rules, he can simply take his fighters to a competing organisation. The number of bodies also makes it hard to determine who is the actual world champion, as each organisation offers up its own 'true' champion.

Boxing had gone through its share of peaks and troughs over the last millennia and has always found its way back into the public's affections. Regulations and convoluted governing systems aside, boxing, a sport of two men slugging it out has always had one great strength – its simplicity. It is this simplicity combined with stories of the pugilists themselves, often before complicated political and cultural backdrops, that gives the sport an enduring legacy.

The Boxers

JACK JOHNSON

To be Jack Johnson was to live a life of criticism and ridicule – his 'lazy' defensive style of boxing, his toothy defiant grin, and his dandyish habit of walking around with a top hat and cane. But beneath the jibes lay a far deeper pool of resentment, which had been stirred by something America had been unprepared for – a black heavyweight champion.

Johnson was born on 31 March 1878, in Galveston, Texas; the son of former slaves. At thirteen years old he began working on the docks and boxing. Under the tutelage of ageing boxer Joe Choynski, Johnson went on to win fifty fights by 1902 and in 1903 secured the World Coloured Heavyweight Championship. But the World Heavyweight Championship was out of bounds to black fighters and the present champion James J. Jeffries refused to face Johnson. Johnson had to wait until 1908, when he followed new world champion Tommy Burns to Sydney, Australia for the title fight.

On 26 December 1908, Johnson laid bare his talent and for fourteen rounds peppered Burns with taunts and blows that Burns had no answer for. In the fourteenth round the referee stopped the fight, seeing that Burns had had enough. Johnson's win simultaneously made him a hero among black Americans and opened a floodgate of white racist outrage. Writer Jack London, who covered the event, described Johnson demeaningly as a 'clown', and compared his 'golden smile' to that of a child. The smile was considered an act of defiance by objecting white Americans, who immediately set about finding what London coined 'a great white hope' to defeat him.

As the title holder, Johnson had to face numerous 'great white hopes' during 1909, including the middleweight champion Stanley Ketchel. By 1910, former heavyweight champion James J. Jeffries himself felt obligated to come out of retirement and 'reclaim the heavyweight championship for the white race', to 'demonstrate that a white man is king of them all.' Critics quickly billed the Johnson–Jeffries fight as the real world championship match as Jeffries had retired undefeated, thus making Burns a false champion.

The match, to take place on 4 July 1910 in Reno, Nevada, was hailed as 'the fight of century'. The papers were full of pro-Jeffries predictions and made no bones of criticising Johnson's boxing style. Johnson was a defensive and tactical boxer who held his fists low and only attacked when he had the advantage. A similar style would be used by greats such as Muhammad Ali in years to follow, but in Johnson's time it was called 'devious'.

As the match grew near it increasingly symbolised the fight between black oppression and white supremacy. The supremacists were to be disappointed. Jeffries, who hadn't fought in six years and was carrying weight, was completely dominated by Johnson. Johnson knocked Jeffries down twice, danced nimbly around his slow, heavy punches and made taunting remarks throughout. In the fifteenth round Jeffries' trainers threw in the towel. The fight's outcome provoked a series of lynchings and race riots around America. Many of these were simply celebrations by black communities, which had gotten out of hand after the police intervened to break them up. Some humiliated whites took their revenge by beating or lynching the nearest black person to hand. Overall, twenty-four black people and two white people died and hundreds more were injured.

But whether they liked it or not Johnson had won the fight. Nobody could dispute his place as legitimate champion of the world, even if it was only acknowledged through clenched teeth. Johnson went on to further enrage white opinion by marrying a white woman, the first of three in his lifetime. With the dividends from product endorsements and advertising Johnson became every bit the high-profile celebrity sportsman. He wore expensive tailored suits, top hats and canes, and raced expensive cars. While he flaunted his fame and fortune for all to see, many white Americans publically seethed.

A minister from the southern states suggested Johnson would be lynched if he showed his face down there.

However, the highflying Johnson was about to experience heavy turbulence when in 1912 he was charged with driving a prostitute across state lines. He was sentenced to one year in prison and jumped bail to flee to Europe. Johnson stayed on the continent for seven years and defended his title three times in France. But the allure of a 1915 championship fight in Cuba proved too great for him. The fight itself would act as an elixir for old wounds in America – challenger Jess Willard knocked out Johnson in the twenty-sixth round. Many believed the match had been fixed. Johnson had dominated every round up until the twenty-sixth and then gone down suddenly. The common theory was that Johnson had taken a secret deal that would keep him out of jail when he returned to the states. If this was the deal, it was not made good. Johnson gave himself up to the US authorities in 1920 and went to prison for one year.

After his release Johnson moved to Harlem, where he opened a nightclub and was treated as its first citizen by its black community. He continued to fight the occasional exhibition match, and at one point even appeared as part of a carnival act. Johnson died in a car crash in 1946, shortly after leaving a North Carolina diner in a rage when it refused to serve him.

The boxer's statistics are formidable – between 1897 and 1928 he won 80 out of 114 fights, 45 of which ended in a knockout. But his impact on the oppression of black people cannot be measured. The first son of slave parents to be born free had shown the world and the black boxers, artists, activists and leaders that would follow him that it was possible to stand up and fight back. This spirit would manifest itself in the next black champion of the world – Joe Louis.

JOE LOUIS

If Jack Johnson had showed the world black boxers were just as good as their white counterparts, Joe Louis would prove they were better. By the time Louis took the heavyweight throne it had been more than twenty years since a black man was champion. Louis would keep the title for twelve, the longest of any heavyweight champion in boxing history. Black boxers would go on to dominate the sport for the rest of the century and into the next.

Joe Louis was born in 1914 in Lafayette, Alabama, and his family moved to Detroit soon afterwards. At twelve years old, Louis began boxing lessons at the Brewster Gym and won his first championship at the Golden Gloves competition in 1933. In 1934 Louis went pro and in 1935 knocked out former heavyweight champion Primo Carnera. Carnera had been photographed giving the Nazi salute, which attracted much publicity to the match and made Louis an overnight celebrity when he won.

Louis would defeat a number of ex-champions while waiting to fight world champion Jim Braddock. But in 1936 he would suffer his first professional loss against the darling of the Nazi party, Max Schmeling. Hitler had promoted Schmeling as a pure specimen of Aryan perfection and his victory proof of the superiority of the 'master race.' Schmeling himself did not support Hitler's doctrine and refused to join the Nazi party despite heavy encouragement to do so. He had simply won the fight by doing his homework. While watching reruns of Louis' fights, Schmeling had noticed his tendency to drop his left fist in defence, a point he ruthlessly exploited. But while Louis' defeat was felt heavily among the black community of America, the victories that followed would more than make up for it.

In 1937 Louis defeated Jim Braddock in the heavyweight championship fight, becoming the first black man to hold the title since Jack Johnson. Then, in 1938, a rematch with Max Schmeling was scheduled. This time around Louis had the hopes of not only black Americans but white ones too. President Franklin D. Roosevelt even met with Louis to tell him America was depending on his fists. The match proved to be a great day for American democracy over German fascism –

Louis punched out Schmeling in just over two minutes.

While America was united in its celebrations, the victory had profound implications for the black community. Unlike Jack Johnson before him, the victorious Louis was portrayed as an all-American hero and not one relegated to racial slurs or innuendo in the press. Louis added to his national hero image by donating the proceeds from his 1942 title fight against Max Baer to the families of those killed at Pearl Harbor. These actions were not flukes, but carefully orchestrated by his manager Mike Jacobs.

Jacobs realised early on that if he was to be successful Louis had to appear as the polar opposite to Jack Johnson. There were to be no racing cars, white women, or flashy clothes, which had so upset the white majority in America. Instead Louis adopted a seemingly moderate and unassuming persona to act in sharp contrast with that of his black predecessor. The non-threatening approach certainly helped Louis infiltrate the American mainstream; by 1942 he had enlisted and acted as a spokesman for the army and was awarded the Legion of Merit. But despite Louis' individual acceptance, racial boundaries still divided America – parks, cafes, buses and the army were all segregated, there was one section for white people and another for black people. It would not be for some years that the next great black boxer, Muhammad Ali, would address these issues of race.

Louis' boxing career peaked between 1939 and 1942

when he successfully defended the heavyweight title seven times. He retired as the undefeated champion in 1949 and was succeeded by Ezzard Charles. Louis would lose to Charles during a comeback fight in 1950, and again to Rocky Marciano in 1951. His second retirement was not an altogether comfortable one, his winnings had been mismanaged and he found himself heavily in debt with tax bills owing.

Louis, the 'brown bomber', who had won 68 out of 71 fights, 54 by knockout and held the title of heavyweight champion for twelve years, would eventually be forced to take a job as a greeter at Caesar's Palace in Las Vegas.

MUHAMMAD ALI

Cassius Clay was a charismatic young boxer who would captivate 1960s America with his clean-cut charm, playful braggadocio, and entertaining buffoonery. But in the late sixties Cassius Clay would metamorphose into Muhammad Ali, an Islamist convert, convicted draft dodger, and vocal spokesman of white oppression of blacks. And while his political and ideological life was inexorably intertwined with his boxing career, his prowess in the ring was undisputed – he is widely considered to be the greatest boxer who ever lived.

Cassius Marcellus Clay Jr. was born on 17 January 1942 in Louisville, Kentucky. His boxing career started when local policeman and youth boxing coach Joe Martin, discovered Clay punching a boy who had stolen his brand new bicycle. Six years later Clay won gold at the Rome Olympics. Following the Olympics, the now professional Clay won public admiration through his shameless self-promotion and amusing antics. He would brag that he was the 'greatest', make up rhyming verse about his exploits, and prophesise the exact round he would knock a opponent out in. Clay's good looks and apparent innocence enchanted TV audiences everywhere. He had taken a page out of Joe Louis' book by playing a safe, undefiant black boxer, unlike the pariah Jack Johnson.

Ironically, Clay's boxing style reminded people of Johnson, whose tactics were once described as 'devious'. Clay held his hands low, backed away from attacks, and only punched when he had the advantage. His speed, agile footwork, and arsenal of punching combinations led Clay to describe his fighting style as, to: 'Float like a butterfly, sting like a bee.'

Clay's big chance to make good his boasts and win the heavyweight title came on 25 February 1964. His opponent was reigning champion Sonny Liston, considered the toughest fighter of his era and 7 to 1 favourite to win. Seemingly indifferent to the odds, Clay taunted Liston at the weigh in, calling him: 'The big ugly bear', and explaining how he would beat him, as: 'Your hands can't hit what your eyes can't see.'

The first three rounds went Clay's way; he had used his speed to dance away from Liston's punches and deliver his own lightening jabs. But in the fourth round Clay's eyesight became impeded by a substance that had either been illegally added to Liston's gloves or had been used to treat the fighter's cuts. It was not until halfway through the fifth round that Clay's eyesight returned to normal, and he began pummeling Liston with a brutal series of combinations. Then, in a shock decision, Liston did not get up from his corner for the seventh round, complaining of a shoulder injury. Clay summed up the win with typical bravado, proclaiming 'I shook up the world!'

Clay would continue this shake up two days later when he announced he had converted to Islam and joined the Nation of Islam, a black nationalist group that advocated Islam as a way of fighting racial oppression. Among the Nation's high profile leaders were Malcolm X and Elijah Muhammad, who bestowed the new name of Muhammad Ali on Clay. The move to Islam was considered controversial at best and often perceived as a hostile act by much of Ali's once adoring mainstream public. Ali was now a spokesman for racial equality, although his comments on the subject would range between outright support for civil rights and complete rejection of integration. Ali once said:

We who follow the teachings of Elijah Muhammad

don't want to be forced to integrate. Integration is wrong. We don't want to live with the white man; that's all.

There would be no ambiguity about Ali's boxing. He knocked Liston out in the first round of a rematch, and went on to defeat Floyd Patterson, George Chuvalo, Henry Cooper, Brian London, and Karl Mildenberger. In 1966 Ali proved his absolute dominance in the ring when he fought Cleveland Williams. Ali landed over one hundred punches, knocked Cleveland down four times, and won in three rounds. Cleveland had only managed to land three punches on Ali.

CONSCIENTIOUS OBJECTOR

Ali would invite a new round of controversy when he refused to fight in the Vietnam War on religious grounds. He had previously said: 'I ain't got no quarrel with them Vietcong,' but had also claimed he would fight in an Islamic holy war, thus giving the draft board enough ammunition to deny his refusal to fight. As a result Ali was stripped of his heavyweight title, had his boxing licence revoked, and received a suspended sentence of five years in jail. Ali made his position clear: 'Why should they ask me to put on a uniform and go ten thousand miles from home and drop bombs and bullets on brown people in Vietnam while so-called Negro people in Louisville are treated like dogs and denied simple human rights?'

His comments outraged the moral majority of the American mainstream, but won him instant acclaim and admiration among white liberals and the anti-war movement. High profile celebrities such as Elizabeth Taylor publically demanded that Ali be allowed to defend his title. His chance would come in 1970 when he was granted a temporary boxing licence to fight Jerry Quarry in Atlanta. Following this victory Ali was also granted a licence to fight in New York, where he beat Oscar Bonavena at Madison Square Gardens.

Ali's real test would be against Joe Frazier, the fighter who had become heavyweight champion in Ali's absence. The match would be fought at Madison Square Gardens on 8 March 1971, and billed as 'the fight of the century'. But despite a monumental build up, it was not to be Ali's night. Frazier dominated throughout and made sure of his victory with a punishing left hook in the fifteenth round, which knocked Ali to the floor. It was Ali's first professional loss. However the fighter was far from finished – he would go on to win eight of his next ten bouts before the rematch against Frazier. Frazier had, in the meantime, lost his title to the powerful puncher George Foreman, so the contest against Ali would not be a championship fight. In a reversal of fortune Ali beat Frazier in twelve rounds, in a show of great technical ability.

Ali's chance to regain the heavyweight title would come on 30 October 1974 against Foreman. The much hyped event was to take place in Zaire and received unprecedented publicity as the 'Rumble in the Jungle.' Foreman had knocked down previous challenger Frazier six times in just over four minutes and nobody seriously considered Ali as a contender.

Speculating pundits thought Ali would fight by dancing around Foreman to avoid his attack. Instead Ali came in hitting, landing nine punches on Foreman in the first round. Then, to further confuse matters, Ali employed his 'dope a rope' strategy, in which instead of dancing around the ring, he fought for long periods by leaning back onto the barrier ropes to avoid Foreman's punches. He then delivered a stinging combination of counter blows. Ali's strategy was to wear the heavy punching Foreman out and outlast him. It worked. In the eighth round Ali knocked Foreman down and he didn't get up again.

The Rumble in the Jungle marked the peak of Ali's career, which began its decline soon afterwards. The last high point was Ali's final fight against Frazier in 1975, which was fought in the Philippines and dubbed 'The Thriller in Manila.' The match lasted for fourteen rounds, which Ali later described as the hardest of his life. The fight looked like it could go either way, but in the end Ali had asserted his dominance and Frazier threw in the towel. The fight would represent the peak for what many consider the golden age of twentieth century boxing.

The once majestic Ali, who had beaten every heavyweight boxer of his era, would not depart the ring with a dignified exit. In 1978 he lost the heavyweight title to the Olympic gold medalist Leon Spinks who only had seven wins to his name and was considered a novice. After retiring in 1980, Ali would return for a comeback against Larry Holmes, a humiliating one-sided fight, that Holmes said even he found sad to endure. Many reported the onset of Ali's Parkinson's Disease was in evidence in his last ever fight against Trevor Berbick in 1981.

As with his black heavyweight champion predecessors Jack Johnson and Joe Louis, Ali's political and social stance against oppression were influential in the battle for equal rights in America, and his legend will always be associated with his objection to the Vietnam War. As a boxer he won 56 of 61 fights, with 37 knockouts. He defeated every heavyweight boxer of his time and was named 'Fighter of the Year' on innumerable occasions. He remains one of the best-known and respected athletes in history.

MIKE TYSON

Mike Tyson, like Muhammad Ali, is one of the world's best-known athletes, but for all the wrong reasons. Tyson was touted as the fighter who would pull boxing out of its slump, transcend racial borders in sport, and give the world an inspirational heavyweight champion to rival the likes of Louis, Dempsey and Ali. Instead, Tyson became the poster boy for an unhinged psychopath with a licence to box – he went to jail for rape, was charged many times with assault and harassment, and even bit off a chunk of Evander Holyfield's ear during a match.

Mike Tyson was born on 30 June 1966 in Brooklyn, New York. His father abandoned the family when Tyson was two years old leaving his mother to raise him and his siblings alone. Tyson was often taunted at school for his high-pitched voice and lisp and fell into crime at a young age. Tyson remembers his first incident with his fists from when he was ten years old, in a television documentary *Taking on Tyson*:

> *I was with my friends and we robbed this person's house. I had, like, sixteen hundred bucks in my pocket, and I was in this pigeon shop, and I wanted these birds so bad... Back then, birds cost seventy-five cents to a dollar, but these birds cost two-fifty. I bought up the whole cage. Seven hundred dollars' worth of birds!*

But somebody had been watching Tyson carry the cages up to the rooftop of a nearby building, and during his next visit Tyson was confronted by two men stealing the pigeons. One of the men decapitated a bird and hit Tyson in the face with it, just to show they weren't messing round.

'So I started fighting. I couldn't fight, but I was flailing away. I hit him more than he hit me, so I guess I won.'

By the time he was fourteen years old Tyson had been arrested thirty-eight times and was sent to reform school for boys. A social worker and former boxer recognised Tyson's talent and introduced him to trainer Cus D'Amato, who had made champions out of boxers such as Floyd Patterson. D'Amato took Tyson under his wing and even became his legal guardian when his mother died. D'Amato trained Tyson to fight with a 'peek-a-boo' style − holding his hands high and staying close to his opponent, while bobbing and weaving to avoid his punches. He would then launch a fast, powerful and aggressive counterattack, which often featured his trademark right hook to the body followed by a right undercut to the chin.

Tyson's fearsome reputation as a knockout boxer would be underscored by his campaign of intimidation before the fight, which included taunts and threats and bad vibes. Many boxers would report avoiding eye contact with Tyson at all times. Tyson's methods made him the youngest heavyweight champion in history after he knocked out WBC defender Trevor Berbick in the second round of their match. After defeating the WBA defender James Smith and the IBF defender Tony Tucker, Tyson became the undisputed heavyweight champion of the world.

He then went on to fight and knock out Larry Holmes, his first defeat in seventy-five bouts, and Michael Spinks, who had until then never lost a match. Spinks was the great hopeful and the 1988 match was eagerly anticipated, but once in the ring Tyson took him apart. After ninety-one seconds of the first round Spinks found himself knocked to the floor and could not get up again. It was his last boxing match. But Tyson, who seemed unbeatable, had already hit the high point of his popularity and boxing ability. What would follow was Tyson's long, hard descent to the bottom.

THE TIDE TURNS

By the time of the Spinks fight D'Amato had died and Tyson sacked his longtime trainer Kevin Rooney soon after. In 1988 Robin Givens, Tyson's wife, filed for divorce amid allegations of battery. Sexual harassment charges were also laid against Tyson from two women who claimed he had groped them in a nightclub. Then, in 1990, came the biggest boxing upset of the decade, when Tyson lost the championship to James Douglas. Douglas, who was not previously considered a contender against the undefeated Tyson, scored a technical knockout in the tenth round.

Tyson won his next four fights, but then in 1991 he was accused of raping an eighteen-year-old beauty contestant, a charge he was convicted of in 1992. Although Tyson served three years in jail, the conviction did little to dim his celebrity status. After winning fights against Frank Bruno and Bruce Seldon, Tyson was set up to fight the two-time heavyweight champion Evander Holyfield on 9 November 1996.

The match was eagerly anticipated and many spectators were hoping for an unexpected twist or bizarre turn from the 'Baddest Man on the Planet.' There was an upset, but it came from Holyfield, who won the fight by technical knockout, defeating Tyson for only the second time in his professional career. At thirty-four years old, Holyfield had been described as 'washed up' by fans and pundits alike, but had defied all predictions to become only the second person after Muhammad Ali to win a heavyweight championship belt three times. Tyson was furious after the match and accused Holyfield of head-butting him, an action the referee had ruled as accidental. The stage was set for an electric rematch, which took place on 28 June 1997.

The match, dubbed 'The Sound and The Fury', was held in Las Vegas and grossed $100 million in sales. Tyson received $30 million and Holyfield $35 million, the highest amounts ever paid out to boxers at the time. The two million television owners who had paid-per-view to watch a piece of history-making controversy would not be disappointed. In the third round Tyson bit Holyfield's ear. The fight was halted but as soon as it resumed Tyson bit Holyfield's other ear, this time taking a piece of it off and spitting it to the floor. The referee immediately disqualified Tyson and the arena exploded into a near riot.

Many considered Tyson's action premeditated, as he had removed his mouth guard before the round started. Some said Tyson wanted to enhance his reputation of being a dangerous and berserk fighting machine. Others said he wanted to be disqualified because he knew he was going to lose. Tyson was punished with a fine of $3 million and his boxing licence was revoked. The ban did not last, and in 1998 his licence was reinstated. But before relaunching his career Tyson went back to jail for nine months, this time for assaulting two motorists in a road rage incident. However, Tyson's incarceration had not cooled his temper – in a 2000 match with Lou Savarese he inadvertently punched out the referee. Then he tested positive for marijuana use after a fight with Andrew Golota.

During this period Tyson tried to schedule a fight against the undisputed heavyweight champion, Lennox Lewis. Following the fight with Savarese, Tyson had outraged the public with his challenge to Lewis, saying: 'I want your heart. I want to eat your children.' Tyson's request to hold the fight in Nevada had been turned down because he was once again facing sexual harassment charges there. Eventually the fight was arranged for 8 June 2002, but not before a prematch press conference had erupted into an all-out brawl between the Tyson and Lewis camps. The match was short-lived and put to rest any suggestion of a Tyson comeback. Lewis twice dropped Tyson before knocking him out in the eighth round.

Tyson would win more fights in 2003, in between having a facial tattoo and hitting the party scene in Las Vegas. But the same year, after making a reported $300 million over the length of his career, Tyson filed for bankruptcy. The boxer retired from professional boxing but was forced to perform in exhibition matches to help pay off his debts. Then in 2007, Tyson avoided a long jail sentence by admitting he was a drug addict after crashing a car while under the influence of cocaine. By 2008 he had put on over 60 kg in weight and was struggling to pay his drug dealers. But in 2011, in an interview to promote *Taking on Tyson*, the former boxer said he had mended his ways and now lived a clean, healthy lifestyle.

Tyson is widely regarded as one of the greatest boxers of the late twentieth century, but his legacy did little to give the sport a boost or rebirth. In the ring his raw power and brutality won him titles, fame and wealth. Yet his was an aggression without control and it led him to assault and rape outside the ring. Then, with a chilling irony, Tyson was allowed to walk back into his celebrity and receive tens of millions of dollars to put his violence on display.

Mike Tyson cannot alone be held responsible for the decline of boxing, but his era belongs to a darker, more cynical age that is far removed from the political and ideological 'golden age' of Muhammad Ali. The sport has suffered ups and downs since it first took over as an alternative to men killing each other in a duel. It is unclear where its future lies, but its appeal – which has fascinated writers, philosophers and artists for centuries – endures. And it has proved an irresistible topic for scores of movies, which all have boxing as their central motif.

Boxing Movies

ROCKY

Sylvester Stallone first got the idea for the 1976 film *Rocky* on his 29th birthday, which found him broke and depressed and spending his last $100 to watch a fight between Muhammad Ali and Chuck Wepner. Stallone said of the fight:

> *Chuck Wepner, a battling, bruising club fighter who had never made the big time, was having his shot. It wasn't at all regarded as a serious battle. But as the fight progressed, this miracle unfolded. He hung in there. People went absolutely crazy. Wepner was knocked out in the 15th and final round, almost lasting the distance. We had witnessed an incredible triumph of the human spirit and we loved it.*

Sylvester Stallone went home and wrote the screenplay for *Rocky* in three short days. He described Rocky as: 'A man of the streets...a twentieth century gladiator in a pair of sneakers.' In the end the *Rocky* franchise was enormously successful and has grossed over $1 billion worldwide.

In the first film, Rocky is introduced as a blue-collar Italian-American who works as a part-time boxer and loan shark enforcer. One day, by chance, he is given the opportunity to fight world heavyweight champion Apollo Creed, and everything changes.

The following six *Rocky* movies are largely about the fighter's ability to 'go the distance' throughout the changing fortunes of his professional and personal life. He wins, loses, boxes in Russia, becomes a trainer and even comes out of retirement as a fifty-eight-year-old to fight the world champion. He doesn't win, but manages to survive the match and remain standing, thus once again proving his worth.

The movies inspirational message about a man who fights his way up from the bottom is reflected in Stallone's own battle to star in and keep creative control of his *Rocky* screenplay. Stallone was offered $300,000 to step aside and let a big name actor like James Caan or Bert Reynolds take the main role, but he would not relent. As a result the movie was produced for under $1 million with the cast and crew taking lower than normal pay. The movie was shot in twenty-eight days, with its iconic montage training shots being filmed on Steadicam camera from the back of a van.

Rocky's boxing style is based, in part, on that of Rocky Marciano's. In *Rocky*, manager Mickey sees a picture of Rocky Marciano and comments the two are similar, as they 'fight with heart'. Rocky Balboa certainly borrows from Marciano's characteristics, both are working class Italian-Americans and both are sluggers. But unlike Rocky Balboa, Marciano was able to avoid punches before landing a killer blow of his own. Rocky Balboa's manifesto was to take any amount of punishment before launching a deadly counterattack. This fighting style was adopted as an analogy for Rocky and indeed Stallone's life up until he wrote the *Rocky* screenplay. As Rocky tells his son in *Rocky Balboa*:

> *It ain't about how hard you hit; it's about how hard you can get hit, and keep moving forward.*

RAGING BULL

Like Rocky Balboa, Jake La Motta was an Italian-American boxer who would take a severe beating before launching his own aggressive counterattack. La Motta is the subject of Martin Scorsese's 1980's hit *Raging Bull*, generally thought to be one of the best boxing movies ever made. While *Raging Bull* and *Rocky* both feature a working class slugger who can absorb punches like a sponge, the similarities end there. Rocky is a brightly coloured, inspirational action movie about one man's ability to beat the odds and win from the bottom up. *Raging Bull* is a dark and disturbing tale about a boxing champion's descent to the bottom, filmed in black and white.

Raging Bull opens with an ageing, overweight La Motta (Robert De Niro) performing his stand-up routine at a club. The action then flashes back to a 1941 fight against opponent Jimmy Reeves. The rest of the movie focuses on La Motta's rise to heavyweight stardom and decline into paranoia, obsession, and violence outside of the ring. In the end La Motta is left estranged from his family and wife and he ends up in jail.

The movie comes full circle to finish on the opening scene, with La Motta about to perform his comedy act. We last see him shadowboxing before he takes the stage.

It was De Niro who convinced Martin Scorsese to make *Raging Bull* after reading La Motta's autobiography. Scorsese rejected the idea for some years but relented after nearly dying from a drug overdose, thinking the movie would be the last he ever made. De Niro trained with La Motta himself for the role and finding he had a talent for the sport entered and won several middleweight matches. La Motta said of De Niro's performance:

> *He is a genius. He got me down pat. We boxed over a thousand rounds together and when I was done with him he could have fought professional.*

After the hard training De Niro was ordered to go soft to portray the older, overweight La Motta. Filming was halted for several months so De Niro could go on an eating tour of France and Italy where he managed to increase his weight from 66 kg (145 lbs) to 96 kg (212 lbs). Scorsese further enhanced the realism of the movie by using Hersey's syrup for the blood, which he thought would look more authentic on black and white film. He made sure the 'blood' was splattered on the ropes, something he had noticed during real fights he attended for research purposes.

Raging Bull is an unsentimental study of a man who uses his aggression and brute force as his raison d'etre inside and outside of the ring. The real La Motta once punched his first wife so hard he thought he had killed her. When asked about such incidents in a 2007 *Sunday Times* article La Motta seemed unrepentant:

> *I never really and truly hit my wives. If I had hit them properly they would be dead. You know how it is: you slap around a broad just a little bit and everything is blown out of proportion.*

While *Raging Bull* goes someway to exploring the pathos of La Motta's violent world the viewer is not left with a fond impression of the boxer. It is harder still to reconcile empathetic feelings of La Motta when considering that De Niro's portrayal is a toned down version of the man himself.

GUNMEN

Fact or Fiction?

It is high noon in a small Wild Western town. Tumbleweed dances along the dusty, dirt road. A saloon door bangs in the breeze. Above the town, a circling hawk lets out a shrill whistle. Then, the slow, deliberate mosey of cowboy boots crunch and ka-ching their way onto Main Street. Once in the middle, the gunman stops, turns, and faces his man. There is around one hundred yards between them. The showdown is set. One throws back his coat tails, exposing two holsters with leg ties, butts facing backwards. The other poises his hand over his Colt .44, twitching for the draw. One narrows his eyes. The other grits his teeth. And then, draw! Six-shooters are yanked out in a flash and a blur. Five shots are fired and plumes of grey smoke wisp through the air. One gunman looks down to his stomach – blood oozes from a round, singed hole. He staggers, spins round, and crumples. Dead in the dirt. A shrieking woman runs out to the corpse. Townspeople huddle, whispering and pointing. The surviving gunman takes a last look, spits and then strides into the saloon. The shoot-out is done.

This is the popular view of a gunfight in the old west, indoctrinated into the public consciousness by TV and movies. But in reality it hardly ever happened. Gunfights of the 'Wild West' were rarely premeditated showdowns in which two famous gunmen squared off against each other because the town just wasn't big enough for the both of them. Instead, gunfights usually took place in a saloon, when two drunken 'nobodys' argued over cards, pulled their guns and tried desperately to hit each other. Most gunfights would take place at close range, and even then both men often missed. Instead, it was more common for a gunman to shoot himself in the foot or leg, or hit an innocent bystander by mistake.

Another fabrication is the 'fast draw' which had little relevance to gunmen of the Wild West. It was not the fastest gun that won most gunfights but the one with the steadiest arm and most considered aim. Many gunmen felt lucky to hit their opponent with even one bullet from the favoured Colt Single Action .44 or .45. These were not the rapid-fire automatic handguns of today. A single action needed to be carefully cocked for each shot, and it wasn't called the 'thumb buster' for nothing. Pulling the hammer back jerkily or at speed caused all sorts of breaks and lacerations. Even more injuries were caused while trying to fire rapidly by holding down the trigger and 'fanning' the hammer with the other hand. While making an impressive amount of noise and smoke, 'fanning' also made it impossible to take proper aim.

For most gunfights a gunman would pull his revolver (often from a pocket or belt), cock it with the second joint of his thumb, steady the barrel, (sometimes on his free arm), and do his best to take careful aim (gunfights were more often fought under the influence of whiskey than not). If ever a gunman found himself squaring off at the Hollywood distance of one hundred yards, the quick draw would have become even more irrelevant. This was too far to even pray for an accurate result and any self-respecting gunman would have simply picked up his rifle or shotgun instead.

The idea that famous gunslingers rode from town to town searching out other gunmen of similar repute is a myth. The real gunmen of the west, that is, the men who gained notoriety and fame as such, usually played a much safer game. They would rarely get into a gunfight unless the odds were stacked highly in their favour. Even then a gunfight was only ever a last resort, and usually only agreed to when a gunman had been 'called out.' Most did their best to avoid other well-known gunmen and would usually ride out of town as soon as one arrived. There were some exceptions. Jim 'Killer Miller' shot between fourteen and fifty people, always went looking for trouble, and boasted he would kill anybody for a fee. John Wesley Hardin's kill sheet is so long it reads like a shopping list, although he made it known that every shooting was in 'self defence.' On the other side of the coin were those who had no business calling themselves gunmen at all. Buffalo Bill was a shameless self-promoter, who made sure the public ate up his gunfighting exploits in dime novels, magazine articles and travelling shows. Not one word was true.

While many notorious gunmen worked as hired guns, almost all others tried at least one other occupation, if not several. Doc Holliday was a dentist and saloon keeper; John Wesley Hardin was a school teacher and lawyer; Wild Bill Hickok was a scout and stage coach driver. Even those who made their money through less respectable means, such as horse thievery, robbing and illegal whiskey peddling, were often happy to jump the fence and pick up a badge from time to time.

It was rightly assumed that troublemakers would think twice about entering a town policed by a known gunman. Once such example was Ben Thompson – a gambler, gunman and convicted murderer who was made marshal of Austin, Texas during a particularly violent phase in 1881. Austin was one of several notorious gunfighting towns during the heyday of the gunman, which lasted from 1860 to 1890. Fort Worth, Dodge City and El Paso also attracted gunfighting troublemakers and famous gunmen such as Wyatt Earp and Doc Holiday were hired to keep the peace in these frontier towns.

However, a gunman was always true to his nature regardless of what side of the fence he stood on. As such, the line between lawman and outlaw often became blurred. Almost all gunmen shared a penchant for gambling, whiskey, or women – and often all three together. One or all of these things was responsible for practically every known gunfight that took place in the west. Gunmen, after all, were largely violent troublemakers who lived hard and died young. They drifted from town to town, drank, gambled, womanised, shot, and were shot at.

The Gunmen

BILLY THE KID

Billy the Kid was a skinny, bucktoothed outlaw with small hands and a reputed kill sheet of twenty-one men. But, as with many gunmen, the legend was larger than the man. In reality, the Kid shot between four and nine men, and was only active as a gunman for four years. Despite his bloodthirsty reputation, the Kid was described as having a personable, cheerful disposition, a way with the ladies and was easily identifiable by his green-banded Mexican sombrero.

Billy the Kid was born Henry McCarty in New York, in 1859. His family soon moved to New Mexico, and despite showing promise as a student, the Kid ended up in jail only months after his mother's death in 1874. The local paper reported the incident: 'Henry McCarty, who was arrested Thursday and committed to jail to await the action of the grand jury, upon the charge of stealing clothes from Charley Sun and Sam Chung, escaped from prison yesterday through the chimney. It's believed that Henry was simply the tool of Sombrero Jack, who done the stealing whilst Henry done the hiding.'

The Kid managed to escape while awaiting trial by

climbing up the guardhouse chimney. He then made his way to Arizona and drifted for a couple of years, taking up work where he could as a ranch hand, gambler and horse thief.

Then, on 17 August 1877, the Kid killed his first man during a bar brawl at a local saloon. Legend has it that local blacksmith, Frank 'windy' Cahill, picked an argument with the Kid over cards, which left the two men wrestling on the floor. Cahill slapped the Kid in the face, who responded by firing his six-shooter into Cahill's stomach. The jury ruled the shooting 'criminal and unjustifiable' and the Kid was incarcerated in a nearby guardroom. But jailhouse walls were notoriously flimsy in the Wild West and guardhouses even more so. The Kid broke out, rode to Lincoln County, New Mexico and changed his name to William Bonney; although most knew him as Billy the Kid.

The Kid soon joined a gang of hired guns who were protecting cattle baron John Tunstall against rivals Thomas B. Craton and the House of Murphy (owner of the local saloon). But Tunstall was killed anyway, and the Kid became unwittingly involved in what was known as the 'Lincoln County War'. On one side were Craton, Murphy, Sheriff William Brady and his posse, who were responsible for killing Turnstall. On the opposing side was the Kid's gang of vigilantes, 'The Regulators', and Turnstall's partner Alexander McSween. The Regulators' first act of vengence was to dispatch Sheriff Brady and his deputy, who they ambushed with shotguns from behind a brick wall. This provocative act was taken at face value, and led to the most famous and unbalanced shoot-outs of the Lincoln County War.

The new sheriff, his men and the local army cornered the Kid, McSween and fourteen of their men in McSween's house and began to lay siege. After five days the sheriff got tired of waiting and so one afternoon he set fire to the house. The Kid convinced the group to wait in the house until nightfall, and they moved from room to room to avoid the flames. As soon as the darkness crept in the Kid and several others jumped out a back window and didn't look back. McSween opted to jump from the frying pan into the fire by shouting out for safe conduct if he chose to surrender. The sheriff called back accepting McSween's surrender, but when he came out with hands in the air the sheriff shot him dead.

It wasn't long before Billy the Kid had become a household name; any gunman who killed him would win instant notoriety. One day the Kid caught wind that one such assassin, Joe Grant, was waiting for him in a Fort Sumner saloon. The Kid walked in and straight up to Grant at the bar, where he began to enquire about his ivory-handled shooter. Flattered and not realising who he was talking to, Grant let the Kid have a look. After a while and few whiskeys the penny dropped. Grant, by this stage flushed and boisterous, pulled his gun, stuck it in the Kid's face, and fired. But the Kid made sure he had pushed the cylinder around to fire on an empty chamber. After Grant's 'click' the Kid drew and responded with a live round.

Meanwhile, in an attempt to clear up the mess in Lincoln County, President Rutherford B. Hayes had made Lew Wallace – hard man and author of *Ben Hur* – governor of Lincoln. A few days later there was a chance meeting in the Lincoln high street between the Kid, another outlaw and McSween lawyer, Houston Chapman, who had been hired by Mrs McSween to sue the state over her husband's death. Within minutes an argument had broken out and Chapman was shot. His body was then soaked in whiskey and set alight. Most accounts agree that on this occasion the Kid was innocent, and he protested this in a letter to the governor. A secret meeting was arranged in the sheriff's office at midnight where Wallace agreed to pardon the Kid if he gave full and truthful testimony about the events of the Lincoln County War. The Kid agreed, but no deal seemed forthcoming. After a period in prison waiting for the trial, the Kid smelt a rat and broke out.

PAT GARRETT VERSUS BILLY THE KID

Furious at his escape, Governor Wallace sent a sheriff after the Kid who would quickly become his nemesis – Pat Garrett. In November 1880, Garrett and his posse tracked down the Kid and his gang and chased them to the Greathouse Ranch in White Oaks. The lawmakers surrounded the house and began passing notes back and forth to the Kid, using a Greathouse Ranch employee, Joseph Steck, as a messenger. After Garrett heard laughter coming from inside the house he realised the Kid and his gang were not going to give themselves up easily. Eventually, the Kid decided to invite deputy James Carlyle into the house to talk terms of their surrender. Carlyle refused at first, and then an agreement was reached: Steck would wait outside with Garrett, and Carlyle would enter the house. However, Garrett grew impatient and angry when Carlyle failed to re-emerge from the house. He shouted to the Kid that unless he released Carlyle, he would stick a bullet in Steck. Fearing he was not being taken seriously, Garrett fired a shot into the air, which was enough of a signal for Carlyle to jump through a side window.

Unfortunately for Carlyle a volley of gunfire followed him out and in the confusion the outlaws escaped. The Kid once again wrote to Governor Wallace protesting his innocence. He said Garrett's posse had killed Carlyle thinking he was an outlaw, and none of his men had fired a shot. Wallace did not pen a reply but instead put a $500 price on the Kid's head.

Garrett's plan was to let the Kid come to him, and he hunkered down in Fort Sumner, hoping the outlaw would eventually return for recreation and supplies. The gamble paid off. One snowy evening the outlaws rode into town, straight towards Garrett and his posse who were waiting inside the saloon. The Kid, who riding at the head of his gang, perhaps had a sixth sense about what was coming; told Tom O'Folliard he needed a plug of tobacco from Wilson at the rear and dropped back. Before O'Folliard could even dismount from his horse he was shot and lay bleeding in the snow. The rest of the gang turn swiftly around and galloped away, followed in hot pursuit by Garrett and his posse.

Garret followed the Kid's horse tracks through the snow, which lead them twenty miles out of town to an abandoned cabin in Stinking Springs. Laying in wait outside the cabin Garrett told his men to hold fire – he wanted to wait until the Kid appeared and then he would shoot him personally. Garrett was anticipating the Kid would sooner or later appear wearing his trademark sombrero with green hatband.

Whether Garrett got a twitch in his eyelid or his trigger finger is unclear, but contrary to his instructions he shot the first man who opened the cabin door, who wasn't wearing a sombrero and wasn't the Kid. Instead it was a man called Charles Bowdre, who upon being shot, fell backwards through the open doorway into the house. Rather than pull him inside, the Kid put a pistol in Bowdre's hand and told him: 'They've killed you Charlie, but you get a few of the sons of bitches before you die.' Then he shut the door on Charlie who stumbled a few paces forward before keeling over face first. The trap sprung, Garrett's only option was to again wait the Kid out and hope the cabin was as cold and desolate inside as it looked from the outside.

The siege eventually ended on Christmas Day, 1880, when the Kid and his gang, hungry and cold, surrendered to Garrett. Governor Wallace was delighted and Garrett immensely pleased with himself. After a few months in a Santa Fe jail, the Kid was transported to Lincoln and tried for the murder of Sheriff Brady. It took no time for him to be found guilty and he was sentenced to hang on 13 May 1881.

While waiting for his sentence to be carried out, the Kid was guarded by deputies Bob Olinger and James Bell. Bell was a mild-mannered man who had no beef with the Kid. Olinger, by comparison, was a loud braggart who made sure to taunt and wind the Kid up whenever he could. One evening when Olinger had gone across the street for dinner, the Kid asked Bell for a bathroom break. Once inside the toilet, the Kid simply pulled his small hands through the handcuffs, walked calmly outside to the gun cabinet, grabbed a pistol and shot Bell. The Kid then walked upstairs and picked up Olinger's shotgun, who was crossing the street to find out what the commotion was about. Opening the upstairs window, the Kid called down, 'Hello Bob,' and emptied both barrels into him.

When Garrett heard about the Kid's escape he appeared to sag like an animal taking a bullet. It took Wallace a period of gentle persuasion for Garrett to cast off his despondency and begin the chase anew. He once again took up residence in Fort Sumner, and hoped the Kid was stupid enough to once again visit the town. He was.

One night the Kid rode in to see a sweetheart, Celsa Gutierrez. At around midnight the Kid was in Gutierrez's room and decided he was hungry. He picked up a butcher's knife and walked barefoot to Pete Maxwell's house next door to ask for the meat-house key. Standing on Maxwell's porch were Garrett's deputies, who did not answer the Kid's question of, '¿Quien es?' ('who is it?'). In response the Kid pulled his pistol and backed into Maxwell's darkened bedroom, where Garrett was sitting on the bed. Garrett had recognised the Kid's voice instantly and had his six-shooter trained on the figure coming through the door. Not making out the dark figure on the bed, the Kid called out again: '¿Quien es?'. The reply was a single bullet, which tore directly through the Kid's heart and killed him instantly.

JOHN WESLEY HARDIN

John Wesley Hardin was a Texan, born and bred, and he once shot a man just for criticising it. Not surprisingly

Hardin is variously described as: 'The meanest man in Texas', 'no more dangerous gunman ever operated in Texas, and, 'John Wesley Hardin – by the time the Texas Rangers caught up with him, he'd killed forty-three men, one just for snoring too loud.'

Hardin, or 'Wes' as he was commonly known, was born to a Methodist preacher in 1853, but by fifteen he had killed his first man – a former slave who wouldn't move out of his way on the road. When three soldiers came to arrest Hardin for the murder he ended up shooting them too. On his Dad's advice he hightailed it out of town and lived a life on the run. He filled the next five years with gambling, saloons, fights and killing – but only in 'self defence', he'd remind people without a hint of irony. The justification of self defence is not always clearly identifiable from the events themselves.

When he was eighteen years old Hardin was tempted into the tent of a pretty circus girl, just to be shaken down by her shotgun-pointing accomplice. As Hardin slowly pulled some notes from his shirt pocket he made sure to drop some of them on the ground. When the man stooped to pick them up Hardin put a bullet clean between his eyes. He did not get far before he was arrested trying to cross into Louisiana, but he shot his captor and galloped off in his usual manner. It wasn't long before he was picked up again, this time by three policemen. But the policeman keeping watch that night dozed off by the campfire, allowing Hardin to pick up his gun and kill him in his sleep.

Deciding a spell in the great outdoors would keep him away from arresting policemen, Hardin then travelled to visit his cousins, the Clements; also of gunfighting fame. Together they set off on a cattle drive across Arkansas, during which Hardin shot three Mexicans and two Native Americans.

Not long afterwards some real trouble started. Two herds of cattle became entangled and after a heated debate between Hardin and the boss of the other herd, they agreed to shoot it out. Hardin and his cousin, Jim Clements, met six of the herders, and when the gun smoke cleared Hardin had killed five and Jim, one. If there was a fast draw gunman of the Wild West, then arguably Hardin would have been it. He would spend hours drawing his guns from special holsters he had sewn into his vest. He preferred to have the butts pointing forwards and would cross his arms across his chest to pull his guns, a move known as the 'cavalry draw'.

It wasn't long before Hardin came up against another famous gunman, and this happened to be the residing lawman of Abilene, Texas: Wild Bill Hickok. Hickok first spotted Hardin at the local saloon, and asked the gunman if he wouldn't mind surrendering his guns. Hardin responded by extending his guns and then using the 'Road Agent's Spin' to flip the guns back into his hands, cocked and ready to shoot. The point had been made and rather than kick the young upstart into the street Hickok bought him a drink. Hickok took Hardin under his wing, offering him advice and joining the younger man for odd bouts of drinking and gambling. The relationship soured one night when Hardin began shooting through his hotel room wall to stop a man from snoring – killing him in the process. Hickok was on his way up the stairs to investigate the commotion when Hardin jumped half dressed from the balcony and made his escape. Hardin later complained of the incident: 'They tell lots of lies about me. They say I killed six or seven men for snoring. Well, it ain't true, I only killed one man for snoring.'

WANTED DEAD OR ALIVE

Hardin ended up in Kansas, Texas, where he married Jane Bowen. In between moments of domestication Hardin carried out several shootings, was arrested, escaped and fled to join his cousins in the violent Sutton-Taylor war. It was during this war that Hardin killed a sheriff, for which there would be long-term reprisals.

It is unclear whether Deputy Sheriff Webb intended to kill Hardin when he travelled to meet him in Comanche for the gunman's twenty-first birthday celebrations. Webb explained to Hardin he was not there to arrest or harm him, but as Hardin turned to buy him a drink

Webb went for his gun. Webb hit Hardin once in the side, but Hardin managed a shot to the lawman's head. The Clements made sure he was dead by riddling his corpse with bullets. It is ironic that this was the one occasion that Hardin had actually acted in self defence. But for the Texas authorities it was the last straw. A $4,000 reward was put on Hardin's head – dead or alive.

Hardin skipped town just in time to escape a lynch mob. They caught up with brother Joe instead. Hardin took Jane and his three children to Florida, where he assumed a new identity and went straight. But $4,000 was a lot of money and after two years, Texas Ranger John Armstrong tracked Hardin down. Armstrong and his men trapped Hardin on a Pensacola Train, where legend has it that Hardin went for his guns, but they became tangled up in his braces.

Hardin was sentenced in 1877. He was found guilty of Webb's murder and given twenty-five years in Huntsville State Penitentiary, Texas. But Hardin's story did not end in prison, instead it marked the beginning of a remarkable transformation. Hardin became an avid bible reader and worked as superintendent of the prison Sunday school. He wrote to Jane that he intended to become a lawyer and set about studying the profession. But by the time the reformed Hardin left prison fifteen years later Jane had died. Nevertheless, he kept to his word and passed the bar exam. He then moved to Junction, Texas where he married a fourteen-year-old girl he had won in a card game. However, the marriage was short-lived and following the divorce, Hardin moved to El Paso to open a law office.

It was in El Paso that Hardin slipped back into gambling and drinking. He conducted most of his legal business from a bar stool, which for the most part involved sipping whiskey and regaling interested listeners with his gunfighting exploits. Then Hardin began an affair with the wife of his client, Martin Morose, and things fell apart. One day two of Morose's friends confronted Hardin in a bar. Instead of killing them there and then, Hardin hired four lawmen to assassinate Morose. But after the deed was done the deal went sour. One of the lawmen, ex-gunman John Selman Snr. came looking for Hardin.

Selman's beef with Hardin is unclear. His son John Selman Jnr had arrested Morose's ex-wife Beulah (now called Mrs Hardin) for drunk and disorderly, which had reportedly annoyed Hardin. Hardin was a full-blown alcoholic by this stage and some reports indicate that he made some drunken threats about shooting John Selman Jnr Another account suggests Selman Snr was never paid for his part in the Morose killing, and thought he'd win it back with a pound of Hardin's flesh. Either way, Selman was after Hardin's blood.

Selman finally caught up with Hardin at a saloon, where he was playing dice with his back to the door. His last known words were: 'You have four sixes to beat,' before Selman's bullet tore through the back of his head. Selman shot Hardin twice more for luck and then left. Hardin's corpse reputedly lay on the floor in a pool of blood for a whole day, so people could come and have a look.

WILD BILL HICKOK

With his long, curly blond hair, frilly silk shirts, fancy waistcoats, and high-pitched voice, Wild Bill Hickok had a reputation as being something of a gunman dandy. But tucked into the red sash tied around Hickok's middle were two ivory-handled Colt .36 Navy Models that had killed at least a dozen men in shoot-outs. A gambler, soldier, performer, lawman and gunman, Hickok would help propagate the legend of the gunslinger duel and the 'quick draw'.

Born James Butler Hickok in 1837 in Illinois, the young gunman was a crack shot and good with his fists. When he was eighteen, Hickok knocked another teenager out and fearing he had killed him, fled the state. He drifted into Kansas and worked in various occupations, including as a soldier, constable and wagon master for the mail service, the Pony Express.

After being injured in a bear attack while delivering mail, Hickok was sent to the Rock Creek station, Nebraska for light duties. It was here he attracted the unwanted attention of nearby neighbour David McCanles, who called Hickok 'duck bill' and laughed at his feminine features. To make matters worse, Hickok was seeing McCanles' mistress behind his back. However, it was on the pretence of settling an account that McCanles, his son and two other men visited the station on 12 July 1861. It quickly became clear they were looking for trouble. McCanles, seeing Hickok standing behind a doorway curtain, threatened to drag him outside. Hickok shouted back: 'There will be one less son of a bitch when you try that,' and shot McCanles dead. He then put bullets into the other two men, who still managed to run away. They were chased down and killed by two station employees armed with a hoe and a shotgun.

Leaving the station for a stint in the army, Hickok found himself in the most famous fast draw duel in Wild West history. The conflict came during a card game at the Lyon House Hotel, Missouri on 21 July 1865. Hickok had been winning big, despite rival David Tutt's every effort to stop him. Hickok was $200 ahead when Tutt demanded he pay off a $35 IOU. Hickok disputed the amount, saying it was only $25, but Tutt responded by grabbing Hickok's pocket watch from the card table as collateral. Hickok told Tutt that he was not to wear the watch, but Tutt replied he intended to wear it first thing in the morning. Hickok calmly replied that if he did so then he would shoot him.

At 10 a.m. the next morning word reached Hickok that Tutt had appeared in the square wearing his watch. Hickok went to talk to Tutt and they both agreed to settle their differences over a drink. But at around 6 p.m. Tutt left the saloon and Hickok was seen walking along the street, gun in hand. It was in the town square that the showdown took place. At a distance of around 65 metres both men turned side on to each other and raised their weapons. Tutt shot first and missed. Hickok used his left arm to steady the barrel of his pistol and squeezed off a fatal shot.

TALL TALES & STAGGERING SHOOT-OUTS

The shoot-out would become legend in an article called 'Wild Bill' by Colonel George Nichols published in *Harper's New Monthly Magazine* in 1867. Nichols was known to use facts sparingly, and the incident at Rock Creek soon turned into an epic gunfight where Hickok had squared off against an army of McCanles' desperados. Naturally, Hickok did nothing to contradict these fallacies. Instead he told another writer he had shot over one hundred men, which in turn inspired a series of 'dime novels' that further embellished Hickok's exploits.

The real Hickok had in the meantime rejoined the army, becoming Custer's 'favourite scout' before taking on a position as sheriff of Ellsworth, Kansas. This position ended after two gunfights, and then Hickok moved on to become marshal of Abilene, Texas.

Abilene was a rough, hard-drinking frontier town, where ranchers and cowboys came to let off steam. Hickok managed to keep the peace, but was often accused of being more interested in gambling and 'whoring' than keeping the town respectable. Hickok had two enemies in Abilene – Ben Thompson and Phil Coe, the owners of the Bull's Head Saloon. Hickok had annoyed the two Texans when he gave into public complaints about the saloon's sign – which featured a bull with an erect penis – and had it painted over. Legend has it that Thompson asked John Wesley Hardin (see page 354) to kill Hickok, but Hardin wouldn't have it.

Instead, the inevitable showdown took place when a group of Texan cowboys rode into town. Coe joined the Texans, who began grabbing people off the street, carrying them into local saloons and demanding they buy a round. Hickok, sensing trouble, alerted his deputy Mike Williams to be on his guard, and went to wait the evening out in the Alamo Saloon. He sat with his back to the wall, as all prominent gunmen were inclined to do.

Sure enough, after a time, the mob of drunken Texans were seen crossing the street towards the Alamo. Then a shot rang out. Hickok pushed open the saloon doors to see Coe holding a smoking pistol. Hickok asked what he was doing, to which Coe replied he had shot a stray dog. In reply Hickok drew his pistols but Coe fired first, hitting Hickok's coat. Hickok then emptied both revolvers into Coe's stomach, knocking him to the ground. Then, from the corner of his eye, he saw somebody running towards him. He turned quickly and fired again, and the man dropped to the ground. On closer inspection Hickok found the shot man to be Mike Williams, his deputy and friend. In a rage Hickok rustled the Texans from the town and pistol whipped any that disobeyed. Coe died three days later.

Hickok took Williams' death hard. The incident had partly occurred because of Hickok's failing eyesight, which was a result of glaucoma. Hickok decided to surrender his marshal's badge and try his luck performing in Wild West shows in the east. He even joined his old friend Buffalo Bill for a period, but he made a dreadful entertainer and soon moved back west. After leaving his wife to try his luck in the goldfields, Hickok drifted into Deadwood, South Dakota on 2 August 1876 – the last day of his life.

Hickok entered the Number Ten Saloon and immediately spied a vacant chair at a poker game, which had its back to the door. Although asking to swap places twice, he reluctantly took the seat and began losing heavily.

Hickok didn't see twenty-five-year-old Jack McCall come in, nor did he see him pull out his revolver and shoot him in the back of the head. No-one was sure why McCall had done it, but they did see Hickok's cards as they slipped to the floor – a pair of aces, and a pair of eights, known forever afterwards as 'The Dead Man's Hand.'

LONG BRANCH SALOON

Dodge City, Kansas was made legendary by its various gunfights. The night of 5 April 1879 would prove no different, as gun smoke filled the air of the infamous Long Branch Saloon. The two men involved, 'Cockeyed' Frank Loving and Levi Richardson were once friends, who had often met for a game or two at the Long Branch.

Loving had come to Dodge City as a wet-behind-the-ears teenager, looking to become a professional gambler. He made friends with several notable gunmen, including Wyatt Earp, Doc Holliday and Bat Masterton, although he was not considered a gunman himself until after the Long Branch Saloon gunfight.

Levi Richardson was a buffalo hunter and gambler, who was rumoured to have shot several Native Americans. He had moved to Dodge City in 1874, where he gambled and was generally disliked. But despite being a rather clumsy, awkward character, Richardson was thought to be handy with a six-shooter.

Over time Loving had become convinced that Richardson had taken a shine to his pretty young bride, Mattie, and decided to take it up with him one spring day on the street. The conversation quickly turned into a fist fight, during which Richardson landed one particularly savage blow to Loving's eye and shouted: 'I'll blow the guts out of you, you cockeyed son of a bitch.' But Loving was not armed, so simply tuned his back and walked away. Richardson, however, was not going to leave it at that.

On the evening of 5 April, Richardson walked into the Long Branch Saloon looking for Loving. Richardson waited for some hours and was getting ready to leave when Loving walked in around 9 p.m. Loving took a seat by a potbelly stove at the end of a long table. Richardson walked over and sat opposite him. 'You wouldn't fight anything, you damn son of a bitch,' Richardson said. Loving replied, 'Try me and see.'

Richardson then stood up and grabbed for his six-shooter, as did Loving. Richardson got off a shot, but Loving's gun misfired, and he scampered behind the potbelly stove to take refuge. Richardson fired another two shots, as the patrons scattered and the saloon became thick with gun smoke. Then Loving started firing slowly and methodically at Richardson, who fell backwards into a table and slumped onto the floor. Within minutes Richardson was dead. Loving received only a graze to his hand, which many witnesses were astounded to learn, considering the gunmen's close proximity.

It was ruled that Loving had acted in self defence and he escaped serving jail time. News of the gunfight spread quickly, giving Loving a new and perhaps unwanted notoriety. It would also lead Loving to another famous showdown, known as the Trinidad Gunfight.

By 1882, Loving had left his wife and children and moved to Trinidad, Colorado. Here, he often played cards with John Allen, a former Dodge City acquaintance and fellow gambler. But one day an argument broke out between the two regarding unpaid IOUs. The two fell into the street shouting and both pulled their guns. They were quickly disarmed by intervening friends, but the matter was far from finished.

The next morning Loving entered the saloon where Allen worked but Allen spotted him first and fired at him. Loving ducked for cover and pulled out his gun, which was then knocked from his hand before he could fire it. Allen fired twice more and burst through the backdoor, as Loving scrambled frantically for his gun. Upon finding his beloved Colt .44, Loving rushed into the back room and fired randomly into the darkness, but Allen was not there. Instead deputy sheriff Jim Masterton arrived on the scene and disarmed Loving. Masterton then went off in search of Allen himself, giving Loving a chance to rearm with a new pistol and resume his mission. Masterton did find Allen, but only after a shot rang out from Hammond's hardware store. Loving had entered the store for more ammunition, but hadn't seen John Allen hiding in a corner, or the bullet that came from his gun. Loving died from his wounds five days later.

John Allen was acquitted of murder, mainly because of Loving's previous record as a known gunman. Allen said he was scared and hiding from Loving and only killed him in self defence. Allen then moved back to Dodge City where he became a preacher and an evangelist.

THE JIM COURTRIGHT-LUKE SHORT GUNFIGHT

The Jim Courtright–Luke Short gunfight is one of the most famous duels to take place in the Wild West. Both men were notorious for being hard living gamblers that were handy on the draw.

Luke Short was 5 foot 6 in height, fond of dressing 'to the nines', and a gambling buddy of gunmen Wyatt Earp and Doc Holliday. Between the three friends it was said Short was the best shot and he carried his gun in a specially tailored vest pocket. After selling bootleg whiskey to the Indians, and working as an army scout, Short decided on a life as a professional gambler in Dodge City. Here, Short, Earp and Holliday formed the 'Dodge City Gang', but Short decided to leave town after a spot of bother known as the 'Dodge City War.' Short moved to Fort Worth, where he immediately bought a partnership in the White Elephant Saloon and went about his favourite activities of gambling and drinking.

Located at the opposite end of Fort Worth were the offices of Timothy 'Longhair Jim' Courtright's Detective Agency. Courtright had been the one-time marshal of Fort Worth, and his reputation with a gun had kept the city clean and under control. But Courtright also had a reputation for being a mean-spirited drunk and he was not re-elected for a second term. After a period away working as a hired gun in New Mexico, Courtright settled back in Fort Worth in 1886. He opened his detective agency, which managed to make some protection money from local businesses.

Courtright and Short were friendly enough at one time for Short to loan Courtright some money, but Courtright wanted a slice of the action down at the White Elephant Saloon. He suggested to Short that he offer his services as a hired gun to keep the saloon free of troublemakers. It was really more of a demand than a suggestion, and Short's curt reply was that he'd rather pay to have Courtright never set foot in the saloon again; of course, he had no intention of doing that either. Short had a reputation for being calm and calculated in strained situations, but now he had thrown down the gauntlet. Courtright stomped off angry, hurling abuse over his shoulder as he went.

After the trouble he'd had in Dodge City, Short figured the best thing was to sell up in Fort Worth and return after Courtright had drunk himself to death. With this in mind he sold his partnership in the White Elephant to co-owner Jake Johnson on 7 February 1887. The next night, Short decided to have a last evening at the saloon.

He was gambling at the tables when Johnson told him that Courtright was outside and wanted to straighten things out. No true gunman would ever go out looking for trouble and Short declined. He was leaving town, after all. But Courtyright had been drinking heavily and would not be dissuaded. He soon appeared on the saloon stairs and shouted to Short that he wanted to talk to him outside. Now Courtright's cards were on the table – he was calling Short out. If he didn't go out to fight he would be branded a coward.

Short reluctantly went outside with Courtright and the two walked slowly down the street. After a few metres they paused and turned to face each other. Courtright said it was time to sort out their differences, to which Short said there was nothing to sort out. He then put his thumbs into his vest armpits, to which Courtright shouted: 'Don't pull a gun on me!'

Short lied and said he didn't have a gun, but Courtright was already going for the draw. As he pulled his gun from the holster, so did Short, from his leather lined pocket.

Short got off the first shot, which practically blew off Courtyright's thumb and disabled the cylinder of his six-shooter. Short fired five more times in quick succession, lighting up the street and knocking his opponent off his feet, killing him dead.

Short handed his gun directly over to the sheriff, who had come running. But after a trial, Short was found to have acted in self defence and acquitted. Short stayed in Fort Worth for six more years, but they were six more years of gambling and heavy whisky drinking, which left his body ravaged. Short was then wounded by buckshot in another shoot-out and finally died a few months later on 8 September 1893.

FRISCO SHOOT-OUT

Elfego Baca was the son of a marshal from Sorocco, New Mexico. Baca's father had gone to jail after shooting two rowdy cowboys, but Baca was determined to follow in his footsteps. When he was a teenager Baca equipped himself with two six-shooters, a mail order badge and began strutting around Sorocco as a gunman. Then in 1884, nineteen-year-old Baca got the chance for his first man-to-man gunfight. The subsequent battle that followed would last for thirty-three hours and go down in history as the most unequal duel of Wild West.

Baca had caught wind of a drunken cowboy called Charlie McCarty who was yahooing his way around the streets of Frisco, shooting randomly and intimidating its citizens. Without a second's thought, Baca pinned on his lawman's badge, rode to Frisco, located McCarty in a bar and 'arrested' him. What Baca had expected was a showdown on the high street, but instead the whiskey-sodden McCarty had surrended his guns quite willingly. But some of McCarty's fellow cowboys from the nearby Slaughter Ranch weren't so passive and demanded Baca unhand their friend. Undeterred, Baca drew both of his revolvers and said he would give the cowboys a count of three to vacate the vicinity. Baca then counted a rapid 'one-two-three' and let both gun barrels fly. One of the cowboys was hit in the knee and the other had his horse rear back on him, killing him dead. The rest scattered.

In the morning, Baca took McCarty to a local Justice of Peace who fined the now sober cowboy $25. Baca left to ride back to Sorocco, job done. But the Slaughter Ranch cowboys weren't going to give this young Mexican upstart such an easy exit, badge or no badge. They must have imagined a pretty easy fight – there were eighty of them and only one Baca. A first shot was fired at Baca, who ducked into an alleyway and made for a small shack inhabited by a woman and her two children. Baca rapidly expelled the residents, and minutes later a rancher called Jim Herne burst through the door with his rifle. Baca fired a shot from each revolver and Herne fell from the house dead. In response to this killing the cowboys laid siege to the shack for thirty-three straight hours.

By the end over 4,000 bullets had shredded the shack's mud walls and tin roof. Nearly 370 bullet holes were found in the shack's door and eight had gone through a broom handle. Luckily for Baca the floor had been dug out to around half a metre below ground level, which is where he lay still for most of the assault, only rising to fire off an occasional shot.

Luckily, Baca's returning fire had shaved the top of one cowboy's head who was approaching the shack behind an iron stove door. Apparently unnerved by this, the besieging cowboys hung blankets between the outside buildings around the shack's perimeter to make themselves less of a target. As night fell the cowboys threw flaming torches onto the shack, and when these did not succeed in setting it on fire they hurled sticks of dynamite. This had the desired effect and part of the roof collapsed onto Baca below. The cowboys stayed until dawn anyway, to make sure their quarry was dead. But then, inexplicably, they saw smoke rising from the back of the shack – Baca was cooking himself breakfast.

The gunfire of the second day was rather sporadic and lacklustre compared to the first, as many of the cowboys had returned to work at the Slaughter Ranch. Finally a deputy called Ross convinced Baca to come out, promising him safe passage to custody in Sorocco and assured him that he could keep his guns. Baca travelled in the back of the wagon driven by Ross, his guns trained the whole time on the cowboys bringing up the rear behind him.

After four months in prison Baca was acquitted for the two men he had killed during the siege. He went onto fame not as a heavy drinking, gambling gunman, but instead a peace officer, lawyer, mayor, sheriff and district attorney. Baca died peacefully in his sleep in 1945 at the age of eighty.

TV and Movies

Movies and TV shows about gunmen are as old as the technologies themselves. The first onscreen gunmen took their lead from the various dime novels and newspaper articles written about them at the time. The writers painted their characters with large colourful creative strokes, furnishing their legends with multiple fabrications and using the facts only as a last resort.

Gunmen were portrayed in one of two ways – good lawmen or bad outlaws. The lawmen were pure, straightforward and moral, and happy to fast draw against any no-good varmint that imposed his ugliness upon the sensibilities of good, law abiding folk. On the other side of the coin were the outlaws. They were all cut from the same villainous cloth – mean, murdering, robbing, gambling, fornicating no gooders, with obvious distinguishing marks that said so (stubble, facial scars, eye patches, sinister black outfits).

The gunfights were as manufactured as the characters, with gunmen fast-drawing smoothly from their tied down holsters in good time to dispatch one or more assailants. In reality, many gunmen didn't use a holster at all, but instead stuck their six-shooters into pockets, belts or waistbands. Those who did don a holster usually wore it high on the hip where it was comfortable, rather than slinging it low. The terms 'gunslinger' was actually coined in the 1920 movie *Drag Harlen*, where the terms 'gunman', 'shootist' and 'pistoleer' were more common in the day. Gun twirling before reholstering is another Hollywood flourish that would not have helped a real gunman's credibility, although the 'Road Agents Spin', was a legitimate move, intended to outmanouvre a gun burglar.

The gunman's character would take several turns in his progression through TV and movie history. The clean-cut lawman of the 1950s, would give way to a new, more complex peacemaker in the 1960s. These grittier, more troubled characters often came from ambiguous origins and made up their own rules to administer justice. It was also acceptable for them to drink, gamble and womanise, as long as they weren't murdering randomly at will, like those they went up against. Clint Eastwood's character 'The Man with No Name' from *A Fistful of Dollars* set the bar – mean, surly and entirely uninterested in chit-chat. Eastwood would later go on to portray an even harder gunman, a cold-blooded killer, now family man, who comes out of retirement for one last job in *Unforgiven* (see page 387).

Today, the lines between good and bad gunmen are even further blurred in movies like *The Proposition,* which mostly concerns itself with outright bloodshed and brutality. A more recent addition, *True Grit* (2010), tips its hat to the adventurous roots of the western genre, while still portraying the violence realistically.

The TV and movies reviewed over the next few pages have been chosen for their depiction of a lone gunman, rather than a duo, group, or family, thus keeping the subject in the context of one-on-one combat.

GUNSMOKE

Gunsmoke was the longest running prime time western TV show in the US, alongside *Bonanza*. It first aired as a radio show before hitting the small screen between 1955 and 1975. Where *Bonanza* concerned itself with the Cartwright boys and family life on the ranch, *Gunsmoke* was focused on the town marshal, Matt Dillon, gunman and keeper of the peace on the mean streets of Dodge City, Kansas.

There would be many gunfights in *Gunsmoke*, as made clear from the first episode. Here, the opening credits showed Dillon in a typical fast draw sequence, after a brief introduction by John Wayne ('No, I'm not in it. I wish I were though…').

The radio show had previously won acclaim for its honest portrayal of life in the west. Most of the show's characters were ordinary hard working folk who barely managed to eke out a living at the best of times. While some of this realism made it onto the TV, other elements had to be sanitised for the viewing public. One example of this is the lead female character Kitty, whose occupation as ex-prostitute and saloon madam was kept deliberately vague and ambiguous (although girls did take cowboys into rooms upstairs). Kitty was not originally allowed to kiss a gunman love interest ('*Gunsmoke* fans would not allow it', a producer said), although this was later amended to allow her four onscreen kisses.

On the other hand, the show did try to stay topical by tackling modern social issues, such as rape, race, the physically and mentally challenged, capital punishment and terminal illness. It would also examine the wider implications of being a gunman, even one like virtuous marshal Dillon, who often needed to mete out justice with his six-shooter. In the episode 'In Bloody Hands', Dillon shoots three wanted gunmen, only for the fourth to surrender with his hands in the air. He looks down at his dead buddies and turns to Dillon, amazed: 'You're alone? You did this all alone? You killed a lot of men… just like so much meat. You're a butcher.'

The words bite, and Dillon becomes instantly troubled by his ongoing occupational hazard: 'Tomorrow there'll be someone else, and the next day, always a man to kill.' Doc Chapman (Pat Hingle) tries to console him: 'I never heard of you shooting anyone that didn't need it.' But Dillon is a burdened man. He wears his gun belt to bed, has sweaty nightmares, and can't pull his pistol on visiting troublemaker Joe Stanger. Dillon decides to resign his post and take some time to smell the roses. But after a few days Stanger is back, and worse still, he has killed a woman. Nevertheless, Dillon stands by his decision and won't be swayed.

But pre-guessing his continued reluctance, deputy Chester Goode (Dennis Weaver) has a speech prepared, which clears up Dillon's predicament: 'I've been thinking lately a whole lot about this. Men like Stanger, they've gotta be stopped, that's all. They gotta be. I'd do it if I could, but I can't. I just ain't good enough – most men ain't – but you are. It's kinda too bad that you are, but that's the way it is, and there ain't a thing in the world that you can do about it.'

And with that, Dillon straps on his gun and rides back to town, lawgiving gunman once more.

THE SHOOTIST

John Wayne's 1976 movie *The Shootist* is about ageing gunman J. B. Books, who is living out his final days in Carson City after being diagnosed with terminal cancer. Books is an old-school gunman who lives by a strict honour code: 'I won't be wronged, I won't be insulted, and I won't be laid a hand on. I don't do these things to other people, and I require the same from them.'

But in Carson City not everybody abides by this code and Books' arrival has not gone unnoticed. As a gunman with thirty-one notches on his belt (although, he 'never shot a man who didn't deserve it.'), there are many keen to be credited as 'the man who shot J. B. Books'. Books realises he won't be left alone by those seeking to exploit him, so decides to take a few of them with him in a final, climatic shoot-out.

This last scene begins with Books entering a saloon and ordering a whiskey. In the mirror behind the bar he spies four other men, all watching him. After slugging back his drink, Books shoots it out with all four men, one after the other. Books is hit, but alive, when the bartender pops up and shoots him in the back. Books' young admirer then enters, grabs Books' pistol and shoots the bartender. He then looks down at the gun, but throws it into the corner, to approving nods from Books.

The movie acts as a eulogy to a legendary gunman, John Wayne (who coincidently died of stomach cancer three years after its release), and the Wild West itself. *The Shootist* is set in 1901 and times are clearly changing – there are motor cars, electric appliances, telephones, and Queen Victoria's death is mentioned several times. As Books' passing symbolises the end of the proud, tough, glory-bound but honorable gunman, Wayne's passing symbolises the demise of this type of character and a general decline in westerns. Perhaps the all-American character Wayne had so often portrayed had little meaning for the movie-going public, who had just lived through the horrors of the Vietnam War.

Wayne's heir apparent, Clint Eastwood, did not continue with westerns, but instead carried on the gunman tradition in a different setting and time, through cop character Dirty Harry. However, it was Eastwood that would revitalise the western genre in the 1990s, with his tribute to the gunman movie, *Unforgiven*.

THE GUNFIGHTER

This 1950 movie is about Jimmy Ringo (Gregory Peck), a tired, regretful gunman at the end of his days. But his fearsome reputation as 'fastest gun in the West' is catching up with him. In the opening scenes, Ringo is drawn into a gunfight against a young wannabe called Eddie, who he kills. But Eddie has three brothers who are out for revenge, and Ringo figures he'd better quit town. He rides to the town of Cayenne, where he spends most of the rest of the movie drinking in the saloon and trying to meet up with his estranged wife.

Sheriff Mark Strett (Millard Mitchel) is an old friend of Ringo's who informs him that his wife has changed her name, become a schoolteacher, and is trying to forget the bad old days when his gunfighting ruined their relationship. Cayenne has its own cocksure youngster,

Hunt Bromley (Skip Homeier), who lets Ringo know that he is king of the heap and a great gunman to be. Eventually Ringo's wife agrees to see him, and says she will consider a reconciliation in a year's time, on the condition that Ringo has kept his nose clean.

By this time, Eddie's three brothers are closing in on Ringo and he makes preparations to leave. But when his back is turned Bromley shoots him. As he dies, Ringo tells Sheriff Strett to blame the shooting on him and say that he drew first on Bromley. Overhearing this Bromley shouts out:

'You don't have to do me no favours pappy.'

To which Ringo replies: 'If I was doing you a favour, I'd let 'em hang you right now and get it all over with. But I don't want you to get off that light. I want you to go on, being a big tough gun. I want you to see what it means to have to live, like a big tough gunnie. So don't thank me yet partner. You'll see what I mean. Just wait...'

Sheriff Strett then takes Bromley into a barn and slaps him around, saying:

'Now listen to me yellow belly. Ringo's fixed you good. You're going to get it exactly like you give it to him, because there are a thousand cheap dirty crooked little squirts like you wanting right now for the chance to kill the man that killed Jimmie Ringo. But it ain't gonna be here sonny, not in my territory. So get going, now. Get killed somewhere else.'

The movie ends with Ringo's wife Molly (Jean Parker) at the funeral calling herself 'Mrs Jimmie Ringo,' therefore giving Jimmie Ringo the reconciliation he so desperately wanted, even if it was posthumously.

The Gunfighter was part of the 1950s film noir western, which dealt with the nastier, unglamorous sides of gunfighting and the inevitable consequences of a lonely death or a bullet in the back. *The Gunfighter* broke new ground and also stands alone. It did not rely on a brassy score to invoke a mood, or moments of humour to ease the tension. Instead it is a thoughtful, melancholic story that stays true to its message without becoming sentimental.

HIGH NOON

This 1952 movie begins with Will Kane's (Gary Cooper) last day as marshal of Hadleyville. He is packing up for the quiet, prairie life with Quaker wife Amy (Grace Kelly). But Kane learns that Frank Miller, a convict that he sent down, is getting out of jail and plans to exact his revenge. Worse still, it seems Miller and his gang will be on the noon train that day.

The townspeople convince Kane to stick to his plan and leave while the going is good, but once on the trail Kane has second thoughts. He decides it is up to him to sort Miller out and turns back for Hadleyville to reclaim his Marshal's badge. But nobody is willing to pitch in to help and time is rolling ever closer to 12 noon. Finally Amy decides to get aboard a train herself, and leaves Kane to fight Miller and his gang alone.

Or so he thinks. As soon as the first shot is fired, Amy leaps off the train unable to let her betrothed die alone. Meanwhile Kane is taking on the Miller gang one at a time as the film blasts itself into a brassy, full-orchestral finale. Most well-known shoot-out devices are utilised – shards of window pane are knocked out with pistol barrels to enable shooting, barns are set on fire with kerosene lanterns, whinnying horses are set free from the flames and then used as decoys. During the action Amy shoots one of the gang in the back and is taken hostage by Miller, but then pokes him in the eye so Kane can shoot him. The couple are reunited as the cowardly townspeople remerge and Kane flings his Sheriff's star disgustedly into the dirt.

In a sense Cooper's Kane was the all-American hero – standing up for justice and freedom in the face of adversity. But John Wayne called the film: 'The most un-American thing I've ever seen in my life.' Wayne did not agree that the townspeople would have deserted its marshal so easily, and felt the film was an allegory against the blacklisting taking place in Hollywood at the time, which he supported. It was no coincidence Wayne's comments came after Carl Foreman was called before the House Committee on Un-American Activities while he was writing the film. In a later movie, the theme of townspeople as frightened cowards unwilling to support their marshal is further explored in Clint Eastwood's *High Plains Drifter.*

CLINT EASTWOOD

Clint Eastwood deserves a special mention because his characters spanned much of the western movie genre – from white-hat cowboy Rowdy Yates in *Rawhide* to killer of women and children William Munny in *Unforgiven.*

Eastwood began playing Rowdy Yates in 1958, but eventually became bored with the role as he told *Playboy*: 'I was tired of playing the nice clean-cut cowboy in *Rawhide*; I wanted something earthier. Something different from the old-fashioned Western.'

Rawhide was cancelled in 1966 and Eastwood moved onto the movies that would make him famous – Italian director Sergio Leone's 'Spaghetti Westerns'. Eastwood starred in three of these movies as the 'The Man With No Name' – *A Fistful of Dollars, For a Few Dollars More* and, *The Good the Bad and the Ugly.* This is where Eastwood was able to develop his trademark western character – the non-smiling, cigar-chewing, sombrero wearing anti-hero, who came from dubious origins, said little, and could shoot the centre out of a flying dime. Eastwood was a non- smoker, but: 'I smoked the cigars only for those films. I didn't really like them, but they kept me in the right kind of humor…they just put you in a sour frame of mind.'

Leone said he liked Eastwood because he had two facial expressions – 'one with the hat and one without it.' For Eastwood the films were a to chance go to Europe and play something different, a hired gun that made up his own rules to pursue money, justice, and the gunman's elusive dream: 'The hero was an enigmatic figure, and that worked within the context of this picture. In some films, he would be ludicrous. You can't have a cartoon in the middle of a Renoir.'

With Leone's mixture of long shots and extreme close ups, and Ennio Morricone's scores featuring whistles, cracking whips, trumpets and electric guitar, the movies stood in a league all of their own. The character of 'The Man With No Name' would further embellish the myth of the fast draw gunman, and would add another element – that of the silent, stoic gunmen. The character, alongside the bleached black Levi jeans, black cigars from a Beverly Hills tobacconist and a Spanish sombrero were all Eastwood additions to the gunman myth: 'My feeling was that the strength of this character was in his economy of movement and what the audience anticipates he's going to do. This builds up a constant suspense. If you can keep the audience's interest in what he's going to do next, you've really got it.'

The critics described Eastwood as being from the

Mount Rushmore school of acting, but this aside, the character's tight lips were still a fabrication of the truth. Gunmen of the west were reported to be great talkers, many liked it as much as gambling.

Eastwood would take a break from westerns throughout most of the 1980s, but almost single-handedly brought the genre back into the public eye with the 1992 *Unforgiven*. The story follows William Munny, an ageing gunman cum broken-down pig farmer trying to eke out a living to raise his two children. Munny reluctantly takes a last job, a hit on two cowboys who have slashed the face of a saloon prostitute in Big Whisky, Wyoming. One gunman has already had a go, English Bob (Richard Harris), but the town's gunman sheriff, Little Bill (Gene Hackman), has beaten him and sent him packing. After he learns William Munny is in town with his old partner Ned Logan (Morgan Freeman) and wannabe gunman 'The Schofield kid', Little Bill shows them who's boss. He beats Munny to within an inch of life, kills Logan, and puts his body on display outside the saloon, with a sign: 'This is what we do to assassins round here.'

When Munny learns Logan's fate, he flies into a silent rage, abandons his reformed ways of 'not drinking or cussing' picks up a bottle and rides into town. He proceeds to shoot every man standing in the saloon and then recounts the event, such as who he decided to shoot first in the room, to a travelling dime story writer who had been riding with English Bob. Munny then leaves, but not before warning those outside the saloon:

'Alright I'm coming out. Any man I see out there I'm going to kill him. Any son of a bitch that takes a shot at me, not only am I going to kill him, I'm going to kill his wife, all his friends, burn his damn house down. Nobody better shoot.'

Unforgiven was praised for portraying the west's nastier, brutal side. It did this by showing a shot man pleading for water, the long-term effects of a brutal physical beating, and how a feared gunman could rule a town with his iron thumb. But it also showed us the contradiction in the gunman himself. Munny, who at one time drank, cussed, and shot women and children, was cured of these things when he married. He then went on to take the final job, not just for the money, but because the cowboys 'had it coming.' In the end those who protected the cowboys in question had it coming too, thus the gunman's sense of justice and duty to restore the natural order prevailed.

Unforgiven also gives a nod to the effect of the dime story, the writer of which is looking for the juicy, sensational details to sell his books. The gunman myths propagated in these largely fictional stories would go on in turn to make up many of the 'facts' present in the westerns that followed.

FIGHTER
PILOTS

Introduction

The terms 'fighter pilots' and 'dog-fights' may bring several popular images to mind – jumpsuited flyboys running across an airstrip; a goggled pilot in a rattling spitfire cockpit; the white condensation trail of a jet fighter reflected in aviator sunglasses. But whether from a sepia toned photograph, television documentary or Hollywood blockbuster, one thing is for certain – no scriptwriter could have created more colourful characters than the real pilots themselves. The young fighter 'aces' who flew in the conflicts of the twentieth century were fearless, larger than life, and often overbearingly arrogant. One pilot that held these attributes in spades is the most famous fighter pilot of all time – the Red Baron.

Manfred Albrecht von Richthofen was the 'ace of aces', who shot down eighty allied planes and painted his aircraft red to let the allies know who was shooting. In Germany he was nicknamed 'The Red Battle Flyer', but the allies knew him as 'The Red Devil', 'Little Red', 'Red Knight' and 'The Red Baron.'

Richthofen began his flying life as an observer, although he hated his first flight – he was cold, his helmet blew off, he couldn't speak to the pilot, and he lost the plane's location, despite acting as navigator. After a few weeks Richthofen was taught to read a map, drop bombs, and draw pictures mid-flight. Richthofen was observing over France when he shot down an allied plane with a portable machine gun, but the kill was not credited as it occurred over enemy lines.

A chance meeting with flying guru Lieutenant Oswald Boelcke on a train changed Richthofen's fortunes. Richthofen asked Boelcke what the best technique was for shooting down planes. Boelcke replied:

'Well it is quite simple. I fly close to my man, aim well and then of course he falls down.' Richthofen shook his head, saying that he did the same thing, but they didn't fall down. However the meeting had an impact, and Richthofen decided to ask his friend Zeumer to teach him to fly. After two failed attempts Richthofen won his wings on 25 December 1915. Despite having only one uncredited kill to his name, Richthofen was recruited by Boelcke to join a group of young, talented flyers on his Jagdstaffel ('Jasta') 2 squadron.

This was Richthofen's big break – a chance to learn from the master himself. It paid off. In September 1916, only a month off joining the Jasta 2, Richthofen made his first kill during the Battle of Somme over Cambrai, France. It was customary for a pilot to receive an engraved beer mug for his first aerial victory, but Richthofen decided to have a silver cup made and engraved instead. He had a cup made for every plane shot down, inscribing on it the kill number, the model of plane, and the date. But after his sixty-first plane the cup makers told Richthofen there was a scarcity of silver in Berlin and rather than stoop to a base metal, Richthofen packed in the tradition altogether.

Later that year tragedy struck Jasta 2 when Boelcke's luck finally ran dry. Richthofen describes the day in his autobiography, *Der rote Kampfflieger*:

> *From a long distance we saw two impertinent Englishmen in the air who actually seemed to enjoy the terrible weather...Boelcke tackled the one and I the other. I had to let go because one of the German machines got in my way. I looked around and noticed Boelcke settling his victim about two hundred yards away from me...Suddenly I noticed an unnatural movement of the two German flying machines. Immediately I thought: Collision.*
>
> *I had not yet seen a collision in the air. I had imagined that it would look quite different. In reality, what happened was not a collision. The two machines merely touched one another. However, if two machines go at the tremendous pace of flying machines, the slightest contact has the effect of a violent concussion. Boelcke drew away from his victim and descended in large curves. He did not seem to be falling, but when I saw him descending below me I noticed that part of his plane had broken*

off. I could not see what happened afterwards, but in the
clouds he lost an entire plane. Now his machine was no
longer steerable. It fell…
Der rote Kampfflieger, translated by J. Ellis Barke in 1918

The death of Boelcke was a major blow to German
morale. The so-called 'Father of Air Fighting Tactics'
had literally written the rulebook for fighter pilots in his
'Dicta Boelcke', which Richthofen followed to the letter.
While pilots such as Richthofen's brother Lothar and
German ace Verner Voss were considered natural flyers
who loved acrobatics, Richthofen played everything by
the book, sticking to Boelcke's carefully thought-out
tactics and building on them.

DAUNTLESS DUELLERS

With his mentor gone Richthofen became the number
one German hero, hated by the allies and built up into
a Titan by the German propaganda machine. Rumours
circulated of a Victoria Cross being awarded to the
pilot who downed him, and whole assassin squadrons
being put together for this task. Richthofen seemed
unbeatable, even against British aces like Lanoe Hawker,
who Richthofen described as 'the English Immelmann.'
The Red Baron would meet Hawker for a historic duel,
described by Richthofen in *Der rote Kampfflieger*.

The Englishman [Hawker] tried to catch me up in the rear while I tried to get behind him. So we circled round and round like madmen after one another at an altitude of about 10,000 feet. First we circled twenty times to the left, and then thirty times to the right. Each tried to get behind and above the other. Soon I discovered that I was not meeting a beginner. He had not the slightest intention of breaking off the fight. He was travelling in a machine which turned beautifully. However, my own was better at rising than his, and I succeeded at last in getting above and beyond my English waltzing partner.

When we had got down to about 6,000 feet without having achieved anything in particular, my opponent ought to have discovered that it was time for him to take his leave. The wind was favorable to me for it drove us more and more towards the German position. At last we were above Bapaume, about half a mile behind the German front. The impertinent fellow was full of cheek and when we had got down to about 3,000 feet he merrily waved to me as if he would say, "Well, how do you do?"

The circles which we made around one another were so narrow that their diameter was probably no more than 250 or 300 feet. I had time to take a good look at my opponent. I looked down into his carriage and could see every movement of his head. If he had not had his cap on I would have noticed what kind of a face he was making.

My Englishmen was a good sportsman, but by and by the thing became a little too hot for him. He had to decide whether he would land on German ground or whether he would fly back to the English lines. Of course he tried the latter, after having endeavored in vain to escape me by loopings and such like tricks. At that time his first bullets were flying around me, for hitherto neither of us had been able to do any shooting.

When he had come down to about 300 feet he tried to escape by flying in a zig-zag course during which, as is well known, it is difficult for an observer to shoot. That was my most favourable moment. I followed him at an altitude of from 250 feet to 150 feet, firing all the time. The Englishman could not help falling. But the jamming of my gun nearly robbed me of my success.

My opponent fell, shot through the head, 150 feet behind our line. His machine gun was dug out of the ground and it ornaments the entrance of my dwelling.

Like many fighter pilots, Richthofen was a great trophy hunter. He would often land next to a plane he had shot down to tear off its serial number or claim one of its guns. By 1917 Richthofen had sixteen kills to his name and was awarded 'The Blue Max', noting that Boelcke had been given the same award for only half the number of victories. He was also made commander of his own squadron, *Jagdstaffel 11*, which he described as 'a beastly nuisance':

> *I must say I was annoyed. I had learnt to work so well with my comrades of Boelcke's Squadron and now I had to begin all over again working hand in hand with different people.*

FLYING FINALE

Richthofen's Jasta 11 immediately went into competition with his former squadron Jasta 2, which he noted was '100 planes ahead.' Enemy planes seemed ripe for the picking during 1917's 'Bloody April', when the allies lost 245 aircraft to Germany's 66. Richthofen, of course, shot down the highest number of planes in April – 21 – bringing his personal tally to 52. He had now bettered Boelcke's total of 40 kills, making him the top German 'Ace of Aces.' In June an announcement was made that five Jagdstaffels would be merged into one super squadron to be commanded by Richthofen. Its name was *Jagdgeschwader 1* ('wing hunter'), commonly dubbed 'The Flying Circus,' or 'Richthofen's Circus.'

But then in July, fate dealt Richthofen an altogether unfamiliar hand – he was shot down. Richthofen described feeling a blow to the head, before losing control of his arms and legs and realising he was blind. The plane began diving, but at 2,600 feet Richthofen regained enough eyesight to crash land it. Surgeons had to remove a bullet and bone splinters from Richthofen's skull and he was grounded for a month. But it would have lasting consequences: headaches, nausea and terminal grumpiness.

The German government did everything it could to keep Richthofen on the ground, as it feared the impact his death would have on German morale. But Richthofen kept flying and shooting down allied aircraft. That is, until the morning of 21 April 1918.

Richthofen had started the morning's sport by chasing a novice Canadian flyer who was doing his best to escape. The Canadian squadron commander Arthur 'Roy' Brown had seen Richthofen from above and ran an attack on him. But Brown did not succeed and Richthofen kept after the novice, who flew as low as he could to the ground. They passed a group of Australian soldiers below, who began firing on Richtofen's red triplane. Brown rejoined the attack and there was a great cheer as the red plane crashed. Richthofen had been killed by a single bullet that entered his right armpit and exited through his chest.

Nobody to this day knows if the bullet came from the ground or Brown's plane. Allied soldiers stripped

Richthofen's plane for souvenirs, just as Richthofen had done himself of his victims' aircraft. One Australian soldier reported that Richthofen was alive when they reached his plane. The top World War I ace, who at just twenty-five years old had scored a total of eighty aerial battles, had only one last word: 'kaput.'

AVIATION ADVANCEMENTS

Richthofen's legacy, and that of every other fighter pilot before or after, was only made possible by a tiny advancement in aviation technology. This was a special synchronisation gear, which allowed the pilot's machine gun to shoot only when the propeller wasn't in front of it. The synchronisation gear not only enabled the creation of a forward-firing plane but also paved the way for aerial combat, or dog-fighting.

Advances in aviation technology have always gone hand-in-hand with the story of the fighter pilot. The pilot himself had little choice but to adapt quickly to new technologies and those of his enemy. Often advances took place during warfare and, as such, came about at an accelerated speed. It was anticipated that many technologies – from the fast World Word II fighter and the jet engine, to air-to-air missiles – would make dog-fighting obsolete. But even modern fighters of today are still trained in this form of aerial combat. And despite the extraordinary capabilities of the modern fighter plane, dog- fighting techniques have changed little in the nearly 100 years they have been practiced.

History

There was a certain amount of heroism involved in just piloting a plane one hundred years ago, let alone trying to bring another aircraft down in combat. And it wasn't long after the Wright brothers' first flight of 1903 that governments began pondering how to make military use of this new technology. Hot air balloons had been used for reconnaissance since the 1870 Franco-Prussian war, and when World War I broke out it was thought aircraft were best suited for the same role.

Aircraft at this time were the flimsy and lightweight biplanes which puttered along at a top speed of 90 mph. Even the weight of the pilot would affect lift, and the two-seater 'observation' planes were not much good for anything but slow, straight travel. In the first weeks of World War I, pilots could do little more than wave at each other, although some tried hurling missiles such as grenades and bricks. It was not long before pilots were arming themselves with pistols and rifles, and from 1915 British Bristol Scout C biplanes were mounted with Lewis machine guns. These were either attached by the pilot and pointed at a 30-degree angle to avoid shooting off the front propeller; or mounted on a swivel mechanism next to the back seat so the observer could provide rear fire.

The role of 'observer', who often acted as back gunner, was highly perilous, as the seat belt would have to be removed to operate the machine guns. Rolls and air pockets caused many observers to simply slip out of the plane and fall to their deaths. The situation was not ideal and everybody agreed the trick would be to add a machine gun to the front of the plane, which somehow avoided the propeller when firing. 'Pusher' planes tried to get around this by simply placing the propeller itself at the back, but these lumbering planes were too slow to catch up to another plane let alone shoot it down. Machine guns attached to a biplane's top wing was a temporary solution, but they proved too difficult to load in mid flight.

French pilot Roland Garros came up with an ingenious solution – a synchronisation gear that would only let his gun fire when the propeller wasn't in front of it. To be safe Garros also added steel wedges to his Moraine-Saulnier Model L's propellers, so they could deflect any stray bullets. Garros' invention was a great success – in April 1915 he shot down three German aircraft behind enemy lines. Unfortunately fire from the ground hit Garros' fuel line and he was forced down. His aircraft was captured by the Germans and studied by Dutch engineer Anthony Fokker, who copied the synchronisation gear and perfected the mechanism. From then on, every new Fokker E1 built was fitted with a synchronisation gear and a Maxim machine gun. The E1 was the first forward-firing monoplane that was light and manoeuverable enough to engage other planes in combat. The age of the fighter plane had begun.

The E1 made short thrift of the heavy British BE 2c biplanes, earning them the nickname 'Fokker fodder.' After the British caught up with the synchronisation gear technology a new type of aerial combat emerged – duels between fighter aircraft known as 'dog-fights.' Dog-fights were considered a sort of chivalrous joust between two knights, or so it was sold to the public. The allies' propaganda department desperately needed inspirational wartime tales to juxtapose against the horrors of the trenches. The fighter pilot provided exactly the right character – a dashing, young patriot onboard his silver flying steed, risking life and limb to rid the skies of the dastardly Hun.

AERIAL ACES

To begin with it was not the British, but two Germans – Ernst Boelcke and Max Immelmann – who made headlines as the first two fighter 'aces'. Ace is the term that describes a fighter pilot who has shot down more than five planes. There were no rules of combat at that time, but there are many stories of courteous pilots who fought according to a gentlemanly code of aviation. An adversary was formally challenged with a couple of warning shots, and would respond in kind if interested in duelling. If an airman was shot down over enemy lines and captured he was often wined and dined by his flyboy captors.

These noble ideals did peter out fairly quickly, after all, there was a world war on. Air tactics were changing too and aces like Boelcke and Immelmann were given carte blanche to take to the skies as lone hunters, seeking, stalking and ambushing enemy aircraft.

The most popular method of ambush was to drop down from the sun, which made an incoming fighter almost impossible to see. If the ambushed aircraft survived, the ensuing dog-fight would see both planes go into a series of turns, rolls, loops and engine stalls to shake each other off. A favourite tactic was to get behind the other plane before lining it up in the machine guns sights. Boelcke became the first pilot to analyse aerial warfare and wrote up eight rules of combat, the 'Dicta Boelcke', which is still studied by airmen today.

The Dicta Boelcke

1. Try to secure advantages before attacking. If possible keep the sun behind you.
2. Always carry through an attack when you have started it.
3. Fire only at close range and only when your opponent is properly in your sights.

4. Always keep your eye on your opponent and never let yourself be deceived by ruses.
5. In any form of attack it is essential to assail your opponent from behind.
6. If your opponent dives on you, do not try to evade his onslaught but fly to meet him.
7. When over the enemy's line never forget your own line of retreat.
8. For the Squadron: Attack on principle in groups of four or six. When the fight breaks up into a series of single combats take care that several do not go for one opponent.

Of course a pilot's tactical knowledge and flying ability was one thing, but his chances were always greatly influenced by the machine he was flying. In World War I a pilot's greatest asset was a fast machine. This always gave him the advantage, both in attack and defence. A faster plane could literally fly circles around a slower one – pouncing from the heavens, delivering fatal machine gun fire and outrunning opposing fire with a hasty retreat. In World War I the faster planes such as the German Fokker Dr. I triplane could reach a top speed of 122 mph. By comparison, World War II aircraft such as the American P-51 Mustang could reach 437 mph and that was before the advent of the jet engine.

But even the fastest aircraft could not equip a fighter

pilot with the required levels of cunning and guile necessary to take to the skies in the first place. Many rookies simply lost their nerve at the first sight of an approaching enemy fighter. Often they would fire their guns too soon and turn into a retreat, giving the opponent a clear shot at their tail. At other times they would deliberately fire wide – a common occurrence in all facets of warfare among novice combatants. Unfortunately for the rookie, their first dog-fighting mistake was often their last. Those pilots who scored 'ace' status were invariably like the best wild west gunslingers – they made sure the odds were in their favour and only then went in for the kill. When two such pilots met, a spectacular dog-fight would follow. One such historical bout was fought in November 1916 between British ace Lanoe Hawker and his greatest adversary Manfred von Richthofen, aka the 'Red Baron' (see page 390).

The man who wrote the rulebook, Ernst Boelcke, won forty victories in the air as well as the coveted decoration of *Orden Pour Le Merite*, commonly know as 'The Blue Max'. But he suffered a rather less glamorous end when his plane collided with his fellow fighter Erwin Boehme. Max Immelmann, also the recipient of The Blue Max, fatally crashed after shooting off his own propeller when his synchronisation gear failed.

It is no coincidence that the last rule of the Boelcke Dicta is directed at those fighting in a squadron, which became a more frequent occurrence as World War I drew on. By the end of the war the large numbers of planes in the sky made flying solo too dangerous, and planes travelled in formations instead. The days of the lone hunter were over, but dog-fighting had only finished its first chapter.

MODERN MACHINES

The Spanish Civil War acted as a testing ground for new aircraft technologies. Faster planes were emerging, including the German's Messerschmitt Bf 109; a closed canopy fighter with retractable landing gear and top speed of 250 mph. The British response would be the Supermarine Spitfire, the backbone of the RAF in World War II, armed with .303 calibre Browning machine guns and a top speed of 251 mph. The Japanese would manufacture the Mitsubishi A6M Zero, the Russians the Yakovlev Yak-1, the Americans the P-51 Mustang, and the Italians the Macchi C.200 Saetta.

While all of these planes represented the height of modern technology, the planes of Britain, Germany and Russia were built with speed and climbing ability over manoeuverability. The reason for this was because it was thought these new faster aircraft would put an end to dog-fighting forever. Simply, it was not thought the human body could tolerate the g-forces involved in aerial combat at high speed. In reality nothing could have been further from the truth, as World War II marked the zenith of one-on-one aerial combat.

It was not just the new fighters that had been tested in the Spanish Civil War but also heavy bombers. Many military minds believed that bombers would take over from fighters as the mainstay of a modern airforce. The RAF was so convinced of this theory that it only started investing heavily in the production of fighter planes one year before World War II began. As it turned out, fighters were more necessary than ever before because without them the bombers were wholly exposed as large, slow moving targets.

Almost all of the dog-fighting in Word War II occurred between fighter planes that were travelling in convoy to protect the bombers. Aircraft would still engage in one-on-one combat but in the context of large aerial battlefields, where dozens of fighters and bombers were brought into play. Because of this, aircraft of World War II were manufactured and destroyed in extremely high numbers. The German Luftwaffe, for example, shot down seven thousand Russian planes during its Barbarossa offensive alone.

The threat of enemy fire did not only come from other aircraft but also the ground. The new, powerful anti-aircraft artillery produced in World War II was responsible for bringing down thousands of bombers and fighters alike. The best-known of these was the dreaded German 88mm FlaK 36, more commonly known as the 'eighty-eight.'

By the end of the war new technologies were fast changing the face of aerial combat. Japanese 'kamikaze' planes were committing suicide by crashing into their targets, in a skewed modern form of the samurai *seppuku*. More pivotal to dog-fighting itself was the emergence of air-to-air missiles and jet engines. Germany had been experimenting with jet propulsion from the beginning of the war, but it wasn't made operational until the introduction of the Messerschmitt Me 262 Schwalbe in 1944. The Me 262 was the first jet-powered aircraft in the world, had a top speed of 559 mph and was heavily armed. While the plane's manufacture came too late to save the Third Reich, jet-powered engines were soon indoctrinated into every major airforce.

The new jet engines would usher in a new era of dog-fighting that was showcased in the Korean War. Here, American F-86 Sabres (sabrejets) and North Korean operated Chinese MiG-15s flew at each other at speeds of around 580 mph, which required a much longer turn for each pass made. The American advantage over the North Korean airforce was their g-suit, which helped prevent blood draining away from the pilot's head to stop g-force blackouts. By the time of the Vietnam War American military chiefs were once again convinced that heat-seeking and guided missiles would make dog-fighting a thing of the past. As such, they stopped arming their F-4 Phantoms with machine guns, which in turn made them easy prey for the Vietnamese MiG-21s.

Despite every technological advancement in aircraft technology nothing has yet made dog-fighting obsolete, although many predict this day is near. The advent of recent technologies such as tail-mounted radar, rear firing missiles and helmet-mounted sights have rendered chasing an enemy aircraft almost impossible. But this state of the art technology has not yet been utilised across the board, and for aircraft without it, the Boelcke Dicta rule number 5 remains the most important for any dog-fighting aircraft: 'In any form of attack it is essential to assail your opponent from behind.' Little wonder then, that so much technology is developed specifically to prevent this form of attack from taking place.

When a dog-fight does occur today, it happens at far lower speeds than the aircraft is capable of reaching. This is to attain the extreme acrobatic manoeuvering, turn rate and cornering speed needed to evade the opponent's missiles and automatic machine gun fire. Often modern dog-fighting etiquette dictates one fly past to give the opponent a chance to 'bug out', which is where a modern aircraft's tremendous speed comes in handy.

But technology has not yet replaced the fighter pilots

themselves, who still risk life and limb to patrol the skies as they did nearly 100 years ago. The following profiles tell the story of some of the greatest fighter pilots in dog-fighting history.

The Fighter Pilots

WILLIAM BISHOP

Canadian fighter pilot William Avery 'Billy' Bishop shot down seventy-two planes in World War I making him the top scoring RAF ace. It is ironic then, that Bishop was considered a mediocre pilot who nearly didn't make it off the ground.

Bishop's childhood was a prophetic warning of things to come. When he turned fifteen, Bishop built a biplane out of wood and cardboard and 'flew' from the roof of his three-story family home. It was the first time Bishop crawled from his wrecked plane after a violent landing, but it certainly wasn't to be the last.

Bishop's next crash landing came in 1917, shortly after he was awarded his wings. This time it was in front of General John Higgins, who immediately ordered Bishop back to flight school. Luckily Bishop's squadron commander pleaded with Higgins to let him have one more day until a replacement arrived. This was fortuitous, as that same day Bishop shot down a German ace. But straight afterwards he experienced engine trouble and was again forced to crash land, this time behind enemy lines. Bishop avoided capture and ran unharmed to the allied trenches where he spent a night in the open air. The next day at the aerodrome Higgins made sure to personally congratulate Bishop and reinstate him. Bishop made another kill the following afternoon and five days later was made flight commander.

What made Bishop such a formidable fighter pilot, even despite his questionable flying ability, was his extraordinary eyesight. Bishop had been a crack shot ever since his father bought him a .22 calibre rifle for Christmas and offered him 25 cents for every squirrel killed. After joining the Canadian Mounted Rifles in 1914, Bishop quickly earned a reputation for bulls-eyeing targets on the horizon that were only specks to other soldiers. According to Bishop, shooting prowess was by far the most important skill needed by a fighter pilot, followed by tactical knowledge, and lastly flying acumen. Bishop's methodology was certainly effective – he quickly won 'ace' status, which his mechanic celebrated by painting the nose of his aircraft blue. German fliers knew Bishop more somberly as 'hell's handmaiden.'

Soon Bishop was flying solo missions as a lone hunter, taking particular pleasure in seeing enemy craft go up in flames, after experiencing this for the first time on 20 April 1917. On this day Bishop was flying his Nieuport 17 biplane over a cloud layer when he spotted a two-seater German aircraft above him. Neither the pilot nor the observer had seen Bishop, so he climbed slowly beneath them to get into position. This was a gamble as it would give the German pilot the advantage if he noticed Bishop. Once in position Bishop let go ten rounds of machine gun fire, all of which missed his opponent but served to grab his attention. The German turned to meet Bishop head-on and a dog-fight ensued.

Both pilots used the common manoeuvres of the day – diving, rolling, and stalling to get into a position where a straight shot was possible. After firing from only two plane lengths away and missing, Bishop tired another tactic – attacking his opponent from the side. This was risky, and the observer began shooting at Bishop from his swivel gun with an unimpeded view. Bishop could feel the bullets whipping past him, but his own bullets were also finding purchase in the German's fuselage. At this point the observer seemed to lose his nerve and fired his bullets wide. Then he slumped and stopped firing altogether. Bishop saw the plane was on fire and it fell, spinning down towards the earth leaving a long black trail of smoke behind it.

Bishop describes his luck as greatly increasing after this kill and in August that year he temporarily became the highest scoring ace in the Royal Flying Corps. To award his bravery in attacking an German aerodrome near the Arras front, Bishop became the first Canadian to be awarded the Victoria Cross. This how the attack was described in the *Supplement to the London Gazette*, 11 August 1917:

Captain Bishop, who had been sent out to work independently, flew first of all to an enemy aerodrome; finding no machine about, he flew on to another aerodrome about three miles south-east, which was at least twelve miles the other side of the line. Seven machines, some with their engines running, were on the ground. He attacked these from about fifty feet, and a mechanic, who was starting one of the engines, was seen to fall. One of the machines got off the ground, but at a height of sixty feet Captain Bishop fired fifteen rounds into it at very close range, and it crashed to the ground.

A second machine got off the ground, into which he fired thirty rounds at 150 yards range, and it fell into a tree. Two more machines then rose from the aerodrome. One of these he engaged at the height of 1,000 feet, emptying the rest of his drum of ammunition. This machine crashed 300 yards from the aerodrome, after which Captain Bishop emptied a whole drum into the fourth hostile machine, and then flew back to his station.

By 1918 Bishop commanded his own squadron, was promoted to major, and had sixty-seven kills to his name. But in June the Canadian Government decided his death would be too much of a blow to Canadian morale and ordered Bishop back to London to become a trainer.

Bishop was furious, but left the air on a high note. Due to leave the aerodrome at midday, Bishop spent the morning on a last solo flight, during which he shot down five enemy planes, bringing his total to seventy-two.

ERICH ALFRED HARTMANN

World War II Luftwaffe pilot Erich Alfred Hartmann was the top-scoring ace in aviation history. During his years of service between 1942 and 1945 Hartmann flew on 1,404 missions, engaged in 825 aerial bouts and shot down 352 planes. Of these, 345 were Russian planes, earning him the Soviet nickname 'Black Devil.' But, to his German comrades Hartmann was 'Bubi' because of his babyish features.

Like many aces, the young Hartmann stumbled at his first flying hurdle. During a training flight in 1942 Hartmann began showing off in his Messerschmitt Bf 109 by performing acrobatics over the airstrip. His superiors were less than impressed: his pay was docked and he was grounded for three months. The stunt could have cost him his wings, but instead it saved his life. On the first day he was grounded Hartmann's plane developed engine trouble and crashed, killing the replacement pilot. Hartmann would develop his own legacy of crash landings, doing so on his first assignment, delivering a Junkers Ju 87 to Mariupol on his way to the eastern front. He would crash another thirteen times, which was surprisingly never caused by machine gun fire but instead engine trouble or flying debris from aircraft he had just shot.

Hartmann would crash land again on his first mission, when desperate for a kill, he abandoned his wingman Rossmann and dropped down on enemy fighters at full throttle. After nearly colliding with the first fighter, Hartmann found himself surrounded and low on fuel. He was forced into belly land. Hartmann was uninjured but had violated every commandment of the fighter pilot code and was lucky not to receive a court martial. After another period on the ground, Hartmann decided to put his head down and learn as much as he could from the veterans in the squadron.

One of these was flying ace Walter 'The Count' Krupinski, the new squadron leader who arrived with a bang. Hartmann was talking to his Wing Commander when a smoking aircraft came in hard, landed, flipped and exploded. Assuming the pilot was dead, Hartmann heard somebody say, 'it is Krupinski', to which a singed Krupinski walked out of the wreckage smiling, and made a comment about the flak over the Caucasus. Krupinski taught Hartmann to get in as close as possible to the enemy before firing, to ensure a kill. This led Hartmann to develop his own mantra of: 'See – Decide – Attack – Break'. He would stalk and then ambush planes, waiting until he was only 20 metres away before firing. Hartmann once said he was sure the majority of those planes he shot down didn't know what had hit them. This method secured Hartmann ninety victories by 1943, winning him the title 'Ace of Aces'.

In August of the same year, Hartmann was forced to land behind enemy lines and found himself surrounded by Soviet troops. Hartmann proceeded to fool the soldiers into believing he had serious internal injuries, who put him on a stretcher and rushed him to a doctor. After also convincing the doctor, Hartmann was laid out on a stretcher in the back of a truck. He proceeded to overpower his guard and ran into a field of sunflowers, dodging the ensuing Soviet gunfire. Lying low until nightfall, Hartmann crept his way to the German front line. Here he was shot by a sentry believing him to be a Russian (the bullet went through his trouser leg), before receiving a lengthy interrogation.

By March 1944, Hartmann had secured 250 victories and was summoned to Berchtesgaden, Barkhorn so Hitler could personally award him the Knight's Cross of the Iron Cross with Oaks' Leaves. Hartmann and his colleagues drank so heavily on the train to Barkhorn that they could barely stand on arrival. At one point Hartmann picked up the wrong hat and was told to put it back as it belonged to the Fuhrer. Hartmann said when he finally did meet Hitler he found him to be: 'an isolated and disturbed man', and later said he found National Socialism: 'sickening.'

From May 1944 the Americans joined the war and brought with them the P-51 Mustang – a plane that had been designed and manufactured in just 117 days, but was superior to the German 109s in every way. Germany was running low on pilots by his stage of the war, and was increasingly sending younger and more inexperienced pilots to the front, and to an early grave.

Hartmann's last air victory was on 8 May 1945 and after blowing up their remaining aircraft, Hartmann and his men surrendered to the US 90th Infantry Division. Then they were handed over to the Soviet troops. Hartmann's fame as a fighter pilot was probably the only thing that kept him alive for the next 10 years after he was detained in various Soviet Gulag camps on false charges of slaughtering 780 soviet citizens. The Soviet authorities wanted him kept alive to spy on his fellow officers and supply information about the German Me-262 fighter jet. Although Hartmann refused all of these demands his status still awarded him slightly better treatment than the other prisoners. Hartmann was finally released in 1955 and died in 1993.

JAMES EDGAR 'JOHNNIE' JOHNSON

James Edgar 'Johnnie' Johnson was Britain's top ace of World War II who was rejected from flight training in 1938 because of an old rugby injury. Johnson's collar bone had been broken and incorrectly set, giving him ongoing pain. But in 1939, with all hands needed on deck, Johnson's reapplication was successful and his training began. It wasn't long, however, that high-speed flying in a spitfire inflamed the old injury. He was told he could either undergo an operation to reset the bone or accept a job as a flight trainer. Johnson did not hesitate with his decision for surgery, but missed the Battle of Britain as a result.

On recovery he joined 616 Squadron at Tangmere led by Commander Douglas Bader. Bader had also overcome personal injury to continue flying after losing both his legs in an acrobatics accident. It was under Bader that Johnson would begin sweeps of Western Europe in 1941.

On one such mission above the French city of Lille, Johnson and twelve other spitfires encountered thirty Me-109s flying above them. Just as Johnson noticed the sun reflecting in the 109s' cockpit windows, they began diving. The spitfires turned sharply left, straightened up and banked right. The 109s couldn't match the turn and climbed back up to rejoin their squadron. But the manoeuvre split the allied group and Johnson's spitfire fell behind.

Suddenly Johnson found himself alone and the sole focus of the 109s, which became intent on picking off the straggler. As four more 109s dived on Johnson he banked hard to the left, pushing his spitfire to the brink of a high-speed stall. The 109s at this stage were so convinced of a kill they began flying badly and firing recklessly from too far a distance. Johnson also fired his guns, just to reassure himself he was still alive. Suddenly a voice crackled over the radio, informing the group that Johnson was alone and under attack. Bader directed Johnson back to the squadron, which was still being tailed by a dozen 109s.

Johnson kept his neck craned upwards to watch their advance and saw two planes dive on the group. He broke right and flew into the attack, making a small turn to end up on a 109's tail. He lined his spitfire up to within 100 yards of the enemy plane, held the handle of his stick tight with both hands, and let go short bursts of machine gun fire. The 109 exploded; a dazzling white-hot centre surrounded by swirling black plumes. The battle was short, with several 109s shot down, and the rest beating a hasty retreat. Johnson flew back across the English Channel with the rest of his squadron, where within minutes they were celebrating with a cup of tea, the sweat not even yet dry on their backs.

From that point on, Johnson's tally of air victories rose

exponentially. By the end of the war he had shot down 34 planes and contributed to seven additional kills, making his personal tally 37.5 – the highest in British aviation history. After the war Johnson retained his commission and retired an Air Vice Marshall in 1966. After writing several books, Johnson died of cancer in 2001.

ROBIN OLDS

Robin Olds was the all-American boy with two aims in life – to play football and become an officer in the airforce. Olds would achieve both of these goals by age twenty-two, and would go on to become one of America's top aces, leading squadrons in World War II and Vietnam with a charisma and swagger that made his name legendary.

Born in 1922 to an Army Air Corps Brigadier General, it was no great surprise when the teenage Olds joined the United States Military Academy at West Point. Here, he played football and trained as a pilot, graduating in 1943. Olds promptly sailed for England and began flying Lockheed P-38 Lightning fighters on missions across France in 1944. Within two missions Olds reached ace status by shooting down two Focke Wulf 190s and three Messerschmitt Bf 109s. He was made a major, squadron leader, and flew the first P-51 Mustangs to arrive in England, further increasing his kill tally. By the end of he war he had thirteen credited aerial victories and was the recipient of a US Silver Star, a British Distinguished Flying Cross and a French Croix de Guerre.

Olds' strength was in his leadership – he led from the front, had no qualms about speaking his mind in front of superiors and always held the respect and admiration of his men. Following the war he was placed in the very first Lockheed P-80 squadron and flew with the Aerial Aerobatic Demonstration Team.

Olds moved steadily up through the ranks becoming a colonel in 1953 and reluctantly serving in several staff assignments until 1955. Olds wanted desperately to serve in the Korean War, but every application was turned down. He also drafted papers on the benefits of tactical bombing and the need for upgrading conventional bombing munitions, but these were rejected by military brass. Olds said it was ironic that the higher his rank the less he was listened to. What Olds really wanted to do was fly, and in 1966 he finally got his wish when he was made commander of the 8th Tactical Fighter Wing in Vietnam.

The Wing was tired, unmotivated and highly suspicious of their new forty-four-year-old leader, who they suspected was a burnt-out relic from World War II. Instead a robust Robin Olds marched through the door and began doing what he did best – leading by example. He put himself on the same schedule as the rookie pilots and began teaching the pilots how to engage in a good old World War II-style dogfight, something he felt was woefully lacking from their flying repertoire.

Next Olds decided to engage the enemy MiGs with the American F-4s by setting a trap. Up until that point the North Vietnamese MiGs would only attack the F-105 Thunderchief bombers and avoid any one-on-one combat with the fighters. Olds' plan, called Operation Bolo, was to get the F-4s to imitate the call signs and routes of the F-105s. This would coax the MiGs into coming out to meet the planes, which, to their surprise would turn out to be a formation of F-4s. The plan worked to stunning effect – Olds got one MiG and the rest of his squadron shot down six more. The ace was back in the saddle doing what he did best: leading from the front and shooting down enemy aircraft.

Olds' fourth MiG kill took place on 20 May 1967 when he and seven F-4s were escorting four F-105s to their drop point. As the formation passed the hills north of Haiphong a group of MiGs suddenly appeared from both sides. The ensuing battle featured so many planes flying at low altitude that there was as much chance of a mid-air collision as there was of being shot down. The MiGs began flying in a defensive 'figure eight' circles so each plane was protected by the MiG flying directly behind it. Every time one of the F-4s would try to go in to fire a missile, a plane from the other side would pull across the circle at full power, guns blazing. By this stage the only fatality had come from one of Olds' pilots, who had managed to explode a sidewinder missile close enough to an MiG that it caught fire and spun into the ground. The fight had already lasted twelve minutes, a long time for modern air combat, and the F-4s were running low on fuel. Olds told the rest of his F-4s to bail out and decided to have one last attempt at an MiG by dropping down behind it. This had the desired effect of panicking the plane and separating it from the rest of the group. The MiG then tried to outrun Olds by performing a series of twists and turns as both planes headed up a narrow valley towards a ridge of hills. The MiG had the choice of crashing into the ridge or flying over it, which would put him in Olds' sights. But Olds' sidewinder did not track, and exploded in mid air. As the MiG turned right Olds let loose another sidewinder, which tracked the plane's exhaust and exploded around five feet from its fuselage. This was enough to knock pieces off the MiG and send it hurtling towards the ground. Olds managed to make it to an aircraft carrier with only enough fuel for a few more minutes flying time.

This fourth kill gave Olds the top aerial victory score at that time and officially ended his combat career at 13 kills. The battle had also proved Olds' theory that the Americans still needed to engage the MiGs in one-on-one combat, as it was too difficult to attack a formation of aircraft. He had no hesitation in explaining this to Air Force Chief of Staff General John D. Ryan, who in 1972 was sent to investigate why the American's air victory rate was so low. Olds, by this stage a brigadier general, even suggested he should be demoted to colonel so he could take on an overhaul of pilot training. This request was refused. So Olds elected to call it a day and retired in 1973.

In many ways Olds represented the last of the dashing, fearless flyboys, who would twirl their moustaches for a last photo before throttling their crates into the big blue battleground. Olds actually did grow a moustache in the airman's tradition of having 'a bulletproof moustache'. It was also an act of rebellious disobedience as it went against military regulations. When Olds returned to America following his tour of Vietnam, Air Force Chief of Staff General John P. McConnell stuck a finger under Olds' nose and said: 'Get it off.' Olds replied: 'Yes sir.'

For many years after he retired Olds continued to call for the airforce to incorporate dog-fighting techniques as part of basic flight training. But with the emergence of stealth, sophisticated radar and guided weaponry, even Olds eventually admitted that one-on-one aerial combat tactics had probably become obsolete. The day of the dog-fighter was over. Olds died of cancer in 2007.

Fighter Pilot Movies

WINGS

Not long after aircraft began to be used for combat, movies began to be made about fighter pilots. The first big budget example of this is *Wings*, which in 1927 was the most expensive film ever made at $2 million. *Wings* brought never seen before images of dog-fighting to worldwide public, and consequently won two Oscars for best picture and best effects.

Wings follows the story of two small-town American boys Jack Powell (Charles 'Buddy' Rogers) and David Armstrong (Richard Arlen) who join the airforce to fight the Germans. But the movie has a bitter ending – David is shot down and steals a German plane. Jack sees this plane, and seeking revenge for his fallen friend, shoots it down. He then lands to inspect the plane and is aghast to see the pilot – David. David forgives him in his dying moments, as does David's mother, who tells the returning Jack that the war is to blame, not him.

Wings was written by John Monk Saunders and directed by William Wellman, both air veterans chosen for their military experience. Saunders approached the US War Department to lend men and materials to the project. The Department saw the movie as a recruitment advertisement and agreed to contribute some money, as long as it had final approval of the film. It is interesting the Department let the final product through, considering its strong anti-war message.

What really wowed the viewing public and critics alike were the dog-fighting scenes, the like of which had never been see before. In 1927 there were no blue screens or CGI effects; all aerial stunts had to actually be performed and filmed at the same time. To enable this the actors went through flight training and cameras were mounted to the biplanes. Real fighter pilots were also used, who were told to use the film as a training exercise. At other times the pilots had to forget all elements of their training and battle against basic human instinct. In one particular scene a pilot had to climb to 6,000 feet and then dive to the ground with his plane on fire. The stunt was recorded by a close-up mounted camera, so the audience would really feel they were in the plane with him with the clouds rushing past. When he reached the required height, the pilot had to switch on the camera, bite down on a blood pellet, release the smoke, kick the plane into a spin, and go limp in his seat – then letting the plane hurtle towards the earth as the camera filmed him acting dead.

The stunts in *Wings* ended up causing one broken

neck and one fatality. The stuntman with a broken neck went on to sue the production company for ruining his reputation after his stunt scene was replaced by one using miniatures. The fatality occurred when a pilot crash landed into the ground. The producer was expecting the military to shut the movie down after this but was surprised instead when the operations officer did not seem fazed. Instead the officer told him not worry, that it was the pilot's own fault anyway and that fatalities happened in training all the time.

Wings is now eighty-four years old but there is no greater movie dedicated to aerial combat in World War I. It is made all the more spectacular for the fact that the dog-fights are actually being performed by real pilots, many of whom had served in the war itself.

BATTLE OF BRITAIN

The Battle of Britain is, of course, considered one of the crucial events of World War II. It pitted vastly outnumbered RAF fighters against the might of the German Luftwaffe, which would attempt to wipe out RAF forces in the south east of England. The destruction of the RAF was considered a necessary precursor to Hitler's 'Operation Sealion' – a ground invasion of Britain planned for September 1940.

The Luftwaffe began by bombing British boats and

seaports before moving to armament factories and RAF airstrips. When this did not have the desired effect the Luftwaffe resorted to terror tactics and dropped its bombs on London. By the end of October the Luftwaffe had suffered heavy losses and had not managed their primary objective. Operation Sealion was permanently put on ice. The defeat was of major significance to the course of the conflict and signalled the beginning of the end of Hitler's war.

The 1969 *Battle of Britain* starts at the end of the German invasion of France and soon moves to Winston Churchill telling the nation 'the Battle of Britain has begun'. To start with things look bleak for the British, until a squadron of Polish fighter trainees defy orders to attack and shoot down a bomber. German bombers then attack London, and RAF bombers do the same to Berlin. An enraged Hitler orders London be razed, which gives the RAF time to repair their airfields and radar installations and come back at the Germans with force. More aerial battles ensue and with heavy Luftwaffe losses for little gain, Hitler is forced to cancel Operation Sealion. The film ends with Churchill's immortal words: 'Never in the field of human conflict was so much owed by so many to so few.'

Production of the *Battle of Britain* began in 1965, with the search for usable World War II aircraft. Eventually 100 planes were found, including spitfires, Messerschmitt

109s, Heinkels and Hawker Hurricanes. The aircraft were mounted with cameras to capture the dog-fighting from the air. Filming took place at old World War II airstrips in Duxford, Debden, North Weald and Hawkinge. The London Blitz scenes were shot at St Katharine Docks, ironically one of the only places in London's east end to escape the bombing at the time.

Great pains were made to make the *Battle of Britain* historically accurate. Consultants from both sides of the conflict were employed, and many of the planes were flown by ex-World War II flyers. There is some creative licence. For example the fighter's transmissions are heard in the Operations Command Centre, when actually the information was phoned in from the airfield. But overall the film stays true to the events, and highlights important points such as RAF command's reluctance to employ foreign pilots, many of whom had more experience than the British flyers. In the end the Battle of Britain could not have been won without the aid of the 595 non-British pilots, and the services of men such as RAF Air Vice Marshal Keith Park, a New Zealander who was known in Germany as: 'the Defender of London.'

Despite its famous cast, which includes Michael Caine and Laurence Olivier, the *Battle of Britain* is commonly criticised for its stilted dialogue and lacklustre script. However, the film has no equal for its portrayal of aerial combat in World War II. It has also become something of a British institution and frequently replayed on television during public holidays.

TOP GUN

Like most movies of the 1980s *Top Gun* is a sensationalist romp through implausible scenarios with one-dimensional characters and clichéd ridden dialogue. But the film is notable for its big budget aerial stunts which, like *Wings,* are performed in America's top fighter planes of the time.

Top Gun features a group American trainee pilots competing against each other on the United States Navy Strike Fighter Tactics Instructor program (commonly known as TOPGUN). TOPGUN is a real training school created as a result of the Ault Report. The report investigated the large number of American fighters lost during the Vietnam War's Rolling Thunder Operation, where 1,000 planes were shot down between 1965 and 1968. A United States Airforce investigation into the matter found that the losses were due to unobserved MiGs dropping down on US fighter's tails, and concluded more observation technology was needed. However, the United States Navy investigation by Frank Ault came up with a different conclusion, one that flying ace Robin Olds had spent years shouting from the proverbial rooftops.

Ault found that the fault was an over reliance on air-to-air missile technology, with virtually no time spent teaching trainee fighter pilots dog-fighting technique. The navy set up TOPGUN for this very purpose, and many similar training centres soon sprang up within the USA and around the world.

In *Top Gun*, Lieutenant Pete 'Maverick' Mitchell (Tom Cruise) is the renegade hero who has something to prove after his flyer Dad was shot down in Vietnam. Despite breaking the odd flight regulation during training, Maverick and his Radar Intercept Officer Nick 'Goose' Bradshaw (Anthony Edwards) are picked to train at TOPGUN.

After some initial posturing with *Top Gun*'s other hot shot Alfa male and rival, Lieutenant Tom 'Iceman' Kazansky (Val Kilmer), Maverick settles into his training and wooing of TOPGUN instructor and astrophysicist Charlotte 'Charlie' Blackwood (Kelly McGillis). But then Goose is killed in training when Maverick suffers an engine flame-out and both flyers have to eject. Maverick feels responsible, and goes through a short period of motorcycle riding and soul searching. Then, a Vietnam veteran who served with Maverick's father reveals to him that his Dad died honourably. This gives Maverick the strength to graduate.

Then all of sudden, there is a conflict situation. A communications ship has strayed into hostile waters near Libya and enemy MiGs have been sighted close by.

Despite Iceman's reservations about Maverick's state of mind the two work together to shoot down six MiGs. Job done, the two shake hands and Maverick decides to become a TOPGUN instructor.

Top Gun is the work of Jerry Bruckheimer and Don Simpson, the producers responsible for many popular 1980s and 1990s blockbusters, including *Flashdance, Beverly Hills Cop* and *Days of Thunder*. To make *Top Gun* the producers requested the help of the US Navy who hired out several F-14s, at a cost of nearly $8000 an hour. Cameras were attached to the pilots' helmets and the fuselages of Learjet aircraft. Professional pilots were used for all of the dog-fighting scenes, including top stunt man and aerobatic pilot Art Scholl.

After performing one particular spin over the Pacific Ocean, Scholl radioed in that he was experiencing problems and crashed into the water – neither Scholl or the plane were ever seen again. Scholl, who the movie was dedicated to, would have been proud of his footage, and *Top Gun's* aerial combat shots are considered some of the best of all time. The *Top Gun* stunts are some of the last actually performed for an action movie. More recent fighter plane movies, such as Jerry Bruckheimer's *Pearl Harbor*, rely heavily on computer generated imagery, thus removing the risk of injury and saving the expense of staging a stunt.

Many of the *Top Gun* audience were so overawed by

modern fighter jet capabilities that they joined up – the US Navy and Airforce reported a 500 per cent increase in recruitment numbers during the *Top Gun* period. Recruitment booths were even set up in cinema foyers to catch enthusiastic Maverick wannabes walking out of the film. Aerial combat scenes aside, the movie was panned for its acting, script, plot and predictability. This did not stop people going to see it – *Top Gun* was made with a budget $15 million, and made over $8 million within its first weekend of its 1986 release. Since then the movie has made over $354 million.

CONCLUSION

One-on-one combat, the brutal contest to kill or harm your opponent, has enthralled and repelled humankind throughout history. Every culture has tried to soften the struggle or limit its horror with rules and regulations, but the brutal reality remains beneath the protocol. Today's society embodies this contradiction as much as ancient Greece or medieval Japan.

A fight to the death is acceptable and treated as normal in warfare, and violent slug-fests are both legal and celebrated in sports such as boxing. But a similar fight in the street, the pub or the home is condemned. Even here, however, our ambivalence is obvious. Television reports the lurid details of knife-fights and killings while maintaining the façade of journalistic 'objectivity.' The news media know that violence is popular even while it is officially forbidden.

The ancient Romans were less hypocritical. They loved the blood and butchery of the gladiatorial games and would reward a gladiator if he fought with bravery and honour. However, a gladiator still came from the lower orders, so while he could win fame, fortune and freedom he would never be allowed to become a Roman citizen. A gladiator could become as popular as a modern rock star, but he could never be respectable. Even in Rome, one-on-one combat stirred a deeply buried unease.

Today's modern gladiator is similarly adored and abominated. Boxers are paid millions to pummel each other in the ring and then expected to behave like gentlemen outside it. And when boxing stars such as Mike Tyson, assault, batter and rape, the public deplores it. The line between officially sanctioned assault and criminal battery is narrow and perhaps even in a sense arbitrary, but it is strict and sternly enforced.

Different cultures and civilisations have tried to disguise the true nature of one-on-one fighting. They dress it up, regulate the violence and insist on codes of conduct invoking 'honour' and decency. Medieval tourneyers performed the jousts according to a chivalric code heavily influenced by the literature of courtly love. The brute contest for power and sexual success was draped with silks and disguised by elaborate rituals. Knights fought for the honour of their refined womenfolk and for their own reputation. The gore was downplayed, the butchery softened. Weaponry became blunter, armour more impenetrable.

The duel had an equally elaborate code of etiquette, which all gentlemen were supposed to understand and obey. Except when they didn't – and instead hacked away at each other like dangerous lunatics. The samurai would similarly punish their own dishonourable conduct, but more ferociously – with ritual disembowelment, the more painful the better. No culture, it seems, can contemplate unvarnished butchery or straight-out brutality. All combat must be regulated, and sometimes the regulation is as savage as the contest.

This story of one-on-one combat has not been one of its rise and decline, but simply its changing form. The contest is likely to continue as long as people exist but it is difficult to predict what shape it will next take.

Books, television, and movies have canvassed various possibilities. The 1996 novel *Fight Club* by Chuck Palahniuk is about an alienated insurance agent who creates a bare-knuckle fighting club as a protest against consumerism and the corporate society. Palahniuk's vision of an underground, unregulated boxing match with no rules was soon being played out for real in America after the movie version was released in 1999. Modern day one-on-one combat sports have followed this lead. Cage fighting, which broke into the public domain in 1993, boasted 'there are no rules.' The contest, once called 'human cockfighting' by US senator John McCain, is a no-holds-barred combination of boxing, wrestling, martial arts and street fighting inside a wire mesh cage. It has been rebranded Mixed Martial Arts in recent years, and instead of 'no rules' there are now thirty-one of them. These include: 'no eye gouging, no biting or spitting, no fish hooking (putting your fingers in an opponent's orifices and tearing them open), and no timidity.'

Mixed Martial Arts is very similar to the ancient Greek pankration – one-on-one fighting without rules. According to Greek myth, Hercules invented it as a way of battling his numerous foes. It is thought the pankration may have existed as far back as 2000 BC, and by 700 BC it was an Olympic event. It seems unlikely that Mixed Martial Arts will make it to the Olympics, as it has been widely condemned by medical experts. The British Medical Association has called for the contests to be banned, as one of its doctors explained to *The Sunday Times*:

> *This kind of competition hardly constitutes a sport,' she said. 'As a civilised society we should be campaigning to outlaw these activities. It can cause traumatic brain injury, joint injuries and fractures. The days of gladiator fights are over and we should not be looking to resurrect them.*

But there is a massive public appetite for these modern 'gladiator fights'. In 2009 the Mixed Martial Arts championship made $200 million in pay-for-view television subscriptions alone and was watched by over 400 million viewers in seventeen different languages.

If genuine gladiator games were resurrected today they would certainly be popular, no matter how much they were officially condemned. They would also be shown on a screen, somewhere. Stephen King's *The Running Man* imagines a future with gladiatorial game shows broadcast live. The contestants are convicted criminals who are chased around the world by 'hunters'. They are paid for every hour they stay alive and for each hunter they kill. But just like the Roman gladiatorial games, King's game show is a form of bread and circuses, an entertainment to distract people from brutal political realities. This is the nightmare possibility: that the gladiator games of the future will be provided and paid for not by an emperor, but a corporation.

INDEX